RESPONSIBLE HISTORY

RESPONSIBLE HISTORY

Antoon De Baets

Berghahn Books
New York • Oxford

First published in 2009 by

Berghahn Books

www.berghahnbooks.com

© 2009 Antoon De Baets

Library of Congress Cataloging-in-Publication Data

Baets, Antoon de, 1955–
    Responsible history / Antoon De Baets.
        p. cm.
    Includes bibliographical references and index.
    ISBN 978-1-84545-541-5 (hbk. : alk. paper)
    1. History—Moral and ethical aspects.   2. Historians—Professional
ethics.   I. Title.
    D16.9.B318 2008
    174'.99—dc22   2008028585

British Library Cataloguing in Publication Data
A catalogue record for this book is available from the British Library
Printed in the United States on acid-free paper.

ISBN: 978-1-84545-541-5 Hardback

To Elly—

For the walks and talks during which many ideas of this book first emerged.

CONTENTS

LIST OF TABLES

FOREWORD

The censorship and persecution of historians, as the present book abundantly illustrates, have been frequent in the past. They continue to be a problem of the present. Given the importance of history and the conditions that govern its political instrumentalization in many parts of the world, they will not go away in the foreseeable future.

Campaigns, petitions, and other interventions by fellow historians can be useful when dealing with urgent cases of persecution that have become known. A systematic analysis of the phenomena of censorship and persecution can be helpful in preparing adequate reactions in the future. To both, Antoon De Baets has contributed a lot.

In practice, he did this as the founder and coordinator of the Network of Concerned Historians in 1995. The purpose of the Network is to provide a bridge between the global community of historians and international human rights organizations campaigning for censored or persecuted historians and others concerned with the past. During the past thirteen years, the Network, under the leadership of Antoon De Baets, has participated in several dozens of such campaigns for cases in countries on all continents. The Network also produces an *Annual Report* covering the domain where history and human rights intersect. As such, the work of Antoon De Baets has supported the endeavors of the International Committee of Historical Sciences (hereinafter "the Committee").

The Committee, founded more than eighty years ago, has always been keenly aware of the crucial importance of the freedom of expression for historians. In the first decades of its existence, however, it was not always able or willing to campaign for individual cases in which that freedom was violated. In fact, the Committee was presented with a dilemma: it had either to speak out in order to help the historians under attack or remain silent in order to avoid conflict with the official delegations of new, abusive regimes that usually tried to downplay the situation. Despite the lack of collective intervention, individual Committee bureau members sometimes made *ex officio* efforts on behalf of their endangered colleagues.

A first change in this "soft" strategy came in 1970. Some delegations attempted to boycott the Thirteenth International Congress of Historical Sciences in Moscow because of the large-scale persecution of Czechoslovak historians unleashed by the "normalization" after 1968. This was prevented, but in meetings of Congress after Congress, the fate of Czechoslovak historians was highlighted. This raised the Committee's awareness. A former Committee President, Karl Erdmann (1975–80), paid attention to these aspects in his history of the Committee, first published in German in 1987 and recently translated and expanded (*Toward a Global Community of Historians: The International Historical Congresses and the International Committee of Historical Sciences, 1898–2000* [New York and Oxford: Berghahn Books, 2005]). And in a dozen essays written between 1984 and 2000, the late François Bédarida, former secretary-general of the Committee (1990–2000), attempted to develop a coherent view of historians' duties.

A further step was taken in the first years of the new century. At the Committee's bureau meeting in Paris in 2003, then Vice-President Romila Thapar gave a detailed report about the difficult political climate for historical research and for historians in India at the time. As the Committee's president, I concluded the discussion following her important report with the words that the Committee had hardly any power to influence the deplorable situation in India for the better. The Committee, on whose behalf Secretary-General Jean-Claude Robert had written letters seeking clarification of the situation in India, would, however, continue to look for ways in which it could be helpful. In this context, it was proposed to add to Article 1 of the Committee's *Constitution* a clause that stated that it was opposed to the misuse of history. In 2005 in Sydney, the Committee's General Assembly unanimously approved that clause. As far as I know, Antoon De Baets is the first to comment on it. He writes that the move was important in that the abuse of history, despite the variety of situations it covers, was finally formally perceived as a meaningful concept in its own right by a recognized universal body of historians.

The present book should be seen as a welcome systematic supplement to the practical work of the Network of Concerned Historians, in accordance with the approach as formulated in the *Constitution* of the International Committee of Historical Sciences. Until this moment, no general theory enabling historians to identify, prove, explain, and evaluate the many types of abuse of history was available. The book's first chapter presents such a theory of wide-breadth. The book's final chapter, a mirror of the first, proposes a universal code of ethics as a guide for responsible historians. The intervening chapters either give illustrations of the theory and the code or explain the fundamental values underlying them. In so doing, Antoon De Baets explores areas of conflict and reconciliation between historians and the world in which they work. He explains why the relationship between historiography and democracy is special. He throws new light on the question of whether history should be solely understood or additionally also judged. He convincingly identifies our elementary duties to the dead and clarifies concepts such as posthumous dignity, posthumous privacy, posthumous reputation, posthumous wrongs, posthumous punishment, and posthumous reparation. He intriguingly shows how freedom of speech ineluctably harbors rights to memory and history and rights to silence and oblivion, but no duty to remember. These novel insights make for compelling reading.

Therefore, I can warmly recommend *Responsible History* to any concerned historian in need of a reliable compass for responsible conduct. I endorse Voltaire's words quoted in this book: "Those who can make you believe absurdities, can make you commit atrocities." Responsible conduct is necessary because irresponsible conduct is dangerous.

Jürgen Kocka, Free University of Berlin

President of the International Committee of Historical Sciences, 2000–2005

1 December 2008

ACKNOWLEDGEMENTS

Any gesture of gratitude to those who have influenced my thoughts should start with mentioning the students of history and international relations who attended my classes on the abuse of history and the ethics of historians through the years. They saw primitive and more advanced versions of parts of this book. Their enthusiasm and perspicacious comments were sometimes memorable. In the same vein, I have benefited from the criticism of, and discussions with, several forums of colleagues.

Jürgen Kocka was an inspiring president of the International Committee of Historical Sciences. Like the late François Bédarida, he has always been deeply concerned about the ethics of the historical profession and about the persecution and censorship to which some of our colleagues fell victim. His moral support gave me the certitude that I participated in a broader movement through which historians express commitment for the wellbeing of their profession. Similarly, sympathetic remarks by Jens Boel, UNESCO's chief archivist, revealed to me that many archivists shared the same concerns and thought along the same lines as I did. I also want to thank the patrons of the Network of Concerned Historians, an initiative so close to the heart and mind of this book. Aside from Jens Boel and Jürgen Kocka, they include Joyce Appleby (United States), Carlos Barros (Spain), Marc Boone (Belgium), Natalie Zemon Davis (Canada and United States), Toyin Falola (United States and Nigeria), Willem Frijhoff (Netherlands), Adolfo Gilly (Mexico), Georg Iggers (United States and Germany), Derek Jones (United Kingdom), Antonis Liakos (Greece), Martyn Lyons (Australia), Shula Marks (United Kingdom and South Africa), Jörn Rüsen (Germany), John David Smith (United States), Sølvi Sogner (Norway), Romila Thapar (India), Hayden White (United States), Daniel Woolf (Canada), and Sacha Zala (Switzerland).

Other colleagues and friends were helpful as to when it came to challenging existing theories and weighing arguments. I thank Jean-Claude Robert, secretary-general of the International Committee of Historical Sciences, for clarifying the amendments to its *Constitution* to me. Peter Burke (United Kingdom), Robert Cribb (Australia), and

Herman Hoen, Sanne van der Kaaij, and Mary Kemperink (Netherlands) kindly commented on my theory of the abuse of history. My colleagues Rik Peters and Frank Ankersmit assisted me in solving some of the puzzles of definition. In the pristine stages of my work on the book's crucial parts about the dead, historian Claire Boonzaaijer provided a welcome echo in our discussions about the merits of some of my theses. I also deeply appreciated comments by Derek Parfit, a philosopher and senior research fellow of All Souls College at Oxford University, on my attempt to understand his theory about future generations in relation to past generations. For questions of law, I was fortunate that Toby Mendel, Head of Law Programme of the Global Campaign for Freedom of Expression *Article 19,* London, shared his insights with me. His views on the relationship between abusive and irresponsible history and between opinions and memories in particular became very dear to me and provided the impetus for important developments in my ideas. My brother Paul De Baets, judge at the Court of Appeals in Antwerp, helped me to appreciate the sort of wisdom aspired to by just judges. I further recall with much pleasure the comments and support of Floribert Baudet, Wouter Beekers, Aernout van Enter, Fred Janssens, Ed Jonker, Chris Lorenz, John Nerbonne, Gorus van Oordt, Bert Overbeek, Stefan van der Poel, Hans Renders, Kees Ribbens, Eelco Runia, Ton Schoot Uiterkamp, Ingrid Sennema, Koen Vangrinsven, Frans Visser, Gerrit Voerman, and Arnold Vonk. My warmest thanks go to all of them and to those whose help I unfortunately do not remember anymore.

I also acknowledge the financial support of the Netherlands Organisation for Scientific Research (NWO) and the Groningen Research Institute for the Study of Culture (ICOG), and the infrastructural support of the History Department of the University of Groningen, the Netherlands. And I appreciated the work of the staff and collaborators of Berghahn Books (Marion Berghahn, Vivian Berghahn, Melissa Spinelli, Ann Przyzycki, Samara Stob, and Cassandra Caswell) very much.

If anyone has observed the birth of this work and accompanied it with intriguing comment and unforgettable encouragement, it was my wife Elly De Roo. At times, our frequent walks resembled a peripatetic academy in miniature. I never knew conversation could unite lives and minds so gracefully. And as, in a sense, Elly was the midwife of this book, I dedicate it to her.

Chapter 1 of this book has not been published yet, although an early attempt to tackle the chapters' two final theses will be found in "History under the Auspices of Power: Political Control and Manipulation of the Past," *Nieuw Tijdschrift van de Vrije Universiteit Brussel*, 15, no. 4 (2002), 17–43, here 30–32. Parts of the remaining chapters were the object of previous publications. However, all of these publications have been entirely revised and, where necessary, thoroughly rewritten. Many old arguments were sharpened, many new ones added. By temperament, I belong to the group of authors who incessantly revise their findings. Chapter 2 originally appeared as "The Dictator's Secret Archives: Rationales for Their Creation, Destruction, and Disclosure," in Alasdair MacDonald and Arend Huussen, eds., *Scholarly Environments: Centres of Learning and Institutional Contexts 1600–1960* (Louvain: Peeters Publishers, 2004), 181–96. Chapter 3 was first published as "Defamation Cases against Historians," *History and Theory: Studies in the Philosophy of History* (Oxford: Blackwell Publishing), 41, no. 3 (October 2002), 346–66. Initially, Chapters 4 and 5 formed a single essay, namely "A Declaration on the Responsibilities of the Present Generations toward Past Generations," *History and Theory: Studies in the Philosophy of History* (Oxford: Blackwell Publishing), 43, no. 4 (December 2004), 130–64. The Code of Ethics at the end of Chapter 6 appears here in print for the first time, although an early Dutch version was posted on the Internet (http://www.vangorcum.nl/CodeDeBaets) in August 2005. Chapter 6, without the Code, was composed on the basis of two parallel texts: "The Swiss Historical Society's Code of Ethics: A View from Abroad," *Schweizerische Zeitschrift für Geschichte / Revue suisse d'histoire / Rivista storica svizzera* (Basel: Schwabe AG), 55, no. 4 (December 2005), 451–62, and "Argumenten voor en tegen een ethische code voor historici" (Arguments in Favor and against a Code of Ethics for Historians), *Tijdschrift voor Geschiedenis* (Assen: Van Gorcum), 118, no. 4 (November 2005), 564–71. The latter essay was followed by a reply of Ed Jonker (listed in the bibliography) and, on pages 581–82, an afterword of mine. I thank all of the publishers mentioned for their permission to reproduce and adapt my texts that appeared in their collections.

I also wrote several pieces on topics identical or similar to those of this book. Related to Chapter 1 is "The Abuse of History: Demarcations, Definitions and Historical Perspective," in Herman Hoen and Mary Kemperink, eds., *Vision in Text and Image: The Cultural Turn in the Study of Arts* (Leuven: Peeters Publishers, 2008), 159–73. Related to Chapter 3 are "Smaadprocessen tegen historici" (Defamation Cases against Historians), *Groniek: Historisch Tijdschrift*, 34, no. 153 (September 2001), 427–50, and "Histoire et diffamation," in Pascal Durand, Pierre Hébert, Jean-Yves Mollier, and François Vallotton, eds., *La censure de l'imprimé: Belgique, France, Québec et Suisse romande, XIXe et XXe siècles* (Québec: Éditions Nota Bene, 2006), 397–428. Related to Chapters 3 and 4 is "Postume privacy en reputatie" (Posthumous Privacy and

Reputation), in Hans Renders and Gerrit Voerman, eds., *Privé in de poli-tieke biografie* (Amsterdam: Boom, 2007), 108–23. Related to Chapter 4 are "Postume straffen" (Posthumous Punishment), *Groniek: Historisch Tijdschrift*, 39, no. 170 (March 2006), 47–60; "Last Rites, Old Wrongs," *Times Higher Education Supplement*, no. 1861 (4 March 2005), 16; "How Humanity Stands on Its Dignity," *The Australian* (13 July 2005), 36; and "A Successful Utopia: The Doctrine of Human Dignity," *Historein: A Review of the Past and Other Stories* (Athens), no. 7 (2007), 71–85. Some other publications of mine revolving around the closely related theme of the censorship of historical writing are listed in the bibliography.

Some essays have still to be published. Close to Chapter 1 is "History of the Abuse of History" (Shanghai); close to Chapter 5 are "A Duty To Remember or a Right To Historical Truth?" (Santiago de Compostela: Historia a Debate) and "La mémoire est-elle un droit ou un devoir?" (Lausanne: Éditions Antipodes).

Over the past few years, I gave several conferences on the topics of this book: on sections of Chapter 1 at the 18th International Congress of Historical Sciences in Montréal (September 1995), at the University of Groningen (October 2005), and at a conference held at East China Normal University in Shanghai (November 2007); on sections of Chapter 2 at the University of Groningen (November 2001); on sections of Chapter 4 at the University of Utrecht (October 2003), at the 20th International Congress of Historical Sciences in Sydney (July 2005), and at the University of Groningen (June 2006); on sections of Chapter 5 at the universities of Santiago de Compostela (July 2004), Ghent (March 2006), Fribourg (October 2006), and Athens (April 2007); on sections of Chapter 6 on a colloquy in Groningen (November 1996), at the 19th International Congress of Historical Sciences in Oslo (August 2000), at the General Assembly of the Swiss Historical Society gathered in Berne (October 2004), at the Royal Dutch Academy of Sciences in Amsterdam (June 2006) , and at the European Social Science History Conference in Lisbon (February 2008).

A Dutch version of the present book appeared as *Gebruik en misbruik van de geschiedenis* (Amsterdam: Boom, 2008).

Antoon De Baets

University of Groningen

1 December 2008

❦ INTRODUCTION

With an almost incurable passion of more than a quarter of a century, I have collected and analyzed data on the censorship of history. The fruits of this labor resulted in many essays and in the book *Censorship of Historical Thought: A World Guide, 1945–2000*.[1] In the process, two areas of interest emerged at the opposite end of censorship of history: the responsible use of history and the ethics of historians. My thoughts about these complementary topics matured in stages. From the pristine days of research, questions about the censorship of history obviously raised questions about the rights and duties of the historical profession either in times of dictatorship or democracy. Gradually, it dawned upon me that some of the cases of censorship and persecution I studied were ongoing still and clearly called for more than research: they also called for action. In 1995, this insight was converted into a campaign, the Network of Concerned Historians.[2] Almost imperceptibly, two questions were raised. The first was whether a code of ethics for historians could play a fertile role in the historical profession. To my great surprise (and to the surprise of some colleagues outside of the historical profession), overall progress in this area was weak. This observation led to a further question: if a code of ethics could be described as a set of rules for responsible conduct, how, then, could its opposite—irresponsible conduct—be conceptualized? With this second question, it seemed that I had come full circle, because the answer to that question obliged me to think about the abuse of history and this, obviously, was the umbrella under which the censorship problem found a home.

During all of the years that I studied this cluster of problems, I made two fundamental mistakes. One was about the subjects of study of historians, the other about historians themselves. I assumed that it would be relatively easy to define the duties of historians to the subjects of their study—the living and the dead—or at least not more difficult than it was for neighboring disciplines. I was wrong. I naively took it for granted that the dead shared many features with the living and the unborn. Some essential common characteristics aside, however, there is no symmetry between past generations and either present or future generations. The question who or what the dead are, whether they deserve respect and why, and which duties we ought to fulfill regarding them, triggered a quest that led me to new vistas and profoundly affected my view of memory and history and even of human life.

This was especially true because I drew much inspiration from the fields of moral philosophy and human rights. In particular, I was influenced by the thinking about time, suffering, and impunity as developed within the United Nations. I made myself familiar with the mass of excellent work done inside the United Nations and by international courts. Little by little, my view on historical truth became impregnated by one single, cruel fact: plagued by the "odious scourge" of gross human rights abuses,[3] millions of persons around the globe yearned to know the elementary truth about their loved ones who were slaughtered or who disappeared in terrible circumstances. Their dramatic stories, of which I read many, left an indelible mark upon me. They made me sadder—and perhaps wiser. Although this did not lead to a "lachrymose conception of history," solely centered on victims, at last I was able to see clearly how important bare existential facts are in discussions about historical truth and how the respect historians ought to have for the living and the dead could and should take shape.

The second mistake consisted in my assumption that the abuse of history and the responsible use of history were bipolar problems, that the former was the opposite and the mirror of the latter. If only, I thought, I were able to map the field of the abuse of history well, this would yield me a negative blueprint for an ideal code. But the abuse of history was part of a broader complex of problems caught under the name of irresponsible history. As it transpired, my attempt to develop a theory on the abuse and irresponsible use of history suggested only two infrastructural principles for responsible conduct, namely the principles of integrity and care. They correspond to what Bernard Williams identified as the two basic virtues of truth: accuracy (to find truth) and sincerity (to tell truth).[4] However refined I tried to make the theory's architecture, my analysis yielded no further direct clues for a code. In contrast, and to my relief, it was replete with subtle signs about how accurate and honest historians should work. But a code of ethics was not a simple black-to-white reversal of a theory on the abuse of history.

This background is helpful to clarify the shell of the book. Chapter 1 is an attempt to sketch a coherent theory on the abuse and irresponsible use of history, with its structures and processes. Such a general theory, which enables historians to identify, prove, explain, and evaluate abuses of history, does not yet exist. The chapter opens with a general discussion of a spectrum of distinctions that are often confused: those between irresponsible and abusive history on the one hand, and non-scientific, incompetent, meaningless, harmful, and dangerous history on the other. It then proceeds to define *the abuse of history as its use with intent to deceive* and the broader concept of *the irresponsible use of history as either its deceptive or negligent use.* After developing the various ramifications of the theory, from a typology of abuses and irresponsible uses, over questions of evidence, explanation, and evaluation, to measures of prevention, the chapter ends with some considerations on the thorny issue of the history of the abuse of history. In particular, I investigate the theses that the demarcation between the use and abuse of history is a modern one and that the abuse of history is on the rise.

The next two chapters deal with instances of (potential) abuse and irresponsible use of history, the second relating to dictatorships and the third relating to democracies. Chapter 2 analyzes the bookkeeping of death, as it is embodied in the secret repression archives of dictators. Given the embarrassing and incriminating content of these *archivos del terror,* an enigmatic question looms: why do dictators create secret records of repression in the first place? A review of motives for creating such archives is supplemented with a look at the feverish debates about the fate of those archives after the dictatorship falls into pieces but not into oblivion. The last part of the chapter probes into the special relationship between democracy and historiography.

Chapter 3 analyzes the conflict between the historians' urge to tell the truth about the past and the equally understandable urge of their subjects to have their reputation safeguarded. Based on a study of more than 160 such conflicts, it wrestles with the clash of two basic rights: expression and reputation. It lays bare the abuse, frequently made worldwide, of defamation laws as disguised instruments of censorship, but, at the same time, it tries to find a method to demarcate the sound curiosity of the historian from obscure voyeurism or irresponsible conduct. It recommends a right to silence for historians, only applicable under strict conditions. And this right to silence also offers the key to solving the centuries-old problem of whether history should be solely understood or, in addition, judged also.

While the first three chapters focus on the irresponsible use of history, the last three concentrate on its responsible use. Chapters 4 and 5 are twin chapters. Both start from the simple premise that, in their works, historians study the living and the dead. As is the case in any profession, the rights of the subjects studied determine the scholar's professional ethics. Once historians know what the rights of the living are, they also know which of these they should respect when they study the living. And since historians are also members of this family of the living, they know at once what basic rights they themselves have. Likewise, if they know what the duties are of the

living to the dead, they know at once what the duties are of historians to the dead. Given that historians are positioned in the same universe as the living subjects they study—a complicating factor often
observed in historical epistemology—it appears as if the question
about the living is more complex than the one about the dead. The
reverse is true. There is de facto consensus about the rights of the
living—formulated in the *Universal Declaration of Human Rights* and
the covenants emanating from it—and by extension, about the most
important rights of historians.[5]

Speaking of the dead, on the other hand, is an operation mined with
paradoxes. Chapter 4 patiently unravels some of them. *I define the dead
as past human beings* and come to the conclusion that the dead do *not*
possess rights, but that the living nevertheless have some definable core
duties to them. I then attempt to determine these duties and explore the
many aspects related to them, including modalities of noncompliance.
In the process, I discuss several relevant concepts: posthumous dignity,
posthumous privacy, posthumous reputation, posthumous wrongs,
posthumous punishment, and posthumous reparation. Basically, I want
to understand why people put flowers on the graves of the dead.

In Chapter 5, I ask two questions that flow from the analysis of
Chapter 4. Is remembering the past a right? And, is remembering the
past a duty? To the first question, I shall answer, Yes; to the second, No.
There is an overwhelming consensus that we have a *right* to memory.
What, then, is the basis of this right, why do we have it, and what are its
limits? That is the first question. The second is whether, in addition to a
right to memory, we also have a *duty* to remember. Both those arguing
in favor and against this thesis have powerful arguments. On balance,
however, historians should join those who reject such a duty to remember. Imposing a duty to remember *on others* is a violation of the latter's
rights. And yet, there are notable exceptions to this fundamental position . . . In the rest of the chapter, I sketch the history of a right to history. This right to history was developed gradually within the United
Nations under the name of "right to the truth."

My overall argument constitutes a strong defense of the rights to
memory and history. As parts of the broader freedom of expression,
they are not new. As tools of survival for the millions of people who
must cope with a legacy of human rights violations, these rights of
memory and history have received international attention only in the
past thirty years. And as enabling conditions for decently fulfilling our
duties to the dead, we have not yet, I feel, fully grasped their value. At
the end of the chapter, I attempt to disentangle the web of relationships
between rights and duties regarding history.

Like the opening chapter, the final one is about the historians them-selves. It deals with the ethics of historians, but only tangentially with the ethics of history. The distinction is that while the ethics of histori-ans refer to the rights and duties of historians, the ethics of history are concerned with the moral evaluation of historical episodes and figures. The chapter has its own prehistory. Twelve years ago, in the fall of 1996, I was invited to a local colloquy to say "something" about the "founda-tions" of the historical profession. When preparing my talk, I jotted down what I thought were unsuspect truisms, such as that historians seek for truth and that they should do this with as much objectivity as possible and with a method called "historical criticism." But, as I soon discovered to my dismay, after practicing my profession and studying problems of the censorship of history for almost two decades, I was not able to give a *coherent* answer to the "vision thing." To make mat-ters worse, a lingering sentiment surfaced: what I called "unsuspect" truisms appeared to be met with reservation, if not plain skepsis, in the profession. I was ashamed for this belated discovery and I revolted against my professional laziness. Eventually, I formulated—tentatively and without knowing much about the pioneering efforts of the Ameri-can Historical Association at the time—a set of five duties for histori-ans. The impossible mission of the colloquy kept haunting me. I noticed that problems of professional ethics were everywhere and awareness of them among historians was high but, as a subject, it was remarkably invisible and even forgotten. And, when discussed at all, the empha-sis was on the duties of historians, while any of their rights remained strangely unmentioned. I began to devote systematic attention to the problem in my annual seminars for last-year students.

The cognac of that experience is Chapter 6. It develops arguments to adopt a code of ethics for historians—but only after a careful appraisal of the many dangers inherent in codification. I perceive a code of ethics as a set of principles about the historians' rights and duties that have to be perfected continuously. It is an instrument that tries to strike a fair balance between the interests of historians and those of others in the universe in which they operate. The road to a good code is long and winding. I believe that it is high time for the his-torical profession to formulate a coherent vision on its four irreducible values: freedom and integrity (of historians), respect (for those sur-rounding them), and the careful and methodically executed search for truth (as the result of the interactions between historians and others). With such a code, historians could convince outsiders and themselves that history is well cared for in their hands. The chapter ends with a proposal for a code of ethics.

A last word. The book is meant as a contribution to understanding and opposing the abuse of history. It is also an attempt to evaluate the risks and advantages of a solid system of ethics for the historical profession. The grasp is wide, but also, I hope, tempting enough as to invite debate.

I

IRRESPONSIBLE HISTORY

✺ 1

A Theory of the Abuse of History

For who does not know history's first law to be that an
author must not dare to tell anything but the truth?
And its second that he must make bold to tell the whole
truth? That there must be no suggestion of partiality
anywhere in his writings? Nor of malice?

—Cicero[1]

It shall defend freedom of thought and expression in
the field of historical research and teaching, and is
opposed to the misuse of history and shall use every
means at its disposal to ensure the ethical professional
conduct of its members.

—International Committee of Historical
Sciences, *Constitution*[2]

The abuse of history is frequently dangerous. It is common under dictatorships and in periods of gross human rights violations. It played
a major role during the genocide in Rwanda (1994) and the wars in
the former Yugoslavia (1991–95). Although the natural habitat of the
abuses of history is a nondemocratic environment, its persistent traces
are also present in many democracies. Not so long ago, religious tensions in India (1998–2004), for example, were partly incited by divergent and distorted views of the past. How can we delineate, with some
certainty, the boundaries of this problem? This is possible only if we
have a theory that provides an insight into what exactly happens when
history is abused and into how such conduct should be judged.

Strangely enough, such an encompassing theory does not yet exist.
This is so because many historians who are informed about cases of
abuse—often historians living in dictatorial countries or their colleagues who were allowed to visit them—do not want to write about
the abuses because they fear research or career troubles or backlash
effects on themselves or their wider circle. The result is broad under-
reporting, with the subject mentioned only in passing. Even if historians find the courage to report about it, they often lack time to make

the evidence conclusive, while those who do find time to become whistleblowers are frequently more fascinated by the painful details of the individual case they are describing and defending rather than by the similarities to other cases. In addition, they generally encounter much disbelief. If they do seek patterns, they rarely have more than a few cases at their disposal, or they only use cases that represent one dimension or type of abuse, thereby hindering broad generalizations and a global view. That is why so many essays about the abuse of history commonly describe the political context of historical writing in certain, often dictatorial, countries. This is useful, but for purely practical reasons.

Even theoretical works broaching the subject are captivated by an inductive approach. They usually describe history as an instrument legitimizing ideology and power (which it often is), but do not systematically test a theory against the abuses they analyze.[3] Only the classic works on the methodology of history and their successors pay some theoretical attention to the question of abuse, specifically in the discussion of the so-called "internal criticism of the lie and the error" (by which the lies and errors of source producers, not of professional historians, are meant), or in the mention of various series of nonscientific motives for the writing of history. Such considerations, however, are seldom supplemented with theoretical reflections on conduct and intention, or with the notions of harm and wrongdoing.

A Note on Scholarship and Profession

When I expound my theory in the lines that follow, I take it for granted that, foremost among several parties, recognized associations of professional historians working under democratic conditions have the authority and duty to decide whether a given use of history is an abuse. My theory is developed to guide them in this area. And if it concentrates mainly on abuses by professional and academic historians, others will obviously benefit from a demonstration of how the profession looks or might look at abuses of history. Clearly, these abuses are only a subgroup of misconduct by professional historians. Misconduct is broader than abuse of history as the former also encompasses violations of professional norms not specifically related to history, such as the abusive reaction to reasonable guidelines from the academic management, the use of offensive language in the lecture room, or the intimidation and discriminatory treatment of colleagues and students.

From the outset, I have to clarify the concepts of historical scholarship and the historical profession. These are very close concepts, frequently used intermingled (also here), but they are not synonyms. Scholarship concerns questions of content and method, questions of truth and reliable expert knowledge. As such, scholarship is the decisive condition for the profession. The profession itself concerns the organizational aspects of scholarship. Although operating under widely divergent conditions across countries, these organizational aspects are quite universal. They are built on two antagonistic core values: autonomy and accountability. Professorial and institutional autonomy is the power to control the academic environment. This includes control of the four pillars on which this environment rests: the curriculum, the awarding of degrees, the admission of students, and the recruitment (selection and promotion) of staff. By accountability, it is meant that universities and their personnel be publicly answerable to the society in which they work. For the moment, it is sufficient to keep the distinction between scholarship and profession in mind.[4]

History is an important, dangerous, and fragile subject. As a universal phenomenon, the abuse of history is infinite in its variety in amount and degree. It is a well-known and obvious area of interest, but at the same time, it is also an underestimated and neglected topic of theoretical research. In 1985, the Slovak Miroslav Kusý, a dismissed philosopher-turned-unskilled worker under "normalization," complained that famous historians, like Marc Bloch and Edward Carr, did not pay any attention to the difficulties and risks of the historical profession and the historian's vulnerability in their highly acclaimed works on the methodology of history.[5] Sadly, both were very vulnerable themselves and became victims of censorship and repression. Carr's multivolume *History of Soviet Russia* has been banned in the Soviet Union for four decades. Bloch's name disappeared from the cover of the *Annales* during the German occupation of France (although he continued to contribute under a pseudonym); he died at the hands of the Gestapo near Lyons in 1944.[6]

Demarcations

It is history that can be abused, not the past. Sources from the past and facts and opinions about the past can be intentionally distorted. But the past itself cannot be affected by acts in the present.

Abusive history is continuously confused with other types of history.[7] Table 1.1 attempts to list some distinctions. Termed demarcations, the boundaries of these distinctions are not clear-cut.

The demarcation between scientific and nonscientific history is, first of all, epistemological, that is, it concerns questions of truth. I profoundly share the views of the sociologist Edward Shils (1910–95) on truth. A professor at the University of Chicago and the founder of *Minerva: A Review of Science, Learning and Policy* in 1962, he was one of the world's leading experts on higher education and academic freedom. His memorable defense of the academic ethic begins as follows: "Universities have a distinctive task. It is the methodical discovery and the teaching of truths about serious and important things . . . That truth has a value in itself, apart from any use to which it is put, is a postulate of the activities of the university. It begins with the assumption that truth is better than error."[8] In the philosophy of science, many theories distinguishing truth from error (including falsity) have been defended. Insights into the epistemological demarcation problem have changed over time and none of the theories has ever gained universal acceptance. I will use one of the theories best suited to the needs of historians (and also perhaps the most famous)—the one expounded by Karl Popper. According to Popper, the central question is whether a given theory—here, a theory about past events—is falsifiable or not, in other words whether a test can be developed to reject that theory. Such a test investigates the relationship between the theory, the available sources, the method applied, and the logic of the argument. The test result decides the status of the theory. A theory before the test is prescientific. If the theory passes the test, it is provisionally accepted as scientific. If it is rejected (that is, if it is not testable or if it does not pass the test), it acquires the status of nonscientific history. When a theory that has been provisionally accepted is tested again with other data or other methods, and rejected after this new test, it receives the status of exscientific history.[9] History that turns out to be of the pre–, non– or exscientific kind is not meaningless. On the contrary, as part of ideologies, myths, legends, or beliefs about the world, it may provide meaning for those who hold such beliefs.[10] As conjecture, this type of history may anticipate or inspire future scientific theories. However, as long as it does not pass the test, this "history" is not scientific history.

Other Demarcations

Another demarcation is drawn simultaneously with the epistemological one. This demarcation has an ethical, professional, and, to a lesser degree, legal nature and fixes the boundary between the reponsible use, the irresponsible use, and the abuse of history. Although the ethico-legal demarcation often leads to an epistemological distinction between false and provisionally true knowledge (and this is the reason why I shall call one classic type of abuse "the epistemological type"), it is partly different and broader, as we shall see. It is concerned less with the theories of historians than with the historians themselves, less with truth than with truthfulness. Of historians who are accurate and honest, I shall say that they use history responsibly; of those who are not honest, I shall not say at once that they are irresponsible or dishonest historians (for this is a judgment about persons rather than about their statements), but rather that they either abuse history or use it irresponsibly.

TABLE 1.1. **Demarcations in Historical Writing**

Prescientific history			
1. *Demarcations of epistemology* (= test of truth) and *ethics* (= test of truthfulness):			
Irresponsible history		Responsible, provisionally scientific history	Nonscientific history
abusive history (deceptive history; pseudohistory)	negligent and reckless history	(when failing new tests →)	(Exscientific history)
2. *Demarcation of competence* (= test of scholarly quality and expertise):			
historical works somewhere on a continuum from incompetent ("bad") to competent ("good") history			
3. *Demarcation of meaning:*			
historical works meaningful not as history but as sources illustrating irresponsible history		historical works somewhere on a continuum from meaningless to meaningful history	
4. *Judgment of morality, professionalism, and legality:*			
always morally wrong	often morally wrong	morally, professionally, and legally right	right or wrong (depending on use)
always professionally wrong; sometimes legally wrong			
5. *Calculus of harm:*			
always harmful		sometimes harmful	
6. *Calculus of risk:*			
frequently dangerous		sometimes dangerous	

Table 1.1 further draws a distinction between professionalism and competence: abusive history can be extremely refined and skillful, hence competent, but it is never professional (because it violates the accountability principle). All types of history lie on a continuum ranging from very competent to very incompetent history. Incompetent (or "bad") history—the product of error, imperfect insight, bias, and lack of training—can be heavily distorting and prejudiced, but it is not irresponsible or abusive as long as it does not transgress the moral boundary of dishonesty or gross negligence. Table 1.1 also distinguishes harm from risk. I maintain that the abuse of history is always harmful (a point elaborated below) and, in addition, frequently dangerous (as briefly illustrated above).

Responsible scientific history and nonscientific history can also be harmful and dangerous, but for other, mutually exclusive, reasons: nonscientific history because it may supply myths that incite hatred and violence; scientific history because it may destroy cherished myths and exploding taboos, at the risk of unleashing retaliatory violence in the process. If the latter is the case, responsible historians risk being treated as destroyers of reputations or as traitors and being persecuted by governments, individuals, or groups. In these matters, the historical perception of the public is crucial: frequently, audiences are not able to distinguish scientific from nonscientific history and are not willing to accept harsh truths over comfortable errors and lies.

Definitions

The irresponsible use of history and the abuse of history are not identical. While the latter is characterized by the lack of integrity, the former is broader and characterized *either* by the lack of integrity or the lack of care (or both). I propose the following definitions:

> *The abuse of history is its use with intent to deceive.*
> *The irresponsible use of history is either its deceptive or its negligent use.*

All abuse of history is irresponsible history, but not all irresponsible history is an abuse of history. "Abuse of history" is an expression reserved for the stronger forms of irresponsible history, as is its synonym "misuse of history." The essential distinction between the abuse and the irresponsible use of history is located at the level of intention. As this will be explained later in the text, for the moment I shall concentrate solely on the stronger and potentially more problematic definition, that concerning the abuse (or misuse) of history.

Critics could reject my definition of the abuse of history because it harbors no reference to the negative consequences that the abuse entails for other persons. After all, abuse without harm is not very interesting. If this is indeed the case, why not reword the definition as *the abuse of history is its use with intent to deceive and resulting in harm to others?* With the term "others," this consequentialist definition introduces the victims of the abuser. Usually, two classes of victims are distinguished. Direct victims are those who have their health, reputation, income, or opportunities damaged. One may think of the people studied, those alive and (insofar as privacy and reputation are concerned) those deceased, and their relatives; authors whose work is plagiarized or falsified and their publishers; those providing information, assignments, contracts, and funding to the abuser; and all of the customers buying the deceptive product. A second class of victims encompasses those with no immediate interest: the community in which the direct victims lived and all of those misled by the deception, including scholars and experts. Although this alternative definition looks plausible, there are many objections to it.

First of all, the alternative definition would diminish the morally and professionally condemnable nature of deception, that is, of malicious conduct as such.[11] Second, the definition would exclude *attempts:* the abuse that was not only prepared but also substantially close to completion, but stopped or disclosed before being entirely executed. Some abuses of history can be committed on the spot, whereas others require considerable preparation. While these first two objections regard conduct, further objections focus on the concept of harm itself. In the first place, the alternative does not take into account abusive conduct that *could* have resulted in harm, but did not because it was unsuccessful. The existence of a *risk* of harm (inferred from the magnitude, likelihood, and imminence of the harm) is itself harmful.[12] Second, the actual harm done to other persons is often not immediately and fully known at the time the abuse is committed (and if it is, it is not always accurately assessable in economic terms). In addition, substantial harm can present itself as an *indirect* effect of the abuse. Third, the alternative definition tends to overlook abuse that profits the abuser, but does not ostensibly harm others. However, if somebody gains an unfair advantage, all of those abiding by legal, professional, and moral rules are harmed proportionally. This third objection thus assumes that abuse *always* produces harm to other persons.

The final and perhaps most important objection is a radicalization of this thought. The alternative definition neglects the argument—weak in legal, but strong in professional and ethical terms—that the intent to deceive *always* harms even when it does not result in harm to other persons. This is so because the concept of victim may be said to encompass a hitherto unmentioned third class: historical writing itself.[13] Arguably, abuses by historians always damage historiography, because historiography is a collective enterprise in which society has an interest. This is all the more so when we deal with professional historians, because society places confidence in their academic and professional qualifications and requires accountability. Abuses threaten that confidence and, therefore, the authority and efficiency of professional historical writing. They engender social costs in terms of the declining credibility of the historical profession and lower the overall quality of the historical discourse.[14] They stimulate beliefs in historical myths and propaganda or induce amnesia concerning previously known history. The harm done to historical writing is a social harm. When postdictatorial or postconflict societies evolve toward democracy, the harm suffered by historical writing during the preceding dictatorship or conflict gradually comes to light. Often, as was the case in postcommunist societies after 1989, history had gained the sad reputation of an unreliable discipline that condoned abuses. Some observers even think that this bad reputation was an important reason for the option of truth commissions to be discarded as a way of dealing with the repressive past in many of these societies. The overall public respect for, and trust in, the historical profession was undermined almost fatally.[15]

In sum, my last two objections support the view that harm consists of both the negative results of an abuse and that abuse itself. For all these reasons, my definition of the abuse of history stands.

The Importance of a Theory on the Abuse of History

The discussion above enables me to answer the question of why the abuse of history is wrong. It is always *morally* wrong because citizens (including citizens who are historians) have the (moral) duty to be honest and, even if there are circumstances where one is not obliged to tell all of the truth (see Chapter 3), the intent of not speaking should not be to deceive. In addition, almost always the aim of deception is to acquire an unfair advantage.[16]

The abuse of history is always *professionally* wrong because, in addition to their moral duties as citizens, professional and academic historians have a duty to apply scholarly and professional standards of care, in particular to search honestly and methodically for the historical truth. Only to the extent that they meet this duty are they granted certain rights, namely academic freedom for themselves and autonomy for the university. Deception, as shown, evades accountability and undermines the trust placed by society in scholarship and teaching. For this reason, abuses of professional historians are worse than those of nonprofessionals. Whereas the responsible use of history—including committing (many types of) error, defending theories before they are rejected as nonscientific, and critically commenting on rival scientific and on pre– and exscientific theories—is protected by academic freedom; abuse is not. And some of the worst abuses are not even covered by the right to free expression.[17]

Finally, abuse is sometimes *legally* wrong, namely when it transgresses the law and in particular when there exists a risk of harm to other persons.[18]

The demarcations and definitions discussed above provide the backbone for identifying the material and mental elements of the conduct of the abuser. Together these elements constitute the evidence for abuse or irresponsible use. Next, an analysis of the motives for the abuse will clarify the explanations that exist for it. And, finally, both evidence and explanation form the infrastructure for the complex process of evaluating the abuse in similar and different historical contexts. The importance of a universally applicable theory of the abuse of history, then, is this: it is a tool to identify, prove, explain, and evaluate the abuses of history, with the ultimate aim of opposing and preventing them.

Evidence of Abuse and Irresponsible Use: Material Elements

In order to prove that a given use of history is indeed an abuse, we need to look into its mental and material elements. The former are related to the mind of the abuser, the latter are not. Material elements comprise the conduct itself (consisting of an act or an omission), the consequences of that conduct, and the spectrum of circumstances (and by extension the context) in which the conduct takes place.

Let us first look at the conduct itself. The irresponsible use and the abuse of history operate at three levels: heuristic, epistemological, and pragmatic. Each level has its specific unit of analysis. At the heuristic level, it is the data perceived as sources or sets of sources (archives). At the epistemological level, it is the data perceived as words or sets of words (statements of fact and opinion, whether or not grouped as theories). At the pragmatic level, it is the data perceived as a whole (the historical work itself) and the use made of that whole by the author and others. When historians collect sources maliciously, they commit *heuristic* abuse. When they dishonestly change the evidential value of their nonscientific theory in order for it to pass the test—for example, by omitting, trimming, or inventing data, by knowingly presenting nonscientific theories as scientific ones, or by distorting provisionally scientific theories—they commit *epistemological* abuse. This is the classic form of abuse. Usually, this type attempts to attach the respect and trust associated with genuine historical writing to itself. The *pragmatic* abuse of history occurs when historians lie about their authorship or the status of their work, or when others irresponsibly interfere with it. The result of abuse deserves the name of "pseudoscientific history," "pseudohistory," or "bogus history."[19] Table 1.2 presents a typology of heuristic, epistemological, and pragmatic types of *conduct*, irrespective of their individual importance.

In principle, the typology is valid for all genres of historical *sources*. Many believe, though, that some historical sources are more amenable to abuse than others. Source editions, genealogies, biographies, memoirs, obituaries, chronicles, chronologies, annals, maps, photographs, bibliographies, historical dictionaries, encyclopedias, statistics, indexes, archive catalogs, and history textbooks have all been mentioned as sources especially vulnerable to abuse.[20]

As for the different historical *periods*, Donald Cameron Watt noted in 1985: "The study of contemporary history has scarcely been undertaken at all by serious historians because of the potential for government manipulation for political purposes. Indeed there has been a strong bias against contemporary history in academic circles because of its frequent misuse."[21] Times have since changed—contemporary history is studied more than any other period—but Watt's remark retains its historical value.

Table 1.2 immediately lays bare the simple fact that many parties are involved in the activity of historical writing. To the extent that this activity becomes more dependent on governments (for example, for salaries or archival infrastructure) or private concerns (for example, of publishers), the interests at stake in history writing multiply, as do the numbers of those willing to participate in its supervision—and as does the risk of abuse.

Most of the time, the conduct constituting the abuse has certain *consequences*—events or states of affairs that can reasonably be inferred from that conduct. The discussion on the definition of abuse made it clear that, in particular, *harmful* consequences are of special interest. The abuse is also embedded in specific *circumstances*, which can be legal, factual, or both. Legal circumstances occur when the law prohibits the abusive conduct. Factual circumstances relate to the modalities of abuse, for example, that the abuser was a student. Some factual

TABLE 1.2. *Typology of Abuses and Irresponsible Uses of History*

Upstream of the historian's work
—heuristic level (archives)—

Heritage and written and unwritten archives

* Intentionally damage and destroy heritage; loot heritage; illegally trade in objects of heritage.

* *Archival cleansing:* Illegally destroy, remove, conceal archives; neglect archives.[22]

* Maintain excessive secrecy or illegal nondisclosure of archives; illegally prohibit access to archives.

* Intimidate and eliminate producers, owners, and custodians of archives.

During the historian's work
—heuristic level (source collection)—

Irresponsible destruction of sources from others

Irresponsible collection of sources from others

* Deceive or blackmail informants and witnesses.

* Accept money from, or give money to, informants and witnesses beyond normal costs.

* *Theft:* Steal work of others.

* *Piracy:* Illegally reproduce or distribute copyrighted work of others (except selections used in research and teaching that are compatible with fair use if source and author are indicated).

Irresponsible use of sources from others

* *Plagiarism:* Deliberately present ideas and words expressed originally by others as own work (that is, without accurate acknowledgement of the source).

* *Falsification:* Falsify work of others, for example, by deliberately changing colophons or data about origin or intellectual property.

* *Bibliography, notes:* Supplement own bibliography or notes with entirely unread works.

Irresponsible use of sources in general

* Monopolize or keep secret information that should be publicly accessible.

Fabrication of own sources (falsification ex-nihilo)

* Invent informants and witnesses.

* Fabricate sources (pseudo-originals).

* Invent provenance of sources (may include falsifying catalogs, certificates, signatures, etc.)

(continued)

TABLE 1.2. *Typology of Abuses and Irresponsible Uses of History* (continued)

During the historian's work
—heuristic level (source collection) (continued)—

* Invent trustworthiness of sources, for example, by presenting them as (really or supposedly) lost sources, long searched for, or a translation thereof, and suddenly discovered.

* Supplement own bibliography or notes with fabricated works.

During the historian's work
—epistemological level (data description and analysis)—

Official and private providers of data, assignments, contracts, funding

* Impose nonscientific provider-favorable conditions on research mandate.

Description of raw and processed data[23]

* Use invented sources and their "data."

* Irresponsibly select and omit data.[24]

* Knowingly deny or minimize corroborated data.

* Misrepresent and falsify data.

* Maliciously present data without any historical context or within a wrong historical context.

* Irresponsibly or defamatorily disclose privacy- and reputation-sensitive data.

* Disclose confidential or embargoed information without permission.

* Falsely attribute information or ideas of others to oneself.

* Falsely attribute information or ideas to others.

* *Bibliography, notes:* omit important read works or purposely annotate them inaccurately.

Data analysis

* *Logic:*

    Purposely misapply logic or research methods and techniques.

    Purposely weigh evidence incorrectly by omitting, ignoring, minimizing contradicting evidence, and exaggerating supporting evidence.

* *Rhetoric:*

    Organize and present arguments in a misleading or deliberately obscure narrative structure.[25]

* *Interpretation:*

    Purposely conclude incorrectly.

    Recklessly disregard implicit moral judgments.

    Make explicit moral judgments negligently or maliciously.

(continued)

TABLE 1.2. *Typology of Abuses and Irresponsible Uses of History* (continued)

During the historian's work
—pragmatic level (publication of work)—

Autobiographical lies

* *Forgery:* Maliciously attributing original own work: (1) to other real (contemporary or historical) authors, or (2) to fictitious or anonymous authors (except pseudonymity or anonymity, either disclosed to the publisher or leaving no doubt as to the author's identity).

* Attribute—after piracy—work of others to third parties or to oneself.

* Misrepresent own curriculum vitae (origin, identity, education, profession, expertise . . .).

Lies about the work (manuscript or publication)

* Purposely draft incorrect preliminary synopsis or abstract.

* Deliberately indicate incorrectly manuscript status in the publication process.

* Submit manuscript simultaneously to several publishers without informing them of this.

* Lack of proper acknowledgement for important or substantial inspiration or help.

* Lie or maintain silence about official and private providers of data, assignments, contracts, funding, and about conditions imposed by them.

* Purposely remain silent about one's perspective or commitment, or about research modalities when the latter are relevant.

* Wrongfully suggest independence, impartiality, or prestige.

* Lie about period of research and time of publication.

* Lie about joint authorship or about contributions of coauthors (mention as authors of persons who did not collaborate; omission as authors of persons who did collaborate.)

* Falsify contracts.

Lack of accountability

* Active resistance against legitimate control of own data or work by others.

Downstream of the historian's work
—pragmatic level (reception of work)—

Censors

* Delete or change authorship without authorial consent.

* Pre– or postcensor text with or without authorial consent.

* Interfere improperly with the content of a teaching course.

(continued)

TABLE 1.2. *Typology of Abuses and Irresponsible Uses of History* (continued)

Downstream of the historian's work
—pragmatic level (reception of work) (continued)—

Official and private providers of data, assignments, contracts, funding

* Pressure to adapt manuscript so as to embellish, or to conceal, unwelcome messages.

Editors, publishers, and their staff

* Abuse editorial control.

* Steal, falsify, irresponsibly omit data from manuscripts or fabricate them.

* Reject work otherwise approved in order to harm careers or favor rivals.

* Deliberately brief authors incorrectly about approval criteria or publication process.

* Intentionally delay publication of approved manuscript.

Peer reviewers of manuscripts, books, textbooks, courses (in the context of publication, employment, tenure, promotion, grants, congresses, and prizes)

* Keep silent about either conflict or harmony of interests between reviewer and reviewed.

* Abstain from reading the entire text; a priori judge favorably or unfavorably; invent judgment.

* Invent data or misrepresent data from reviewed text.

* Lie about authorship of reviews.

* Commit piracy or plagiarism of data submitted by the reviewed.

Beneficiaries of the historical work (mass media, audience, leadership)

* Invent, plagiarize, intentionally distort data.

Sources include American Historical Association, *Berne Convention*, Bernheim, Bloch, Broad & Wade, Brugioni, Chubin & Hackett, Eco, Fischer, Grafton, Haywood, Jaubert, Kurz, LaFollette, Langlois & Seignobos, Ouy, Pradel, and Vansina.[26]

circumstances are more conducive to abuse than others, for example, heavy moral or material pressure from outside, blackmail, the weight of schedules, and workload. A good example of a factual circumstance deeply influencing abusive conduct is censorship. Censorship is abuse in which the content or exchange of historical facts or opinions is systematically controlled (often by deliberate suppression) by others (usually the government, but also colleagues, sponsors, source providers, or pressure groups).

The *context* of the historian's conduct is an extension of the circumstances. It is obviously relevant to know whether the abuse was committed, for instance, during a war or under a dictatorship, or in the twelfth or the twentieth century. One of the most important context variables is whether the abuser acted alone or was part of a larger group, and whether the activity of that larger group—most probably the government or an organism linked to it—was an exception or part of a widespread or systematic pattern. I recognize, however, that my theory is better suited to analyze situations of individual abuse than situations in which a large group of leading historians abuses history for a "greater" cause.

Evidence of Abuse and Irresponsible Use: Mental Elements

In the description of material elements, it is almost impossible to avoid qualifications of intent (like "purposely," "deceptively," "irresponsibly," "carelessly," "in good faith," or "malafide"). Strictly speaking, intent is dual: it consists of the desire that a consequence occurs (the volitional aspect) and of the foreseeability of that consequence (the cognitive aspect). Depending on the varying presence of these two components, usually four gradations of intent are distinguished.[27] In the stronger gradations, the conduct is malicious; in addition, the harm inflicted is more under the control of the abuser than in the weaker gradations. *Direct intent* means that the consequence of the abusive conduct is certain or probable, foreseeable, and desired. We speak of *indirect intent* when the consequence of the abusive conduct is certain or probable, foreseeable, and accepted, although not especially desired. Whereas the first two degrees of intent are called "specific intent" because they express determination and purposiveness, the third and fourth degrees are sometimes taken together as "general intent." The third form, then, is *recklessness:* the consequence is not certain but still possible, foreseeable but not desired, and the considerable risk of its occurrence is taken. A variant of this is called "willful blindness." The fourth form is negligence (or carelessness): the consequence is possible, foreseeable, and not desired, but the risk of its occurrence is neglected.[28] Recklessness is sometimes called "willful negligence."

Intent lies between motive and purpose. On the one hand, it is associated with, but clearly different from, the motive lying behind the intent (see below). On the other hand, it is closely connected with purpose, but only in the stronger gradations where the consequences of the conduct are certain (or highly probable), and desired or accepted. The four degrees show that the meaning of "intent" in "intent to deceive" is far larger than the meaning of "intention" as commonly understood. Hyman Gross, who developed a theory of criminal justice, made this clear as follows: "Acting intentionally is often not a matter of fulfilling an intention."[29] Responsibility for committing an abuse and displaying "intent to deceive," then, is dependent on the degree of *control* by the abuser.

This enables us to explain and refine the distinction, already mentioned, between abusive and irresponsible history: abusive history is done purposely or knowingly; irresponsible history is done recklessly or negligently. To use the same concept for extremes, such as historical propaganda that incites genocide on the one hand, and negligent microabuses on the other, although theoretically defensible because they are covered by the same roof (intent), would be seriously confusing. All reckless and much of the negligent conduct is sufficiently blameworthy to fall within the two lowest degrees of our definition of intent, but to differentiate it from the stronger abuses, I shall call it "irresponsible use."

Evidence of Abuse and Irresponsible Use: Material and Mental Elements

Judges will often rule against historians accused of abuse on the basis of proof for the latter's premeditation or their deviation of generally accepted standards of care that prudent historians should observe (see Chapter 3). The search for evidence, in this case for the material elements of abuse and irresponsible use, is also the daily business of historians. Through the ages, they have developed rules of historical criticism to verify the authenticity of sources with respect to their form and content.[30] Hence, they routinely search for internal and external inconsistencies and anachronisms in sources.

Proof of the mental element is less obvious. Of course, some acts *automatically* imply malicious intent (*mala in se*), for example, stealing a manuscript. Usually, however, intent is inferred from the relevant material elements (conduct, circumstances, consequences), and, to a lesser degree, from abuser confessions. Judges, for example, may infer it from the choice of language, the one-sided nature of statements, or the precise moment of their utterance.[31] It is not easy to base proof of intent to deceive on convincing, let alone compelling, evidence. This means that the demarcations (1) between the abuses of history and the irresponsible uses of history, and (2) between the irresponsible and responsible uses of history, are not always clear, especially in two areas: the difference between deliberate omission, reckless omission, and negligent omission of data, and the difference between recklessness and negligence. As far as the latter area is concerned, even if there is a clear difference between the reckless disregard of the truth and a simple error, the boundary between blameworthy negligence and simple negligence can be thin. There are gray areas and degrees of appreciation between error, exaggeration, and lie.[32]

Explanation of Abuse and Irresponsible Use

After the abuse of history is defined and described, the theory should now focus on problems of explanation and on those of motivation in particular. Motives are sometimes called "ulterior intent."[33] *Black's Law Dictionary* explains: "While motive is the inducement to do some act, intent is the mental . . . determination to do it."[34] From the accumulated knowledge about motives, two assumptions are important for our theory. First, a given conduct can have one motive, but can have also none or several. Second, actors are often barely conscious of their motives, and, when asked to formulate them, they do not necessarily provide clear answers or real motives. Rationalization of motives is a frequent practice. Almost always, writing history rests upon a *combination* of motives that spring from personal or collective needs, emotions, and interests. In Table 1.3, I distinguish two main groups: scientific (or intrinsic) motives and nonscientific (or instrumental, consequentialist) motives. These motives partially overlap. Nonscientific motives are very common and sometimes overriding. They are acceptable to the extent that they remain compatible with intrinsic motives.

It is time for an example. Historians can (and many do) write history to discover the historical truth (scientific motive), satisfy their curiosity (nonscientific, recreational motive), tell a story (nonscientific, literary motive), and earn money (nonscientific, economic motive). Historians who study the past of their national state and want to show how a certain royal house came to power have a legitimate motive. If, however, they intend to conceal criticism of the predecessors of the present king out of monarchism or in order to guarantee future employment as the palace's archivist and court historian, their political, professional, and ideological motives prepare the ground for malicious intent. Again, the point here is that nonscientific motives do not necessarily lead to nonscientific history, though in certain circumstances they may ignite negligence or malicious intent. Only two rules of thumb can be given. First, the *risk* of abuse is enhanced when scientific motives are less central. Second, among possible combinations of nonscientific motives, some tend to focus exclusively or mainly on favoring oneself

TABLE 1.3. *Motives for Historical Writing*

Scientific or intrinsic motives

Primary-scientific (history-related)

Search for and disclose true historical knowledge.

Secondary-scientific (history- and memory-related)

Search for and disclose true historical knowledge *as* a struggle against oblivion, historical taboos, or denial of the past.

Nonscientific or instrumental motives

Educational

Acquire historical awareness and orientation in time.

Acquire insight into processes and structures.

Moral

Document good and bad conduct as examples (*historia magistra vitae*).

Apportion praise and blame.

Prevent repetition of past crimes and conflicts.

Didactic

Learn lessons from the past.

Cultural

Stimulate cultural knowledge.

Conform to dominant or minority cultural group.

Philosophical

Enhance self-understanding through orientation in time.

Clarify human existence and endow it with meaning.

Explain identity (origin, continuity, and destiny) of individuals and groups.

Participate in the story of humanity.

Predict the future.

Religious

Develop an acceptable religious version of the past.

Defend a religious doctrine.

Metaphysical

Pay a debt to the ancestors.

Pay tribute to the heroes and victims of the past.

Racial, ethnic

Demonstrate racial or ethnic superiority, inferiority, or equality.

Conform to dominant or minority ethnic or racial group.

(continued)

TABLE 1.3. *Motives for Historical Writing* (continued)

Nonscientific or instrumental motives (continued)

Therapeutic

Seek consolation and courage.

Heal old wounds and promote postconflict reconciliation.

Recreational

Seek pastime and amusement.

Satisfy curiosity.

Literary

Tell stories.

Esthetic, artistic

Create beauty and atmosphere.

Psychological

Regarding oneself:

Clarify genealogy and identity.

Satisfy nostalgia and escapism.

Feel oneself attracted to the strange and the old.

Seek recognition and fame, including posthumous recognition and fame.

Project aspirations into the past.

Leave a legacy.

Regarding others:

Convince skeptics of own viewpoint.

Display sense of mission (unique insight into the truth).

Show admiration, loyalty, chauvinism, idealism.

Satisfy resentment (envy, hatred, revenge); settle scores.

Economic, commercial

Earn income, subsidies, profit.

Professional

Realize professional ambition, reputation, and prestige, career advantage, power.

Ideological, political, social

Acquire group spirit.

Determine group identity and origins.

Construct social cohesion and identity.

Build ethnic groups, nations.

Build institutions (states, sub- and supranational entities).

(continued)

TABLE 1.3. *Motives for Historical Writing* (continued)

Nonscientific or instrumental motives (continued)

Ideological, political, social (continued)

Contribute to reparation of historical injustice, to peace, reconciliation, tolerance, democracy.

Create acceptable ideological and political versions of the past.

Legitimize ideologies, practices, traditions, institutions, policies (including status quo, territorial expansion, and human rights violations).

Legal

Historians writing as or on behalf of:

citizens: Prove claims of genealogy, reputation, law, privilege, profession, property.

victims: Prove crimes, guilt, claims for reparation of historical injustice.

perpetrators: Prove innocence; seek rehabilitation.

judges: Judge guilt and innocence.

Sources include Bernheim, Bloch, Feder, Gallie, Grafton, Haywood, Kurz, Langlois & Seignobos, and Vansina.[36]

or favoring or excluding others and, therefore, are the most prone to induce malicious intent.[35]

Table 1.3 further demonstrates that the abuse of history does not always mean the *political* abuse of history. Certainly, political motives are powerful; nonpolitical motives often appear to possess a political background or dimension; and, governments are frequently the ultimate cause of the most serious forms of abuse of history. But the abuse of history springs not only from political sources.[37]

Motives provide an answer to the question: why do historians use history with the intent to deceive? They are important to explain and evaluate the abuse, including to determine sanctions, but, in contrast to intent, they do *not* play a role of significance in determining whether a given conduct is an abuse. Historically, many abusers acted with noble or acceptable motives. Noble or acceptable motives, however, do not make the abuse less abusive; what matters most is the intent to deceive.[38] Finally, it should be remarked that it would be a mistake to think that we have explained the abuse of history completely once we have identified the motives of the abusers. This is necessary, but not sufficient. The analysis of the material elements must also play a considerable part in any attempt at clarification.

The Intrinsic Importance of Abuses

The rest of the theory is a commentary on the question of how to evaluate abuses and how to handle them. Not all abuses of history—let me repeat this point—have the same weight. Judging the importance of different types of abuse and comparing them are the first elements of a broad evaluation procedure. Unfortunately, this is a vexing exercise because the application of evaluative principles sometimes leads to contradictory results. I will demonstrate this now.

The first evaluative principle is related to the degree to which the abuse makes testing it either possible or impossible: *traceability*. This principle prescribes that, under conditions of an equal mental element, abuses that make data (sources, statements, and works) untraceable are more harmful than others. This is so because the stronger the untraceability, the harder it is to recognize and measure the abuse and its harm. The logic of the principle implies that heuristic abuse is worse than epistemological and pragmatic abuse, because manipulating sources is often harder to trace and less reparable than manipulating statements or historical works. At the heuristic level itself, it means that abuses involving unique sources (e.g., diaries) are worse than those involving nonunique sources, and that abuses committed after monopolistic access to sources are worse than those committed after free access to them.[39] On this principle, destruction is worse than falsification, and falsification worse than invention.

A similar principle is *refutability*. On this view, under conditions of an equal mental element, abuses are more harmful than others when they make refutation impossible. At the epistemological level, this principle suggests that abuses of data description are worse than those of data analysis. This means that, if we divide historical statements into (descriptive) statements of fact and (analytic) statements of opinion, the distortion of facts is worse than the distortion of opinions.[40] The rationale behind this is that if facts are distorted, it is impossible to check the plausibility of opinions based upon them, whereas if opinions are distorted, it remains possible to formulate alternative opinions on the basis of facts that are accurately described. Some critics of this "fact-oriented" version of the principle may reply that facts that are distorted must be important and that if they are important, they are known by several people who can rectify the factual allegations of the abuser. In its absolute form, this argument seems to invest too much responsibility in experts and too much confidence in the self-healing powers of historiography. Other critics say that the "fact-oriented" version of the principle is not valid, because a distorted overall historical opinion (or representation) in a historical work is worse than the distortion of singular facts. It is, they say, precisely this overall representation rather than particular facts that stick in the minds of people. This is an important objection and if it is correct, the principle is useless for the distinction between facts and opinions.

This does not mean, however, that the refutability principle cannot serve as an indicator for other important problems. For example, at the level of data description, it suggests that irresponsible omission of factual data (for example, by prior restraint) is worse than falsifying or inventing them, because omission renders refutation more difficult (similar to the destruction of sources under the traceability principle). Andrus Pork contended the opposite. He writes:

> Are there any *substantial moral differences* between using 'direct lie' [that is, falsification in my terms, *adb*] and 'blank pages' [that is, omission in my terms, *adb*] methods? Although it is clearly a choice between two evils, it seems to be that from the point of view of most historians' intuitive ethical understanding, the 'blank pages' method is morally more acceptable. After all, the selection of facts for a narrative is inevitable.[41]

Obviously, selection of facts is not only inevitable, but also obligatory for historians, let alone history textbook authors. I believe that Pork, however, misses the main point, namely that a selection stemming from a particular perspective containing an often inevitable cognitive bias is different from an irresponsible or abusive selection that *is* evitable.

There is another evaluative principle that works in the opposite direction of the traceability and refutability principles. This principle prescribes that abuses significantly diminishing the overall *trust* in historical writing and its practitioners are more harmful than others. On this principle, falsification and fabrication arouse more distrust than omission precisely because they are generally more visible and traceable. Application of the trust principle and application of the traceability or refutability principles thus lead to opposite results. From this discussion, I conclude that principles for determining the importance of abuses *as such* form a necessary but unsatisfactory part of the evaluative process, because, although certainly enlightening, they do not cumulatively support each other.

The Importance of Abuses Relative to Textual Context

The importance of *epistemological* abuses can also be gauged by evaluating them in their textual context. The question here is this: how to determine whether, in a given text (T) consisting of n statements (S), the presence of a single statement Sa (a statement shown maliciously to be false or fabricated) justifies an overall judgment of "abuse of history" in relation to T? Suppose T consists of one hundred true S and only one Sa, can T in its entirety be called an abuse of history or not? Is the author an abuser of history or not? To complicate matters: one should consider that skillful and subtle abusers do not blatantly falsify the historical record, but leave intact as much of the past as they can and only alter key passages so as not to arouse suspicion about their purposes.[42] Therefore, the answer to the question will depend on the importance of the abusive statement, Sa, within the entire argument, T.

The Importance of Abuses Relative to Frequency

There is another problem, closely connected to the demarcation issue: the frequency of irresponsible uses of history, on the one hand, and abuses, on the other, may reverse their relative importance. Indeed, the lighter forms of irresponsible use occur far more frequently than the worst abuses. In addition, some of the lighter forms are barely visible and detectable. Furthermore, a continuously high frequency of lighter forms affects the work climate; it makes the environment more condoning and the work habitus sloppier. If that is the case, the lighter forms tend to involve more people. And once condoned, they may have a slippery-slope effect and make the occurrence of grosser abuses more likely. In addition, this mechanism is transsystemic, that is, active in democratic as well as nondemocratic systems.

Seen from this angle, the lighter forms of irresponsible use are the most important of all of the questionable uses, and the more serious forms of abuse, because of their lower frequency, are less important. This conclusion implies that negligence—as the mental form that lighter forms of irresponsible use adopt—is far less innocent than its low degree of intent suggests. On the other side, this conclusion creates a possibility for effective remedy, because it demands structural attention for preventive strategies that focus on the many lighter forms of irresponsible conduct.

Justifications and Wrongdoing

The lesson to be learned from the preceding discussion is that judging abuses should be done with a broader evaluative horizon that includes the parties involved: victims and abusers. The three categories of victims were already identified at the outset of our theory. When we turn our attention to the abusers, a first necessary step is to consider grounds for *justification*—reasons showing that an alleged abuse was not an abuse. Distortions of history effectuated *in good faith* are such justifications. They are not abuses, for there is no intent to maliciously deceive, and they are not irresponsible uses, for there is no blameworthy negligence. Examples at the heuristic level include the restoration under scientific conditions of objects and manuscripts (such as facsimiles, transcriptions, and translations) and the *bona fide* reproduction of lost or damaged originals. At the epistemological level, one should think of scholarly corrections, revisions, and interpolations. Stylistic exercises of imitation and homage, when openly acknowledged, belong to this category. At the pragmatic level, voluntarily relinquishing the economic profits of copyright is such an instance.[43]

Many other *bona fide* deformations are not mentioned here, as they are relatively rare in professional historical writing, for instance, parodies or other techniques of historical novels with their large margins of appreciation of historical reality. These deformations are often deceptive, but they are not abusive if their authors do not intend to keep secret the possible deception at all costs. Therefore, the deception cannot be said to be malicious. And some liberty in dealing with historical facts is a normal feature of these literary genres governed by different criteria and expectations.

Can other grounds for justification be invoked as a defense? Can historians argue that they did not know that what they were doing was abusive (ignorance) or that they committed an abuse unintentionally (mistake)? Since we are talking here about professional historians, trained to act consciously as experts and to be acutely aware of the limits of their knowledge, ignorance is often a poor defense. Judges usually react with impatience when confronted with false statements of fact due to ignorance (see Chapter 3). The other defense, mistake, is more serious. No historian is perfect; like others, they commit errors or forget or underestimate relevant facts and arguments in favor or against their theory. These are cases of *simple, inadvertent negligence*. But what if the number or nature of the mistakes is "unreasonable"? What if negligence takes place on a large scale (brought about by laziness, haste, incompetence, credulity, self-deception, bias)? Large-scale negligence by academic historians who are supposed to act with accuracy results in bad history transgressing the boundary of blameworthy negligence (the lowest degree of intent and of blame). In short, it is at least an irresponsible use.[44] "Accuracy is a duty, not a virtue."[45]

If no justifications can be invoked, the question of wrongdoing arises. Any accusation of wrongdoing should be substantiated; allegations alone are not sufficient. False complaints should lead to rehabilitating the accused and sanctioning the complainant. Assuming that the complaint is accepted, guarantees for fair treatment and due process apply. These include presumption of innocence of the accused, burden of proof for the complainants, written case files with the right to reply, defense opportunity, and appeal. Once the evidence for the abuse is accepted, general principles for apportioning blame and guilt are applicable. First, the higher the degree of intent, the larger the wrongdoing will be. Also, the more the harm was desired, foreseeable, imminent, or, when inflicted, serious, the larger the wrongdoing will be. In particular, harm resulting from crimes attributable to the abuse of history—for example, when historical propaganda directly and publicly incites hatred, discrimination, and violence, or the commission of genocide[46]—maximizes wrongdoing. Second, abusers, as well as those aiding and abetting them, are responsible, but the former are usually more so than the latter. Special attention should be given, however, to the role of the masterminds who planned and organized the abuse and of the censors or providers of contracts and budgets who exerted pressure and, by so doing, had a dominant influence on the abusive conduct.

Excuses and Pseudo-Excuses

The next problem is how to sanction the abuse once it is determined. Sanctions are excluded entirely or partially if valid excuses exist. In two situations, these excuses are responsibility-denying. To begin with, there is the situation, just mentioned, of coercion: in such circumstances, the abuse was sometimes inevitable because it took place under severe pressure. For example, historians were forced to commit abuses on orders of third parties, such as censors, and refusal of compliance signified a substantial threat to their or their family's life or safety or to their career and income prospects (as is rather common under dictatorships). The extent to which autonomy was lacking determines the excusability. The second excuse is mental abnormality, either chronic or episodic: the abuser suffered from a mental illness or from intoxication (*furiosus furore solum punitur*). There is also a harm-denying excuse: the abuse was so small that punishing its abuser would do more harm than the abuse itself (*de minimis non curat lex*). One must think here of cases where the abusers are history students at a stage in their education at which they were not yet fully aware of professional ethics or did not yet master fully the techniques of historical research. Precise information in history courses can play a preventive role and reduce this comparatively large group of cases substantially.

Statements of abusers about their motives and intentions, although valuable in many respects, are not always transparent, logical, or true. Pseudo-excuses are of two types. Some are dishonest justifications or

TABLE 1.4. *Pseudo-Excuses for Abusing History*

Abusers are:	and typically they say:	Their defense regards:
exceptional	I have a special mission exempted from normal procedures.	their person
mediating	I am guided by irresistible super-natural forces.	
good	I have a good character.	their character
compulsive	I could not help it.	
cryptomnesiac	I unconsciously borrowed informa-tion from others.	their memory
clean	I had no motive to commit abuse.	their motive
noble	I had a noble motive (*pia fraus*).	
ignorant	I did not know that it was an abuse (*ignorantia legis non excusat*).	their knowledge
reluctant	It does not need examination.	their conduct
euphemistic	It deserves another name than "abuse."	
occasional	It was an accident.	
respectful	It was a tribute.	
denying	It was no abuse but responsible use.	
futile	It was insignificant compared to my complete works.	
defensive	It prevented grosser abuses from being committed (*lesser evil*).	
misunderstood	Others did not appreciate my work; therefore, I took revenge.	others
victimized	Others abused my work also.	
innocent	Others committed the abuse, not me.	
accusing	Others now exposing me produced abusive work themselves (*first stone*).	
ordinary	Others committed abuses also (*tu quoque*).	
better	Others committed worse abuses.	
democratic	Everybody commits abuse.	all

forms of self-deception—excuses which may be valid as such but which are invoked improperly in the case at hand. Many abusers typically use defense pleas, such as: "I was distracted, sloppy, stressed, playful, temporarily out of control; my abuse was inadvertent; it was a jest," while, in fact, this was not the case. Such dubious assertions, of course, complicate the task of providing a substantial evidential base for the abuse. Other excuses are manifestly ill-founded most of the time. Table 1.4 offers a tentative list of the second type.

Mitigating and Aggravating Circumstances

In addition to (legitimate) excuses, there may be mitigating factors at work *after* the abuse occurred. The first of these is the regret expressed by abusers either implicitly when they repent and abandon attempts to abuse, or explicitly when, once the abuse has occurred, they cooperate, confess, publicly apologize, and/or amend the harm inflicted. The second is an estimation of the abusers' new situation, in particular, whether the sanction imposed would lead to unreasonably grave consequences for them. Finally, there are two time-related factors. Limitations, statutory or other, may apply when the disclosure of the abuse occurs several years or decades after the facts and sanctions become superfluous when the abuser is deceased.

Three responsibility-related factors may have *aggravating* effects. The first factor occurs when the abuser is a professional historian. The second is the case of the mastermind manipulating others to commit abuses. The final factor is repetition of the offense leading to serial abuse or serial irresponsible use.

Sanctions

Sanctions for abuses should be applied wisely and with restraint, and should pursue four goals: to force or stimulate abusers to change their conduct (if, at least, the abuser's identity is known); to deter others from imitating them; to repair harm done to victims; and, to encourage all historians to take preventive measures and to help preserve the integrity of historiography. The principles guiding the operation are well-known. Sanctions should not cause more harm than the abuse did. They should take into account abuser motives, excuses, and mitigating and aggravating factors. They should be proportional to the degree of intent, to the risk of harm, and to the harm effectively inflicted. The burden of reparation should be distributed equitably over various abusers and the benefits of reparation distributed equitably over different victims. Sanctions should also apply to attempts to abuse, but be less strict than those applied for completed abuses: attempts may be counted as abuse only if it can be shown that the intent to deceive was clearly present. Finally, sanctions should be limited in time and offer, if possible, some perspective beyond them.

In practice, these principles are not always applied strictly. There are three types of sanctions: symbolic, professional, and legal. The first type is the most frequent. *Symbolic sanctions* are imposed by victims or third parties. A first scenario is that the identity of the abusers is known to their victims or to third parties, but not to the public. The effect of this on the abusers is unpredictable: their loss of reputation may encourage them either to express regret or to commit further, more subtle, abuse. Victims may find selective disclosure frustrating or, alternatively, see it as an instrument to exert pressure on the abuser and demand reparation. As for the public ignorant of the abuse, it may still be harmed by it. *Confidential symbolic sanctions*, often imposed without a fair and full examination of the facts, serve two purposes: satisfaction for the victim through private confession, excuse, or reparation by the abuser, and, consequently, a clean slate for the latter. They often take the form of a friendly settlement backed up with the threat of exposure. *Public symbolic sanctions* may entail satisfaction for the victims and make the public aware of the abuse and the abuser. Typically, they take the shape of an investigation culminating in the disclosure and refutation of the abuse in a journal or on the Internet, or of a public discussion with the abuser. This scenario is often accompanied by a request to the abuser for public rectification and apology.

Professional sanctions are imposed by an association of professional historians or the home academic institution of the abuser. They range from withdrawal of the malicious publication and a requirement for rectification in future writings, to reprimands or suspension for shorter or longer terms. *Legal punishment* is imposed by the law or by a judge. It consists of the seizure of copyright infringing copies of a work, injunctions restraining publications, and demands for rectification in the press, in future editions of a book, or in a future issue of the journal where the problematic text first appeared. Other judicial measures include penalties and compensatory payment for damages, and criminal prosecution and imprisonment of the abusers, their superiors, and accomplices.

Almost all of the sanctions listed above are controversial among professional historians. Some are even strongly reminiscent of the darker periods in which responsible historians, not abusers of history, were forced to publicly recant their deeds or works. This is even more so the case with stronger categories of sanctions than the ones listed above. Measures such as stripping abusing historians of their doctoral degrees or credentials, refusal of promotion, demotion, dismissal, early retirement, blacklisting, and so on, all echo reprisals against honest historians under dictatorships. All of this results in a dilemma: on the one hand, no one wants abuses of history or large-scale irresponsible uses of history to go unpunished, especially because indulgence toward the "agents of oblivion, the shredders of documents, the assassins of memory, the revisers of encyclopedias, the conspirators of silence"[47] invites repetition but, on the other hand, almost any type of sanction and almost any adjudication procedure seem to possess awkward echoes of past unjustified repression of historians and they meet, therefore, with hesitation or resistance. This dilemma is what I call the *trap of the just judges.*

Prevention

Abuses can also be opposed preventively on four levels at least. Prevention of abuse is fostered through the formation of a careful and honest work habit in the first place, especially by acknowledging intellectual debts in notes and literature and by clearly distinguishing quotation and paraphrasing. A second level is the furthering of a process of awareness through the explicit teaching of students about ethical questions for historians, including teaching about past abuses of history (see Chapter 6). At the same time, it is important to fight incredulity in scholarly circles. Many clichés circulate: "I do not know of any affairs of abuse, therefore their occurrence is low; if they occur, I would know; there were more abuses in the past than now; they occur, but not here; alluding to abuse tarnishes the reputation of our department." Clichés such as these hamper vigilance. The third level is the level of institutional safeguards. The temptation of abuse decreases where academic freedom and institutional autonomy are respected; the selection of, access to, and disclosure of information are well-regulated; a critical and objective method is taught; and a climate of impartial peer review and free and pluralist debate about the past is established.

The fourth level is standard-setting, through the development of norms in professional codes of ethics. Such codes should clearly state that all historians have a responsibility to oppose abuse (see Chapter 6). At the global level, the International Committee of Historical Sciences is the profession's umbrella organization. In 1926, when it was "created in order to promote the historical sciences through international cooperation," the Committee drafted a Constitution, Article 1 of which contained the Committee's purpose.[48] To that Article 1, a sentence about the rights and responsibilities of historians was added in 1992. And in 2005, the General Assembly of the Committee unanimously amended Article 1 again by adding the clause that "it is opposed to the misuse of history"; in French: "il s'oppose à l'usage abusif de l'histoire." The precarious situation of historical writing under the Bharatiya Janata Party that ruled India from 1998 to 2004 had been the immediate cause for inserting this clause.[49] The move was utterly important in that finally, a recognized universal body of historians formally perceived the abuse of history, despite the variety of situations it covers, as a concept in its own right.[50]

Opposing Abuses

This brings us to a difficult question: how wrong is failing to oppose known abuses? There are three situations. The first is the case of historians participating in abusive operations themselves. Not opposing such operations is clearly wrongdoing. The second situation arises when works of historians are abused against the latter's will. These historians cannot, of course, be held accountable for the abuse of others. *If*, however, they become aware that their published work is being abused by third parties and *if* they are free to speak, they should stand up and denounce the abuse of their work. The third case is the most difficult: do historians in general have the duty to oppose known abuses of colleagues? It seems reasonable to restrict the category "historians in general" to those who are experts in the field in which the abuse occurs. Thus, the initial question can be reformulated as follows: do specialized historians have the duty to oppose a known abuse in their field? In principle, failing to oppose a known abuse and bogus history is failing to exercise the professional duty of accountability. In practice, however, circumstances are sometimes less simple. First, there may be tough psychological factors at work: inertia, the underestimation of the phenomenon of abuse, ill-conceived collegiality, or the incredulity that abuses occur in one's own branch of specialization. Second, there is the sheer volume of work resting on the shoulders of individual historians, which may delay exposure of known abuse, especially because standards of proof are—and should be—high. Third, the experts in question are often rivals or colleagues of the abusers. And sometimes they find themselves in positions of subordination vis-à-vis the abusers.

Disclosing abuses, therefore, usually requires exacting courage. This is obviously so under dictatorships. It even is in more open surroundings when disclosing means reporting these abuses confidentially to an ombudsperson or to some ethics advisory committee. The experience of whistleblowers—those releasing well-founded information on wrongdoing—in democracies is not very reassuring. All too often, they risk becoming targets of campaigns themselves (and some of these campaigns may be instigated by powerful abusers). Fear of being sued for defamation or other tactics of intimidation have traditionally been powerful motives not to react to abuse.[51] Experts, therefore, can sometimes invoke attenuating circumstances. From this discussion, two conclusions follow. First, it is important to see the subtle but important distinction between opposing abuse and disclosing it. Opposition to abuse encompasses several activities: disclosure, refutation, sanction, and prevention. Second, the fact that even individual specialists need much courage to denounce abuse, renders the collaboration among historians in terms of organization and procedures necessary.

History of the Abuse of History

When we compare the abuses of history over centuries and place them in their historical context, two important problems arise. The first problem, discussed at the International Congress of Historical Sciences in Oslo in 2000,[52] is whether the demarcation between the use and abuse of history is a traditional one that has always existed or a modern one. The second problem is whether the abuse of history is on the rise at the dawn of the twenty-first century. In trying to offer a solution to these problems, I will proceed as follows. First, I will address the challenges for such an investigation. Then, I will identify constants and variables in the history of the abuse of history. Finally, I shall weigh these constants and variables against my theory and address both problems themselves.

Challenges for an Investigation of the History of the Abuse of History

The study of the history of the abuse of history is an attempt to compare abuses in different historical settings and, therefore, also an instrument to evaluate them. Confronted with such large-scale comparisons, the first impression is discouraging. The field is so wide and the literature so vast that it seems impossible to learn any clear lessons.

For indeed, much of the literature in which forgery, plagiarism, fraud, and other abuses are studied from a historical perspective is also relevant to the particular field of abuses of history. In order to prepare the ground, three preliminary observations must be made. Whereas the first expands the comparison, the others limit it. First, the further one moves away from the present and from countries with firm historiographical traditions, the less obvious is the classic definition of the historian as the professional expert who methodically studies the past. *Griots* and scribes fulfilled many of the functions of historians in the past. Consequently, any comparison over time obligatorily applies not only to professional historians, but also to other practitioners of history. Second, most of the *general* literature about abuses concerns Western situations.[53] Only insofar as non-Western historical writing operates in ways similar to Western historical writing are lessons from the latter applicable to the former. Finally, I will consider the abuse of history only and exclude other forms of irresponsible history. Much that can be ascertained for the abuse of history can be ascertained for the negligent and reckless forms of irresponsible use of history also, but weighing over time honest against abusive history is different from weighing careful against irresponsible history.

Constants

The constants of the history of the abuse of history, presented here without any exhaustive pretense, ostensibly meet with near-consensus in the field. I summarize them in staccato.

1. Although no single abuser profile exists, the subtler abusers display great skill and sharp historical awareness. Usually, considerable knowledge of history is required to successfully abuse it.[54]
2. Furthermore, the works of abusers, however corrupt, can be considered as historical sources in their own right. They merit preservation in an archive (see also Chapter 2). These works do not inform us about the period they pretend to treat, but about the period in which they were created and the decades and centuries in which they were accepted as true and received as authentic. They are sources for the history of the psychology of abusers and mythmakers, and their audiences.[55]
3. To the extent that the deceptive sources and the bogus theories emanating from them were believed by many, they sometimes had important consequences as people could and did act upon

them. In general, these consequences were negative.[56] As we saw, however, as part of ideologies, myths, legends or other beliefs about the world, nonscientific history may provide meaning for those who hold such beliefs.[57] Falsity is often more appealing than truth, in particular when believing it is easier than searching for truth. Truth, therefore, possesses no inherent ability to gain general acceptance.[58]

4. To the extent that the deceptive sources and the theories they contained were *not* believed, they elicited skeptical responses. Unintentionally, false testimonies stimulated the development of the historical-critical method of separating truth from lie.[59] Moreover, the concept of false information played a key role in two major scientific theories: the free speech theory of John Stuart Mill and the philosophy of science of Karl Popper. For Mill, it was wrong to suppress information thought to be false for two reasons: the refutation of false information constituted an intellectual challenge for those searching for truth. Moreover, some of the supposedly false information could turn out to be true after all.[60] And as we saw, Popper believed that the identification and elimination of error and falsity brought us nearer to the scientific truth.[61]

5. At the level of motivation, the reasons for exposing abuse are as mixed as those behind the abuse itself. Personal rivalry and bias often provided an important impetus to unmask untruth.[62]

6. Wherever there are traditions of textual criticism and criteria for science, discussion about the epistemological and ethical demarcations of knowledge emerges. This means that in areas and countries with strong historiographical traditions (such as the West, China, and Japan), this discussion is very old. [63] Epistemological and ethical demarcations of knowledge are necessary to think in terms of use and abuse. Hence, the abuse of history has been recognized, condemned, prohibited, and punished from early times, although also sometimes ordered and condoned.[64] In *La divina commedia*, Dante put all the fraudulent in the eighth circle of Hell, *malebolge*. Within this last but one circle, falsifiers and liars were to be found in the tenth and deepest ditch, or *bolgia*. Fraudulent types, who were driven by motives and convictions that they perceived as noble and just, sometimes entertained the illusion that they were not abusing history. Most abusers, however, including those acting from noble motives, were very well aware of what they were doing. Many were not marginal; on the contrary, they belonged to the cultural elite.[65]

7. Perhaps the most fundamental insight—obvious but worth repeating—is that truth is a basic value for persons and societies. Everyone possesses a conception of truth.[66] "There is no social order without trust and no trust without truth . . . [I]t is . . . impossible to be human without having a concept of truth."[67] And the search for truth lies at the core of the academic ethic. Naturally, truth has a provisional, plural, and perspectival character. There are many truths about the past, because there are many different perspectives with which to look at the past and many different ways to make sense of that past.[68] But these tentative truths—the only ones to which we can ever aspire—are intrinsically better than error and lie.[69] Those who do not agree with the thesis that truth is superior to falsity, defend a self-defeating view: they say, in fact, that their claim that truth is *not* superior to falsity, has the status of a truth.[70] In addition to its intrinsic value, truth has an instrumental value. Indeed, truth is a chief condition for attaining many goals: human dignity, communication, science, democracy, and personal and social survival.[71] The alternative is social disorder, misery, war, and death.

The conclusion from this survey of seven constants is clear. Tampering with historical sources (heuristic abuse), historical facts and opinions (epistemological abuse), and entire works (pragmatic abuse), and the awareness that this was not, or not always, justifiable in moral terms, are phenomena of all times.

Variables

Time-dependent variables qualify the picture of the long-term occurrence of the distinction between the responsible use and the abuse of history. Even though this distinction has long been known in many places, it became sharper when science was professionalized and institutionalized in the nineteenth century. Variables related to truth conceptions, to method and evidence, to motives, and to the individuality of authors were markedly different before and after 1800.

First, oral societies and societies in transition to a written and printed culture entertained several coexisting notions of truth. The notion of *factual truth* meant that a true statement about the past corresponded to past reality. In its most primitive form, this old realist theory—incessantly attacked and always in retreat but never entirely defeated—was known as the correspondence theory. For the West, Bernard Williams has traced the idea of an objective conception of the past back to Thucidydes.[72] Along with this scientific notion, two other powerful conceptions linked historical truth not to past reality, but to its observers. The notion of *moral truth* made truth dependent on the intention of its observers: a true statement about the past was a statement made by trustworthy persons. Truth did not reflect what *had* happened, but what *ought* to have happened according to the insights of these honest persons.[73] Still another notion, that of *orthodox truth*, made truth dependent on the status of the speaker. It was associated with authority and, therefore, with tradition. According to this conception, a true statement about the past was an old and authoritative statement. The example rather than the original set the tone.[74] Whenever moral and orthodox truth prevailed, imitation and quotation of past masters, acknowledged or not, were not only inevitable but also desirable; these were signs of respect instead of disrespect.[75] Both truth conceptions often encouraged authors to write anonymously or pseudonymously. And in this context of highly valued tradition, the wisdom of old masters was conveniently adapted (and sometimes the old masters themselves were invented) to satisfy the needs, emotions, and interests of the moment.[76] Although the three truth conceptions described above coexisted over centuries and cultures (and still do), the relative strength of moral and orthodox truth, that is, of nonscientific truth conceptions, was greater then than now.

The second aspect, the slow development of the historical-critical method necessary for unmasking and proving abuse, has been studied by Herbert Butterfield. Historians, he maintained, have always been acutely aware of the fact that people, including source producers and storytellers, make mistakes or are capable of being dishonest. This, however, did not prevent historical criticism from evolving unusually slowly and with great fragility into the sophisticated method we know today. For centuries, human beings did not see clearly how they might correct untrustworthy history or reconstruct forgotten history. The analytic achievements of the seventeenth century or the hesitant transition of history into a recognized form of scholarship in the nineteenth century eventually led to the necessary level of training, technical insight, and bias control.[77]

Third, nonscientific or instrumental motives for writing history were welcomed with less reservation than today. For example, tolerance of esthetic motives such as embellishing historical narrative with semifictitious speeches was generally high.[78] In particular, the view that history was philosophy by example and constituted a large storehouse of moral lessons had huge appeal and received an unreserved welcome unthinkable today.

Fourth, the individual, authentic, and original character of author-ship received very uneven appreciation over time. Such appreciation was, for example, greater during the Hellenistic period than in the western middle ages, especially during the so-called golden era of forgery, the eleventh and twelfth centuries.[79] Indeed, during these two centuries, the shift from oral to written testimony brought about a situ-ation of restricted literacy (the term is Jack Goody's). At the same time, nagging uncertainty persisted about entitlements formerly based on oral testimony. This often provoked a need to commit forgeries.[80] In contrast to oral forgeries, however, forgeries that were written down and printed tended to become permanent.[81] More generally, the rise of written communication is associated with precision and coherence that are more easily verified than they are in oral discourse.[82] David Hume, for example, said that printed books obliged historians to be more careful in avoiding contradictions and incongruities.[83] Therefore, the staggering increase in written documentation in the centuries after the advent of printing, with its unprecedented circulation ranging across borders, gradually changed the perception of the individuality of authors and sharpened criteria for determining their authenticity and originality. Bernard Williams located the breakthrough of the notion of personal authenticity in the eighteenth century.[84]

What, then, changed around 1800? Several converging developments in the wake of the scientific revolution of the seventeenth century and the Enlightenment of the eighteenth century made the scholarly aspect of the four variables we are considering (truth conceptions, historical method, motives, and authorship) definitively more prom-inent. Around 1700, the modern footnote, perceived as an acknowl-edgement of intellectual debt, had been invented.[85] More or less at the same time, at least in England, licensing of the press was abolished, the first copyright law took effect, and the terms fabrication (in the sense of falsification) and plagiarism made their appearance.[86] In the early eighteenth century, the *systematic* use of evidence, especially nonliterary evidence—formerly mainly an activity of antiquarians and erudites—became accepted practice among historians.[87] Concom-itantly, the standards of historical criticism gradually reached a more refined level. In the nineteenth century, history became more scientific through its greater emphasis on authentic sources. The parallel pro-cesses of professionalization and institutionalization compelled his-torians to think more deeply about good and bad history—and about their practitioners inside and outside the craft and academe.[88] Another important milestone was the adoption of the *Berne Convention for the Protection of Literary and Artistic Works* in 1886. It carried an important clause about the moral right of authors as part of their copyright. In its last revision (1979), the principle stated:

> Independently of the author's economic rights, and even after the transfer of the said rights, the author shall have the right to claim authorship of the work and to object to any distortion, mutilation or other modification of, or other derogatory action in relation to, the said work, which would be prejudicial to his honor or reputation.[89]

Today, copyright protection is seen as an incentive for intellectual creativity. Much attention is given to the balance between authorial rights and the public interest in education, research, and access to information.[90]

The Thesis of the Modern Demarcation

From this overview of constants and variables, it can be inferred that the distinction between the use and abuse of history is not a modern one, but an ancient one, and, at the same time, that it changed radically over time. This is a poor conclusion that needs further testing against our theory and its four levels: definition, evidence, explanation, and evaluation.

The *awareness* of abuses and the will to call them wrongs (the level of *definition*) were present of old, but the concept of malicious intention so crucial in our definition was interpreted less strictly in various earlier epochs, mainly because nonscientific truth conceptions were stronger. In past times, this generally less strict application of the concept of deception excluded much conduct from the definition and scope of abuse. Admiration of the skilful liar, for example, seems to have been common in pre-industrial societies.[91] The eagerness to prove truth and expose abuse (*evidence*) was also an age-old characteristic; the *critical tools* to carry out these operations were, however, less developed in earlier times—and only gradually became more rigorous. At the third level (*explanation*), the role of nonscientific motives was less contested in earlier centuries. They served as a basis for condoning and excusing abuses to a degree unacceptable today. According to our rule of thumb, the risk of abuse is enhanced when scientific motives are less central. The fourth element (*evaluation*), finally, was also understood differently. Not only was much conduct excluded from the definitions of abuse at the time, also the evaluation of the remaining wrongs falling under those definitions deviated significantly from the norm of today.

The fact that present evaluations of present abuse differ considerably from past evaluations of past abuse, should make us very cautious in present evaluations of past abuses.

At all levels—definition and scope; historical method and evidence; motives and explanation; evaluation and comparison—things were done differently in the pre– and early modern past. However, because the absence of sophisticated evidential tools for centuries hampered the detection of many abuses, and because the presence of nonscientific motives is always a matter of degree of compatibility with the search for truth, the differences appear widest at the levels of definition and evaluation. Therefore, the abuse of history as defined here is a concept that can be applied appropriately to traditional and premodern times *if and only if* the different modes of definition and evaluation are weighed against each other with considerable care. Three successive major shifts in history—the transition from memory to written and printed record; changing perceptions of truth, evidence, and authorship; and the professionalization of history—mark a watershed in defining and evaluating abuses before and after the nineteenth century. As is obvious from my hesitant chronology, however, it remains difficult to identify any single key factor between 1500 and 1800 that is most responsible for this watershed.

The Thesis of an Increase in Abuses

Part of our conclusion for the first thesis will help us to investigate the second thesis. It is open to debate whether the abuse of history is on the rise at the dawn of the twenty-first century. The thesis of an increase is buttressed by two arguments that I shall call *demography* and *technology*. According to the *argument from demography*, as the world population increases and the general level of education rises, more groups than ever before claim that they have a separate identity. These groups incorporate history to support their claims, tailoring it to their needs in the process. The result is an explosive increase of mutually incompatible, and often partially falsified, histories. In addition (and this is the *argument from technology*), the omnipresent mass media and the easy (instant, informal, cheap) and virtually global access to the Internet endow historical discussions with potentially large-scale resonance. Furthermore, current information and communication technology allows abusers, including manipulative governments, to execute their abuse anonymously, leaving few, if any, traces.[92]

Two other arguments, I shall call them *perception* and *democracy*, are two-sided: they may serve to buttress *or* to counter the thesis of an increase. What is meant by the *argument from perception?* As we revealed in the discussion about the modernity of abuse, some practices identified as abuses today were perhaps perceived as wrongs in the past, but were not defined nor evaluated as abuses at the time. What looks *prima facie* as an increase in abuses of history in recent decades, therefore, could well be nothing more than the *trompe-l'oeil* effect caused by ever stricter contemporary criteria. In contrast, due to the shortage of historical sources and to the imperfection of methods to detect abuses at the time, we are certainly also under-informed about many practices in the past that were recognized and evaluated as abuses even then. In addition, scientific truth conceptions and motives were generally less central in the past and this enhanced the risk of abuse.

The *argument from democracy* is also two-sided. The twentieth-century downfall of many dictatorships notorious for their rewriting of history resulted in the spread of democracy, and, with it, better conditions for writing and teaching history truthfully. In 2005, the United Nations asserted that at the closure of the twentieth century, and for the first time in world history, the majority of countries were democratic.[93] Democratic procedures cannot, however, ban many types of abuse—and in a paradoxical sense may even be said to enhance the likelihood of their occurrence, if not on the scale of states, then on smaller and less systematic levels. Simon Blackburn formulated this effect as follows:

> [T]here is no reason whatever to believe that by itself freedom makes for truth . . . Freedom includes the freedom to blur history and fiction, or the freedom to spiral into a climate of myth, carelessness, incompetence or active corruption. It includes the freedom to sentimentalize the past, or to demonize the others, or to bury the bodies and manipulate the record.[94]

At the same time, the democratic effect tends to encourage the early exposure of abuse. By definition, democracies favor free expression, unfettered debate, and ethical awareness, and thus the chances increase that abuse is detected and opposed early. The more democratic the political context, the less unobserved and uncriticized the abuse.[95]

After weighing the arguments (demography, technology, perception, democracy), the thesis of an overall increase of abuses seems defensible in absolute terms and undecided in relative terms. The growing numbers of producers of nonscholarly versions of history and digital technology obviously enhance the risk of abuse in absolute terms, but they do not necessarily imply that in the past there were fewer abuses in proportion to the quantity of versions of history then available. An absolute increase of abuses, then, does not imply that today humanity is more inclined to lie about its past and identity than yesterday—or the opposite.

There is, however, no reason to be confident. Therefore, the historian who formulates the academic ethic, when trying to sum up what is really at stake in cases of grave abuse of history, should remember the words of Voltaire: "Those who can make you believe absurdities, can make you commit atrocities."[96]

❀ 2

THE DICTATOR'S SECRET ARCHIVES

In December 1992, a judicial team raided a police station on the outskirts of Asunción, the capital of Paraguay. It was the first of a series of raids during which five tons of sensitive documentation were discovered and confiscated. This mass of files (700,000) was soon called the *archivo del terror*, as it appeared to belong to the nerve center from which the repression under General Alfredo Stroessner's 35-year dictatorship (1954–89) was organized. The archive contained two types of documents. One group concerned materials confiscated or stolen by the security forces: identity documents, personal correspondence, subversive political literature, or membership lists of political parties. The other group dealt with materials produced by the security forces themselves, such as surveillance reports (including photographs and transcripts of bugged telephone conversations), 8,369 files on political detainees, transcriptions of 400 statements extracted under torture, and records describing the internal administration of the repression apparatus, including personnel lists and documents of the pre–1954 years (the *archivo muerto*). In addition, records were discovered about *Operation Condor*, a secret criminal plan devised by six military governments in the Southern Cone in the 1970s and 1980s to eliminate political refugees from each other's states.[1]

When dictatorships are toppled, they leave a painful legacy of human rights abuses. A curious part of this legacy is the dictator's secret archives, with their embarrassing and incriminating content. Often they are disclosed, even if selectively, as in the Paraguayan case; sometimes they are destroyed. The intriguing question is: Why? Why are these explosive archives disclosed or, alternatively, destroyed during or after the fall of the dictatorships? And why are they created in the first place?

Definition

When speaking about "the dictator's secret archives," I follow the classification elaborated by the Spanish archivist Antonio González Quintana, who headed an international team that studied the archives of the security services of former repressive regimes. They include the archives of two broad categories of repression-related institutions: first of all, traditional parts of the governmental bureaucracy such as the armed forces, police and security bodies, civil tribunals, and the Interior, Defense, and Justice Ministries, and, second, those specifically created for repression purposes: intelligence services, paramilitary bodies, special tribunals, concentration camps, special prisons, and psychiatric centers for "re-education."[2]

The Spanish Inquisition archives (1478–1820) are frequently mentioned as the forerunner of such contemporary repression archives.[3] The tendency of dictators to keep secret records appears to be systematic and widespread despite the potential of these records to undermine the dictatorship once these records are captured by its adversaries. Contemporary repression archives are generally well documented. This comes as no surprise for the two classic cases, Nazi Germany and the former Soviet Union. In Nazi Germany, meticulous records were kept, but relatively intact sets of Gestapo records have been preserved only for Düsseldorf, Würzburg, and a few other cities. (However, sets of Gestapo case files from former East German cities are possibly to be found in Moscow.[4]) In the case of the Soviet Union, the Chief Archival Administration was under direct control of the secret police, NKVD/KGB, from 1938 to 1960. A similar situation existed in Romania, where the General Directorate of State Archives operated under direct *Securitate* control even longer, from 1948 to 1990. Furthermore, also regimes less known for their traditions of bureaucracy—the Czechoslovak Communists (1948–89), Guatemala's governments waging civil war (1960–96), Brazil's dictators (1964–85), Ethiopia's Dergue regime (1974–91), Cambodia's Khmer Rouge (1975–79), Iraq's Baathists (1963–2003), or Stroessner in Paraguay—created extensive repression archives.[5] One of the biggest secret services, the East German State Security (Stasi), had around 100,000 staff members and at least 150,000 informal collaborators. Its present archives contain six million individual files (180 kilometers of shelves).[6] The Romanian *Securitate* had 500,000 staff members and millions of informers, amounting to as much as one quarter of the population. More than a million files (12 kilometers of shelves) became accessible in 2005, but many remain in the hands of the Romanian Intelligence Service.[7]

Historical Criticism of Repression Archives

In order to judge the value of these repression archives, they should be subjected to critical external and internal scrutiny. The so-called *external* criticism verifies their coverage and completeness. Repression archives reflect the activities and the organizational structure with which dictatorial security services reacted to dangers. Not all dangers are monitored—only perceived ones. Perception depends on the systematic character of the observation, the perspicacity of the observer, and the visibility of the observed: activities endangering the regime may not be detected or not detected in time. Also, the generally prevailing atmosphere of censorship discourages the expression of opinions from the opposition. In addition, the archives do not reflect all of the perceived dangers, only those to which the security services attach sufficient importance or respond to for some reason. Finally, the selected perceived dangers do not necessarily reflect all stages of repression. Several exceptional but important moments of repression are particularly ill-suited for recording: for example, the very moment that crucial high-level decisions about repression campaigns are taken; the moment that the worst violations are being committed; and the moment of large operations, when the scale of the indiscriminate violations is so large that there is not enough time for recording them. Recording of repression typically requires stability and routine. Regarding the completeness of the archives, the question is how they have been stored, how much of them have been destroyed during or after the dictatorship, and how much is still hidden. In this context, the French historian Marc Bloch pointed to the advantages of discontinuity, when he wrote: "Contrary to what is generally believed, peaceful continuity of a social life without fever peaks is much less favorable to transmit memory. It is revolutions that break safe doors open and force ministers to flee before they found time to burn their secret notes."[8]

Even where crises favor the survival of records, it remains to be seen how accessible and reliable the available archives are. This is the domain of the so-called *internal* criticism. It differentiates between the two main types of data mentioned in the beginning. The first type consists of materials confiscated or stolen by security forces to document, if only partially, the political opposition, or more precisely, those individuals and groups perceived as opposition.[9] The second type of sources, the materials produced by the security forces themselves, raises several questions. First, how accessible are they? Are they found sorted or disordered? Were heuristic tools such as catalogs compiled and have they been saved? Second, how uniform are they? Robert Gellately, a specialist in the history of the Gestapo, tells us that the surviving Gestapo dossiers are extremely heterogeneous: "[S]ome contain only a tiny scrap of paper, while others run to many pages, complete with the transcript of interrogations, so-called confrontations between the accused and witnesses, an account of trial and punishment meted out, and even at times correspondence from the concentration camp."[10] Third, and most important, how reliable are the different subtypes of information produced by the institutions of repression? The first subtype is the telltale report. Political denunciations from citizens whose identity is mostly unknown or undisclosed give rise to the thought that many testimonies are false.[11] As Henry Kamen, a specialist in Inquisition history, reminded us, denunciations based on suspicion lead to accusations based on conjecture. Observation reports, the second subtype, elicit questions of the observer's status, interest, and language. Was the observer an agent or an informer? Was the report the result of coercion, pressure, or cooperation? Was the information paid for? Was it in the observers' interest to shield themselves or to impress their superiors with their efficiency? What does the observer's often densely coded or ideological language exactly mean? The risks of distortion or fabrication are high. Observation reports tell us as much, perhaps more, about the observers than about the observed. Internal reports, the third subtype, pose interpretation problems similar to observation reports. How reliable, for example, are reports *about* telltales? Confessions by prisoners, whether handwritten or not, or signed or not, constitute a fourth subtype. Are they spontaneous, extorted, or entirely concocted? Torture reports are a special category of this subtype and their availability is widely divergent. According to Kamen, Inquisition records give us *verbatim* reports of torture, while Gellately signals that there is no mention of torture or even of the officially condoned "intensified interrogation" in the Gestapo records.[12] A fifth, equally explosive, subtype is personnel lists. Who was an effective member of the secret service and who a potential member? Equally important, who *knowingly* collaborated with it? All these questions will allow us to make a judgment about the informative value and reliability of the repression archives.

The Value of Repression Archives

As incomplete, chaotic, and corrupt sets of sources, repression archives are utterly ambiguous, but are also utterly fascinating. The archives, however corrupt, can be considered as historical sources in their own right and they deserve to be preserved. They inform us less about the persons they treat than about the persons that create them. This means that, when perceived as evidence, they will be useful for a general historical analysis of the dictatorial regime. An accurate history of the dictatorship and the opposition against it requires, however, that they are supplemented with other sources: archives collected by national and international human rights groups during the dictatorial regime,

TABLE 2.1. *Rationales for Creating, Destroying, Accessing, and Disclosing Secret Repression Archives*

During the dictatorship		
Creation and secrecy	*Destruction*	*Disclosure*
		Opposition to dictatorial regime:
	Members of dictatorial regime:	
1. Obtain information on opposition outside and inside the regime.	6. Remove evidence of abuses and their perpetrators.	8. Provide evidence of abuses and their perpetrators.
2. Provide infrastructure for the security system.	7. Remove evidence of command chains and of repression and surveillance mechanisms.	9. Provide evidence of command chains and of repression and surveillance mechanisms.
3. Support ideology of just war.		
4. Exert control over collaborators.		
5. *Repression personnel:* Prove obedience and zeal.		

After the dictatorship		
Preservation without access (nondisclosure)	*Destruction*	*Preservation with degrees of access and disclosure*
	Members of old or new regime:	
10. Hide incriminating evidence to ensure impunity.	17. Destroy incriminating evidence to ensure impunity.	
	Members of new regime:	
11. Hide information contradicting new official view of history *(see 18)*.	18. Support ideology depreciating remnants of old regime *(see 11)*.	21. Pursue *political* interest: intrigues and leaks *(see 15)*.
	Transitional society:	
12. Avoid risk of abuse of *memory* (reopening old wounds).	19. Safeguard reputations *(see 16)*.	22. Pursue *moral* interest of former victims and their relatives (right to the truth).
13. Avoid risk of abuse of *history.*	20. Ritual cleansing after an explosion of popular rage or out of shame or fear.	23. Pursue *legal* interest of all implicated in the archives (documentation of rights, claims, charges, defense against charges).
14. Avoid risk of *legal* abuse.		
15. Avoid risk of *political* abuse: intrigues and leaks; recycling when dictatorial relapse *(see 21)*.		24. Pursue *social* interest (vetting of former collaborators).
16. Safeguard privacy *(see 19)*.		25. Pursue *cultural* interest (patrimony).
		26. Pursue *historical* interest (research).

and archives that are the product of postdictatorial criminal justice and other truth-seeking efforts (including forensic evidence from mass graves).[13] Considerable care in treating the documents is necessary if the aim is the collection of biographical details about those individuals who, according to the archives, belong to the side of collaboration or opposition. At the same time, even from the most distorted files enough truth can be squeezed to tell us something about the cast of mind of the observers—those executing the repression and their superiors—and about the fate of the victims of repression.

With this preliminary conclusion about the value of repression archives in the back of my mind, I have tried to identify rationales for the creation, destruction, access, and disclosure of secret repression archives in Table 2.1. This table is chiefly based on post-1945 data about worldwide repression archives compiled within a broader framework.[14]

Rationales 1–5

The most enigmatic question is why dictators create secret records of repression in the first place. The reasons are complex and partly contradictory. To begin with, there is the obvious need to be informed about the opposition outside and inside the regime, and about its motives, plans, and actions *(1)*. Illegal and illegitimate regimes maintained by force and continuously challenged by forces of resistance and subversion need a system of security, surveillance, and repression for their survival. This system will largely function in secret to avoid criticism and further loss of legitimacy. Secret records sustain it and make routine procedures possible *(2)*.[15] In addition, secrecy is often justified by the view these regimes have of themselves: usually they cultivate a self-portrait of an avant-garde taming chaos and fighting a just war against internal and external enemies of the state. The unshakeable conviction this "avant-garde" has of doing the right thing leads to feelings of untouchability and overestimation of the duration of her own absolute power *(3)*.

The archives, however, also serve very different ends. Given the atmosphere of distrust common under dictatorships, they are tools of control over the collaborators of the repression, who are pressured to leave traces of their actions and who are sometimes blackmailed with them *(4)*. During their daily work, military, security, and police officials for their part utilize the archives as proof of their obedience, formalism, and zeal. There is sufficient evidence that many of them—interrogators and documentation workers alike—became obsessed with the bookkeeping of death.[16] A prime example is the Holocaust archive at Bad Arolsen, Germany, which was opened to survivors and scholars in late 2006. It contained 50 million pages of information (26 kilometers of shelves) on 17.5 million people (Jews, slave laborers, political prisoners, homosexuals). The files were discovered by the Allies in dozens of concentration camps in the spring of 1945. Chief archivist Udo Jost called them the "bureaucracy of the devil." When asked why the Nazis kept all of these records, American Holocaust scholar Paul Shapiro said that they probably wanted to show that they were getting the job done *(5)*.[17]

All of this may not sufficiently explain the presence of such explosive documents as torture reports, confessions, and lists of torturers. Why are they kept? The deeper rationales for this, if they exist at all, escape systematization. Robert Conquest, specialist in the history of the Great Terror in the Soviet Union, describes how confessions, preferably handwritten (and sometimes even posthumous!), were obligatory in Stalin's prisons—as the reflection of a legalism meant to impose on everyone the acceptance as authentic of the forged confessions.[18]

In his study of the Tuol Sleng torture center in Khmer Rouge Cambodia, David Chandler reports how forced confessions of prisoners were meticulously preserved, despite the fact that their contents were kept secret, much of the material was untrue, and all of the prisoners were killed after their confession. He suggests that, in this case, a master motive was at work. The Tuol Sleng archives, he contends, provided the leaders with the raw material for a massive, yet unwritten history of the Khmer Rouge through confessions that gave detailed evidence for numerous but ineffective conspiracies planned by enemies of the regime. In addition, they testified to the Khmer Rouge's omniscience and power over their opponents, thus assuaging the fear of their leaders and appealing to the regime's need for reassurance that it was really in control. Interrogators at Tuol Sleng acted like therapists for their leaders, vindicating them by excavating the buried "memories" of their prisoners. Reading the confessions, Chandler says, takes us inside the thought processes of the regime: they provide a narrative of the leaders' evolving fears and obsessions as they centralized control.[19] These Khmer Rouge archives confirm that repression archives reflect the mind of the instigators of violence rather than the mind of their victims.

Rationales 6–9

Some examples prove, not unexpectedly, that dictators sometimes order the destruction of their secret archives during their rule, notably in times of instability. We are not dealing here with destruction as a normal feature of responsible official information policies, for reasons of insufficient space or budget, but the willful destruction of secret records for political reasons (although such destruction normally occurs under nonpolitical pretexts). South Africa is a case in point. From 1978, but particularly at the end of the apartheid era, many state records, especially on the inner workings of the security apparatus, were destroyed in an attempt to remove incriminating evidence and, in the words of the Truth and Reconciliation Commission, to "sanitize the history of oppressive rule."[20]

In a democracy, archives are the property of society; in a dictatorial system, they are an instrument used capriciously for the purposes of absolutist power. This tension only dissipates at the moment of final crisis, when it is clear for all that the dictatorship will tumble. Therefore, a classic censorship case is the archival cleansing during last minute interventions in the turmoil of the dictator's downfall. For example, in the weeks before the overthrow of the Iraqi government by the Coalition Forces led by the United States in March–April 2003, Iraqi government officials destroyed scores of documents. They also removed many sensitive documents for safekeeping.[21] Reasons for destruction are straightforward: at the individual level, the removal of the traces of abuses and their perpetrators (6), and, at system level, the removal of the traces of command and obedience chains, and of repression and surveillance operations and mechanisms (7).

Despite all measures to protect the dictator's secrets, repression archives do not seem to be immune to leaks or theft by personnel or by outsiders who illegally gain access to them. Since 1976, Dmitry Yurasov (at the age of twelve!) had been compiling a file of victims of the Stalinist repression from archival and published sources. In 1981–82 and 1985–86, he worked in several Soviet archives, secretly recording and smuggling out information about the Stalinist repression. In November 1986, his activities were discovered and he was dismissed. In September 1987, 150 notebooks and 15,000 to 20,000 index cards were confiscated from his apartment. Although frequently interrogated and harassed, he started lecturing on Stalinism all over the country after a television appearance in the autumn of 1988 (it was the era of *glasnost*), acting as a liaison officer for the Historical Enlightenment Society *Memorial*. There are other examples of secret archive copying and smuggling. Once the secret records are copied or smuggled out of the archives, they may be published abroad, either by the smugglers themselves, if they are fleeing the country, or by their contacts, if they stay. The main problem in these cases remains how to determine the authenticity of the smuggled material.

In Brazil, a team of thirty-five lawyers working with the Catholic Church secretly photocopied and microfilmed the complete records of the archives of the Supreme Military Court covering the 1964–79 dictatorship years. Duplicates were stored outside of Brazil. The copying and analysis of the materials in 1979–85 had to be done in complete secrecy, because the 1979 amnesty law deterred investigation into the truth about the repression. If caught, the lawyers would run the risk of reprisals and the archives would be in danger of destruction. The team maintained its anonymity even after the 1985 publication of its analysis, *Brasil: Nunca mais* (*Brazil: Never Again*), which became a bestseller. Another example was the 2001 publication of the *Tiananmen Papers*, which allegedly contain secret documents from the Chinese Communist Party in the period of April–June 1989 concerning the Tiananmen massacre of 4 June 1989. They were collected and smuggled abroad by Zhang Liang (a pseudonym), who said that he was a party member.[22]

A special case is the case Bloch alluded to: the seizure of archives in periods of political upheaval. In Iraq, eighteen tons of state documents, especially from the secret police, were captured by Kurdish parties in the March 1991 uprising (after the Gulf war) and shipped to the United States for safekeeping and analysis. They contain evidence of genocide against the Kurds, particularly during the 1988 Anfal campaign, and would play a key role in the trial against Saddam Hussein and his accomplices in 2006–7.[23] The examples illustrate that reasons for disclosure are the reverse of the reasons for destruction: documents are captured to provide evidence of the abuses and their perpetrators *(8)* and to provide evidence of command and obedience chains, and of repression and surveillance operations and mechanisms *(9)*.

Rationales 10–16

Once a dictatorship falls, the successor regime may reveal itself as being either democratic or dictatorial. It may be eager or reluctant to deal with the traumatic past. Part of the archives may remain in the hands of representatives of the old or new regime, who hide them for reasons that are not hard to determine. A first possibility is the silent intervention by members of the old or new regime, when they prefer (or are obliged) to hide, instead of to destroy, incriminating evidence *(10)*. In 2002–3, the South African History Archive of the University of the Witwatersrand, Johannesburg, discovered the existence of many thousands of military intelligence files that had never been sent to the Truth and Reconciliation Commission.[24] In similar ways, Guatemalan military, intelligence,

and security officials refused to turn over internal files to the Historical Clarification Commission in that country on the grounds that they
had supposedly been destroyed during the civil war (1960–96) or simply
did not exist. This claim was refuted by the discovery in July 2005 of
50 million pages of National Police files (covering a century of police
operations)—said to be the largest and most revealing collection of
"dirty war" documentation ever unearthed in Latin America.[25]

Almost every postconflict or postdictatorial regime is confronted
with the task of writing a fresh version of history. If it is animated by
democratic intentions, it will carry out this task with historical truth
at the forefront of its attention. Otherwise, the new regime will dedicate itself to remove any challenges to its rewriting of history *(11)*. The
Vietnamese who drove out the Khmer Rouge from Cambodia allowed
no exhaustive examination of Khmer Rouge records (except those
from Tuol Sleng), perhaps because these records did not reflect sufficiently the demon theory the Vietnamese sought to teach.[26] In Nasser's
Egypt, documents pertaining to the pre–1952 history of revolutions and
national movements were kept under lock and key in the presidential
palace archives because, as official historian Muhammad Anis pointed
out, "they are seething with snakes and scorpions and the authorities
do not want to have accidents."[27]

When the successor regime was engaged in a democratic transition,
for example, in Spain after 1975 or in Central and Eastern Europe after
1989, it was not so strange that, in light of the explosive and unreliable
character of so many secret archives, fierce debates about the degree
of their disclosure and accessibility took place. Every conceivable
option—complete access; restricted and conditional access; complete
sealing; and destruction—found advocates. In most cases, such debates
resulted in a compromise, usually some formula of access for selected
user groups to specific and partially censored documents.[28]

In late 1997, President Eduard Shevardnadze of Georgia categori-
cally opposed the opening of the former KGB archives by appealing to
the dangers they brought to the collective memory *(12)*. He argued that
access would lead to "a new wave of resistance, mistrust and hatred"
and would "reopen old wounds."[29] This argument should be taken seriously. In the long term, archives, with their dubious contents, might
poison the climate and, given the ever-present risk of witch-hunts, be a
catalyst for political revenge and conflict, not for reconciliation. Much
depends, of course, on who exactly appeals to memory and with what
intentions (see also Chapter 5).

Others doubted the historical accuracy of the archives' contents and
found their files incomplete, unsorted, and corrupt *(13)*. Former Czech

President Vaclav Havel and Polish historian and journalist Adam Michnik often emphasized this point.[30] Still others, like political philosopher Bruce Ackerman, questioned the evidential value of illegally seized sources *(14)*. He pleaded not to admit this evidence at trials because the dictatorial apparatus had captured it in violation of constitutional guarantees of privacy and dignity of the victims of the secret services.[31] Writing on East Germany, he also pointed to the risk of political operations whereby reputations were damaged or incriminatory material was leaked to the press, leading to the risk of trial by newspaper *(15)*. "In my moral calculus," Ackerman wrote, "the risk of damaging living reputations outweighs whatever insights the future may gain in an encounter with the Stasi's version of the historical facts."[32] If the leak was traced, it sometimes appeared that poorly paid archivists or other secret security personnel sold the records, or that personnel from the old regime—still in service due to limited means—corrupted the files.[33] Before the Stasi files were officially opened in Germany, there existed a black market for files stolen by former Stasi agents and for those provided by the KGB (which had copies of many of them).[34] Sometimes, representatives of the new regime blackmailing the opposition, or alternatively, key members of the *ancien régime,* were behind the maneuver.

Another political risk occurs if repression archives are recycled when society relapses into dictatorship. After the Bolshevik Revolution of 1917, the newly established special services recycled many of the archives of the tsarist political police *Okhrana*. And in what was called *Operation Spider,* Czechoslovak Communist officials in the 1950s ordered their secret police to assemble lists of Czech and Slovak Jews in order to put pressure on them: the lists were partly based on registers dating from the Nazi occupation.[35] The recycle risk covers three rather different situations: either the archives are reused by the successor regime (as in the examples above), or they are in the possession of the successor regime but recaptured by those staging a coup (to which could belong representatives of the old regime), or they are never discovered in the first place because members of the old regime keep them hidden while biding their time. This last possibility was the very reason why the *archivo del terror* still existed for almost four years after Stroessner's downfall in Paraguay: the old guard expected to return to power.[36]

Finally, privacy is another strong rationale for nondisclosure *(16)*. In July 2001, a Berlin judge decided that the Gauck Authority (managing the former Stasi archives) could not make public 2,500 pages of tapped telephone conversations by former Chancellor (and historian) Helmut Kohl for reasons of privacy. The conversations concerned Kohl's reportedly illegal activities as president of the political party Christian Democratic Union. The decision was confirmed on appeal in March 2002. In March

2005, some of the Kohl files were released but these did not include information gathered from illegal wiretaps.[37] The Holocaust archive in Bad Arolsen, already mentioned, was opened to survivors and scholars in 2006—more than sixty years after it was established—because the German authorities for decades kept it closed for reasons of privacy: it reportedly contains sensitive information such as who was subjected to cruel medical experiments, who were thought to be homosexual, and which Jews allegedly collaborated with the Nazis.[38]

The risk of disclosing privacy-invading information entails questions about its preservation and accessibility. An illustration of the first question, about preservation, comes from the European Court of Human Rights in a case assigned "importance level 1."[39] In 2000, the court ruled that the right to privacy of a Romanian applicant was violated by information held on him in secret archives. It said that the Romanian law had not made sufficiently clear under which conditions the Romanian Intelligence Service could store and use a file containing personal information on Aurel Rotaru, born in 1921. The law did not place limits on the age of information held or the length of time for which it could be kept. Since 1993, Rotaru had claimed that parts of the information stored was false and defamatory (namely his supposed membership in 1937, when he was barely sixteen, of an extreme-right student movement), and he requested that the file be destroyed or amended. Romanian courts had confirmed the falsity of Rotaru's extreme-right past in 1994 and 1997, but did not order destruction or amendment of the file because they saw the Romanian Intelligence Service as a mere depository of the *Securitate* archives. Moreover, the judgments of these national courts were not added to the file. In a joint concurring opinion, seven judges of the European Court stated the following:

> [D]ata collected under a previous regime in an unlawful and arbitrary way, concerning the activities of a boy and a student, going back more than fifty years and in one case sixty-three years, some of the information being demonstrably false, continued to be kept on file without adequate and effective safeguards against abuse. It is not for this Court to say whether this information should be destroyed or whether comprehensive rights of access and rectification should be guaranteed . . . But it is hard to see what legitimate concern of national security could justify the continued storing of such information in these circumstances . . . [T]here was no legitimate aim for continuing an abusive system of secret files.[40]

Recently, the European Court of Human Rights also illustrated the second question (accessibility). In February 2006, in *Turek versus Slovakia*, it ruled against Slovakia because Ivan Turek, accused of having been a collaborator of the former State Security Agency StB, could not access a secret guideline that was used for the accusation. The court said that the denial of access to the classified information violated Turek's privacy.[41]

Rationales 17–20

Reasons for destruction are partly identical to reasons for nondisclosure. Ackerman, for example, would prefer the repression archives to be burned and, if that option was excluded, to be sealed. He offered the same set of arguments for both. As he put it succinctly: "The secret police should not be allowed to rule liberal revolutionaries from the grave."[42] Many rationales for nondisclosure are valid for destruction as well, but the latter disposes of an additional array of motives. Destruction is the only secure way for representatives of the old or the new regime to remove unique pieces of embarrassing information and thus prevent future blackmail or leaks (17). During the transition period from apartheid to democracy in South Africa in 1990–94, the deliberate destruction of secret archives occurred systematically and massively. In June 1993, the transitional cabinet even explicitly sanctioned the destruction. According to the Truth and Reconciliation Commission, it was designed "to deny a new government access to apartheid secrets through a systematic purging of official memory." In mid-1993, archivist Verne Harris disclosed the destruction to the press. Lawyers for Human Rights challenged the governmental authorization in the Supreme Court. A September 1993 agreement between all parties involved was later violated. In defiance of two government moratoria, the National Intelligence Agency destroyed scores of records in as late as November 1996.[43] While the interest of the old guard in destruction is rather obvious, members of the new regime may have participated in the old regime or committed abuses during the takeover itself and thus they may be keen to remove any incriminating traces.

The new elite's ideology is often markedly different from the old one, or at least it pretends to be so, even when that new regime displays dictatorial traits itself (18). Normally, the historical perception of the abolished, often demonized, regime by a new dictatorship oscillates between indifference, rejection, and hate, and its remnants are depreciated. Such reactions are sometimes found where Islamic regimes (Khomeini's Iran, ul-Haq's Pakistan) take over from secular ones. But by no means is it limited to this type of regime. A notorious case of archival neglect for political reasons was Nasser's authoritarian republic, which replaced the Egyptian monarchy. Nationalist archive custodians regarded pre–1952 history as a long period of foreign domination, the sources of which were allowed to perish.[44] Likewise, under Equatorial Guinea's first president, Francisco Macías Nguema, school textbooks of the colonial period and large parts of the national archive were branded as "imperialist" and publicly burned.[45]

A powerful motive for destruction in transitional democracies is the interest in saving reputations, because like privacy (16), reputation is a universal human right (19). This motive, however, is not unproblematic (see Chapter 3). In Greece, for example, the documents of repressive bodies operating under the junta of the colonels (1967–74) were used afterward as evidence for vetting those responsible for the repression. Once the vetting operation was finished, the documents were destroyed: it was judged undesirable to keep references, in registries and public archives, relating to people who had been vindicated concerning "illegal" activities under the previous regime.[46] This was not the only time that such a view prevailed in Greece. On 29 August 1989, the fortieth anniversary of the official end of the civil war (1946–49) was celebrated by burning all of the police files from the postwar period (16 million files). Greek historians denounced this as an act of historical vandalism.[47] Although it draws a line under the past, this drastic solution obviously imposes a burden of frustration upon the future (as we shall soon see).

The last motive belongs to the realm of collective action. When the liberated masses feel the winds of change, their actions become unpredictable. Collective rage or shame about the past repression and fear aroused by the possibility of recycling the archives may lead to ritual cleansing (20).[48] A famous example was the occupation, in January 1990, of the Stasi archives, seen as a hated symbol of East German repression. In the Dominican Republic, after the assassination of Rafael Trujillo in 1961 ended a 31-year-old dictatorship, records were burned to "cleanse the country of all traces of the hated tyrant."[49] During Saddam Hussein's downfall in Iraq in 2003, occupying troops sometimes failed to protect security archives from random looting and destruction, despite the fact that these archives contained the key to identify by name tens of thousands of former security agents and informers. Countless other records were destroyed as a result of the wartime aerial bombing campaign. An unknown number of documents were offered for sale. The illegal appropriation of these archives by unknown nongovernmental parties enhanced the risk that these files would be abused to incite to retaliatory violence and vengeance killings. Nevertheless, millions of documents remained intact as sources of information about the practices of the Saddam Hussein government and would serve, together with witness testimonies and the forensic evidence from 259 mass graves, as the basis for prosecuting former Baathist officials.[50]

Rationales 21–26

Rationale *(21)*, political intrigue, is the mirror of rationale 15. Disclosure of authentic or forged evidence of complicity in the repressive structure is often a form of blackmail. The most notorious example was perhaps the *noc teczec* (night of the long files) in Poland. In December 1991, former dissident and historian Antoni Macierewicz became interior minister in the cabinet of Premier Jan Olszewski and in June 1992, he sent to the *Sejm* (parliament) a list with 64 names of politicians and officials—including the prime minister's most important political adversaries, such as then-President Lech Wałesa—suspected of having been agents of the security police during the period of 1945–90. The list was drawn up on the basis of secret police files. In the controversy that followed, the cabinet fell (partly due to other factors too), and Macierewicz was expelled from the political party ZChN. In July 1992, a *Sejm* committee investigating the list concluded that only six of the 64 persons had signed any agreement to collaborate. It accused Macierewicz of actions that could have led to the destabilization of the state. In September 1993, he was charged with publishing state secrets. Twelve years later, Macierewicz was in charge of restructuring the military intelligence under the new Kaczynski government.[51] Shortly before this government came to power, in January 2005, a new file scandal exploded. Unknown persons leaked an alphabetical list of 240,000 people kept on file by the former Communist-era secret service UB and in the possession of the state-run Institute of National Remembrance, Warsaw, onto the Internet. The (highly unreliable) list included names of both former agents, informers, and employees of the secret service and their victims, but did not identify who belonged to which category. The leak was traced back to Bronisław Wildstein. This journalist reportedly gained access to the names legally—available to historians, journalists, and others cleared for access to the institute—and admitted copying the list from the institute archives to distribute it to some of his colleagues. He was dismissed from his paper *Rzeczpospolita,* although he denied having posted the list on the Internet.[52]

Other transitional societies abounded with similar scandals. For example, in March 2003, a list identifying 75,000 spies and informers who had denounced friends and neighbors to the Czechoslovak Communist regime was posted on the website of the Czech Ministry of Interior and was also made available in print. The list revealed that approximately 1 in every 130 Czechs had worked with the secret police.[53] Presidents, premiers, and foreign ministers of several Central and Eastern European countries were accused, often unjustly, of collaboration with the secret police.[54] Again, Poland is a good example. In January 1996, Prime Minister Józef Oleksy resigned after he had been accused of spying for the KGB since 1983. Three months later, however, prosecutors dropped the charges after they had established that the evidence was flawed and insufficient. Oleksy accused former President Wałesa of having concocted the charges. In January 2005, however, Oleksy resigned again, this time as chairman of the *Sejm*, after he admitted that he had not reported, as was obligatory for those in public office, that in the 1970s he had collaborated with a special military unit. And in 2000, the *International Herald Tribune* wrote that, in the early 1980s, the secret police had formed a special team, including professional forgers, to doctor documents so as to be able to discredit then-Solidarity leader Wałesa as a secret police agent. Aleksander Kwaśniewski, president between 1995 and 2005, was similarly cleared.[55]

Other rationales for access and disclosure were more related to the democratic calibre of society. Most of them apply as criteria in any archival access policy, but they figure poignantly in times of transition to a democratic society. Ruti Teitel remarked that "opening the *ancien régime's* files offers an appealing symbol of the open society," but she also described the classical friction between privacy and freedom of information in such an open society—two fundamental rights so notoriously absent under the old regime.[56] There exists, first, a considerable moral interest of former victims of surveillance or repression to know the truth *(22)*. By 2006, for example, there had been two million requests from individuals for access to the Stasi files.[57] Victims and relatives are entitled to know the answer to such questions as: Who spied on me? Who tortured me? What is in my file? Can I rectify lies? Are our disappeared relatives dead or alive? If they are alive, where are they? If they are dead, how and when did it happen? Can they be (re)buried? The answers found in the archives may contribute to the reparation of injustice and facilitate the rehabilitation or mourning process (see Chapter 5).

Closely related is another rationale: the legal interest of citizens looking for evidence as the support for asserting their rights *(23)*. A telling case comes from Saddam's Iraq. During his rule, hundreds of thousands of Iraqis were internally displaced or deported. Baathist officials destroyed or confiscated documents in the possession of the victims—

including citizenship and nationality documents and the expulsion or deportation orders themselves—leaving them unable to prove their identities and property titles. For many, other government records formed their only chance to prove these titles.[58] Hence, access may be vital to exercise individual rights. The legal interest also extends to the substantiation of charges against members of the old regime and its security forces. More broadly, all of those implicated in the archives— not only the victims—may want to restore their reputations.[59]

A further rationale is the social interest in screening and disqualifying those bearing responsibility for past human rights violations whenever they occupy or seek public office *(24)*. In the first four months of its existence, the Gauck authority, for example, received half a million requests for information about state employees. By 2006, there had been three million requests for background checks.[60]

Underlying rationales 25 and 26 is a last fundamental question that may be illustrated with an example from Portugal. In April 1996, a controversy took place in that country about the accessibility of the secret PIDE archives of the Salazar-Caetano epoch (1932–74) and the possible restitution of stolen letters, secret photographs, and telephone conversation recordings in these archives.[61] The question that arose was about who owned the files: the victims who had been robbed of their data or who were recorded in the files, or society at large?[62] The victim-related parts of repression archives can be perceived either as illegally confiscated private property or as an inalienable part of the national cultural patrimony and the world's documentary heritage *(25)*. Applying again the principle evoked above, the documentation in repression archives, however corrupt, can be considered as historical sources in their own right, which merit to be preserved. If restitution of these archival items to their former owners is allowed, however, this particular source value is lost. Indeed, what would prevent some individuals or groups at the receiving end from destroying, then or later, those traces of an unsavory past? Respect for private property, expressed in restitution, threatens the survival and integrity of record groups and constitutes an obstacle for their treatment as cultural property. However, combining the presence of these records in the archives with solid privacy guarantees could help solve the dilemma.

One vital reason to regard repression archives as cultural (and not individual) property to be preserved is that the questions asked by future generations will probably differ from those asked today. A generation that believes that all has been said already about the traumatic past, displays a low historical awareness. Preservation for future use points to a further rationale for disclosure: these files constitute a vital substratum for research into the history of the dictatorship and the opposition to it *(26)*. Research questions emerging sooner or later are the following: How did the repression apparatus, including its secret services and death squads, work? What were the objectives and strategies of their superiors? How were national security doctrines translated into day-to-day practice? How did the dictator take power, survive crises, and finally disappear? What was the place of the dictatorship in the international arena? Was there an opposition of significance? How strong was the resistance at different moments? With the help of repression archives (among other sources), official and private research into these questions may in the end uncover some truths, and refute at least the worst lingering lies on the repression, those that deny or falsify the dictatorial past. Remarkably, the desire not to forget the pains of the past is also visible in the highly symbolic gesture to locate former archives of repression into the very premises that were used by the repression apparatus during the dictatorship. This was done, among other countries, in Germany, Russia, Argentina, Brazil, and Mexico. Thus, spaces of repression were converted into spaces of remembrance of repression.

Conclusion

In 2005, after almost fifteen years of discussion, the former United Nations Commission on Human Rights adopted a series of principles that provided guidance for combating impunity. Some of these so-called Impunity Principles regulate the treatment of repression archives.[63] According to these principles, discussed more in depth in Chapter 5, repression archives should be preserved in order to give a people the opportunity to know the history of its oppression as a part of its heritage. Access to such archives should enable victims and their relatives to claim their rights, and enable other persons implicated in them to prepare their defense. The interest of historical research is another ground for access, subject to reasonable restrictions aimed at safeguarding the privacy and security of victims and other individuals. Access may be denied on the grounds of national security only in exceptional circumstances. All persons should be entitled to know whether their name appears in the repression archives and to challenge the validity of biographical information about them by exercising a right of reply. The challenged document should include a cross-reference to the document challenging its validity and both must be made available together whenever the former is requested. Other countries are expected to cooperate with a view of communicating or restituting relevant archives for the purpose of establishing the truth.[64] This is what the Impunity Principles prescribe.

This chapter abundantly showed that such principles are badly needed. Secret repression archives are widespread and the range of rationales for creating, destroying, accessing, or disclosing them is impressive. Two conclusions can be drawn from our analysis. First, however tempting it is to conclude that dictatorial rationales are less numerous, diverse, or complex than postdictatorial ones (confirming in passing the stereotype that dictatorships are simpler political systems than democracies), some of the former may nevertheless be hard to identify without extensive and intimate knowledge of the dictatorial system, as the reflections of Chandler for Cambodia and Conquest for the Soviet Union suggested. When repression archives become the subject of an open debate in a transitional society, they reflect not only the evidential concerns central to the moral, legal, and historical motives, but also the political, psychological, and cultural considerations of numerous decision-makers, professionals, and lobbies.

Second, a comparison of post–1945 data with those of pre–1945 repression archives from the Inquisition, NKVD, and the Gestapo allows for the hypothesis that rationales for the creation, destruction, or nondisclosure of repression archives are basically the same in different historical periods. In contrast, rationales for access and disclosure seem to be linked to a relatively recent human rights awareness, developed during the last sixty years. The International Criminal Court, established to combat the impunity of dictatorial regimes worldwide and keen on collecting evidence from various sources, including repression archives, will not alter the needs of these regimes to create their secret archives, but it may, paradoxically, induce tyrants to professionalize their strategies for keeping and destroying sources.

After the fall of dictatorships, secret repression archives become invaluable historical sources and this makes imperative their preservation in safe conditions. The manipulations to which almost all of them were subjected constitute a warning: professional archivists should develop sound safety standards for their preservation, access, and disclosure. To regulate access to individual records, the protection of former victims and their relatives should be the governing criterion. Considerations of privacy and reputation for all persons who are the subject of these records and for those who created them should be duly balanced against the public interest in disclosing them. The analysis of groups of records should be taken care of by experts. *Archivos del terror* are crucial for historical research, because they may yield answers to tantalizing questions about life and death.

Afterword: The Special Relationship
Between Democracy and Historiography

Long ago, Bertram Wolfe described the relationship between dictatorship and historiography as follows: "Shall the Dictator . . . be less harsh
with facts and records than with men? Should he be more tender with
the traditions and men of other lands and other times than he is with
the men of his own land and time?"[65] A dictatorship needs historiography as a source of legitimation. During this legitimation process, history is frequently abused. The relationship between democracy and
historiography is very different. Let us look more closely into what is
surely a *special* relationship.

The first observation is that democracy and historiography have
common determinants. Both are fostered by a culture of human rights,
in particular by the freedom of opinion and expression. That freedom
is a cornerstone of both democracy and the search for, and transmission of, the historical truth.[66] In the *Universal Declaration on Democracy*,
perhaps the most authoritative text on democracy, the interconnected-
ness between democracy and human rights is so pervasive that a democratic society is virtually co-equal with a society that recognizes and
respects human rights.[67]

The second observation is that democracy and historiography are
each other's conditions.[68] Democracy is necessary (though not sufficient) for historiography. Strictly speaking, the condition is "quasi-necessary," because historians can exercise their duty under a dictatorship,
albeit under far less favorable circumstances. Democratic principles
of transparency and accountability enable historians to claim access
to official archival information and to organize autonomously their
investigation and education. These two principles also encourage citizens to claim the right to memory (the right to mourn and commemorate) and the right to history (the right to know the truth about past
human rights abuses). Indeed, a democratic regime—strengthened by
the right to culture and science mentioned in article 27 of the *Universal
Declaration of Human Rights*—does not in principle restrain the search
for historical facts nor for the supporting evidence thereof. Equally, a
democracy does not limit the range of opinions about these historical facts nor the public and critical scrutiny of these opinions in an
open debate. This evidence-based search for facts and open discussion
of opinions is exactly what is lacking in a dictatorship. In a repressive system, key facts are suppressed and deviating historical versions marginalized or censored—sometimes with amazing accuracy.
Dictatorships abuse, and therefore harm, historiography. And even if

democracy cannot ban the abuse of history and the harm it inflicts, even if democratic freedoms offer possibilities for abuses, its climate increases the chances that abuses are disclosed and opposed early, thus making unlikely the transformation of abuse into a large-scale phenomenon (see Chapter 1).

Conversely, a sound historiography, either seen as a form of scholarship or as a profession, *reflects* a democratic society. Sound historical *scholarship* constitutes a practical demonstration of the values—freedom of expression and information, plurality of opinions, and an open and critical debate—that are central to democracy. And the same is true for the core values of the historical *profession*—autonomy and accountability. This demonstration of democratic values does not mean that each proposal to fill in the historical truth has to be given the same attention. As Bernard Williams remarked:

> [I]n institutions that are expressly dedicated to finding out the truth, such as universities, research institutes, and courts of law, speech is not at all unregulated. People cannot come in from outside, speak when they feel like it, make endless, irrelevant, or insulting interventions, and so on; they cannot invoke a right to do so, and no-one thinks that things would go better in the direction of truth if they could.[69]

Democracy in scholarship and profession means equality *and* distinction. Furthermore, a sound historiography *strengthens* a democratic society, because its result—a provisional form of tested historical truth—rejects historical myths once believed in and replaces them with more plausible historical interpretations. Even if truth-seeking is imperfect and in its daily practice it is troubled by many alien interests and needs, in essence it supports the democratic principles of transparency and accountability.[70] This is also the case for archival science: by making documents of former regimes accessible, it supports the same democratic principles. On its turn, knowledge of historical facts and their interpretation is a condition for exercising the rights to memory and history (see Chapter 5). A sound historiography, then, is a necessary (though not sufficient) condition for a *sustained* democracy.

The third observation is that the special relationship between democracy and historiography is *procedural* rather than *substantial.* It is obvious that democracy is a necessary subject of research and teaching for historians. If the goal of those historians is to promote democracy through its study as an historical subject, however, I am inclined to state several reservations. The first is that democracy can be promoted through the study of other subjects as well, such as dictatorships, because they function as a contrast to democracy, as this chapter has shown. The next reservation is that the current political system is often conveniently decreed synonymous or confused with democracy and that, in fact, democracy is not promoted, but the current system is instead. Another reservation is that if the emphasis on democracy as a subject of study is uncritical or finalistic, the goal may not be reached. The final reservation I have is that even a critical historical study of democracy does not necessarily promote it: democracy's many failures and weak performances, which will unavoidably rank among the findings of such a study, may discourage rather than encourage readers and students to embrace it. In short, the goal of historiography should *not* be the *direct* promotion of democracy—nor the *direct* promotion of human rights, peace, tolerance, or international understanding. The *direct* goal of historiography should be the methodical and critical search for historical truth (and, through this, as I shall argue in Chapter 5, the creation of conditions for the right to history and the right to memory of the general public). To the extent that this search for historical truth is carried out properly, democracy is practiced *directly* and promoted *indirectly*.

The fourth observation is that the above analysis of the special relationship between historiography and democracy may have wider implications. This is so because historiography is only one form of dealing with the past, namely, its methodical and cognitive form. I am convinced that there is a similar, even stronger, mutual relationship between democracy and the proper dealing with the past in general—and with recent and perhaps more remote past injustice in particular. Dictatorships do not deal properly with the past. Not dealing properly with the past continues past injustice; continuing past injustice denies democracy. A democracy must offer a truthful critique of past dictatorships and conflicts.[71] The risks are not small, though: revealing painful truths about the past may reopen old wounds and revive these old conflicts.[72]

Among the rights of the *Universal Declaration of Human Rights*, some are of particular importance for dealing properly with the past: equality of all citizens (articles 1–2), free expression for searching the historical truth (article 19) and education and culture to teach about it (articles 26–27), a fair trial for former perpetrators of human rights abuses (articles 5–11), and an effective remedy and reparation for their victims (article 8). Sooner or later, therefore, any democracy must deal with the recent and perhaps more remote traumas of the past, come to terms with them, incorporate them as accurately as possible into the historical account, and, if applicable, issue a public apology to make closure possible. In Chapter 5, we will discuss the duty of democratic governments to investigate past abuses as a condition to enable the right to the truth for their citizens. All present democracies, not only incipient but also stable ones, go through such processes. Again, the authentic search for historical truth and the proper dealing with the past are acts of democracy. It is democracy in practice.

✿ 3

DEFAMATION CASES AGAINST HISTORIANS

More than may be expected, historians land in the dock.[1] Among the charges leveled at them, those involving defamation constitute a separate category. Some persons think that their reputation is tarnished because they are critically portrayed in works of history and they may seek redress in court. Often, prominent people—in many countries even incumbent heads of state—are among the complainants.[2] For the scholar who wants to study the use and abuse of defamation laws against historians from a comparative perspective, collecting the scattered and incomplete relevant information is not easy. In this chapter, a worldwide survey of the phenomenon is taken nevertheless. Thereafter, I will focus in depth on a series of contemporary defamation cases in Western Europe.

Definitions and Defenses

Honor and reputation are basic human rights enshrined in the *Universal Declaration of Human Rights,* together with the right to privacy.[3] It is essential to distinguish these three rights from each other. Privacy is the right to respect for one's private life, home, and correspondence. Honor, a concept halfway between privacy and reputation, is a person's self-esteem. Reputation is the appraisal of a person by others, a person's good name or fame.[4] Defamation is usually defined as the act of damaging another's reputation ("fame"), in oral (slander) or written (libel) form. The distinction between defamation and the cognate term "insult" (a term denoting an emotion rather than a reputation) is often not clear. In practice, defamation laws are frequently applied to conflicts that concern insult.[5] In most countries, defamation is a criminal as well as a civil offense.[6]

Privacy, honor, and reputation belong to the group of so-called "personality rights." Under strict conditions, they are generally considered legitimate grounds for interfering with the right to free expression of others. Unjustified charges of defamation, let alone unjustified punishment, however, have a chilling effect on the freedom of expression and on public debate.

When they are accused of defamation, historians have different legal defenses at their disposal: we will call these defenses "truth," "due care," "fair comment," "public interest," "privilege," and "good faith."[7] Not all of the defenses can be used all of the time. This is so because statements found to be defamatory by the judge can be divided into two fields: "facts" and "opinions." This basic distinction is sometimes clouded in practice because in their place other, more or less synonymous terms, are used. Facts are also called "information," and opinions are called "thoughts," "ideas," "beliefs," "comments," "views," or "value judgments."[8] Judges perceive statements of fact very differently from statements of opinion; while facts are susceptible to a truth/falsity proof, opinions are not.

Therefore, the first and most important defense for historians charged for defamatory facts is the defense of truth, also called the defense of justification or *exceptio veritatis*. It means that historians can prove that the disputed fact is true. If the proof succeeds, it is effective because a true fact cannot, in principle, be defamatory, otherwise the reputation of the complainant would be undeserved. Hence, a true factual statement cannot constitute an attack upon reputation. It is a strong defense—if it is allowed. There are three exceptions to the defense. In some cases, judges will rule that a proven true fact was defamatory after all, for example, when it was formulated in a biased or misleading manner.[9] In others, they will maintain that the facts are too old for their truth-value to be of any relevance—many of these cases are of interest to historians. And finally, the truth defense is far less effective in privacy cases than in defamation cases because true revelations about someone's private life may still be invasions of privacy. As Frederick Schauer notes:

> Information that interests the public is not necessarily information whose dissemination is in the public interest . . . It is superficial to say that all knowledge is necessarily valuable. Knowledge as to the affairs and past of purely private persons serves little if any public purpose. Moreover, disclosure of private facts, in addition to causing embarrassment and humiliation, infringes on the individual's interest in controlling certain aspects of his life . . . [I]t is hard to see why truth *per se* entails an unrestricted right to speak.[10]

If historians made an untrue factual statement that is allegedly defamatory, they have another defense at their disposal, that of reasonableness (or "prudence" or "due care"). They will maintain that even if the allegedly defamatory fact turned out to be false, it was still formulated, though erroneously, after reasonable efforts to verify its accuracy. The historians will make it clear that they did not know that the fact was false and that they showed no reckless disregard as to whether the fact was true. This is a good, but less strong and less effective, defense. Indeed, judges will deal impatiently with the ignorance and mistakes of historians, because as scholars the latter have a duty to be accurate and to check thoroughly their factual statements. Historians have sometimes invoked another defense (with little success), the defense that they were not historians but "text specialists," "journalists," "writers," or the like, in an attempt to circumvent any duties of scholarship demanded from them by the judge.[11]

Opinions are not susceptible to a truth/falsity proof. Demanding a truth proof for opinions uttered by historians is seen as a requirement impossible of fulfillment.[12] Judges maintain that opinions are expressions of pluralism crucial for a democratic society. Therefore, opinions enjoy greater protection than statements of fact: facts should be as accurate as possible, opinions may vary widely. This does not mean that determining whether a statement is one of fact or of opinion is always easy, the distinction will often depend on the context. Nor does it mean that historians are allowed to make unfounded speculations. On the contrary, their opinions should have sufficient factual basis. If these opinions are nevertheless disputed, historians can invoke a defense of fair comment. They will then say that the opinion was formulated as an honest contribution to a public debate about matters of general interest in the historical sphere.

There are other defenses that can be invoked for either statements of facts or opinions. The first is public interest (close to the "fair comment" defense). On this view, historians maintain that it was their duty to inform public opinion about a certain case and that it was the public's right to be informed about it. The second defense, intimately connected with the idea of public interest, is the defense of privilege for those cases in which a defaming statement has to be reiterated. Literal repetition of allegedly defamatory words of others with the aim of serving the public interest enjoys various degrees of protection according to the context in which the repetition took place (parliamentary or judicial proceedings, press reports, or a chapter such as the present one). The last defense, and the most important of all, is good faith. Historians then typically say that they did not formulate their facts maliciously or recklessly; that they honestly believed that the facts proven to be untrue were true; that they took due care; that they made every effort to verify the truth of their facts; that their opinions constituted fair comment; and that their statements were uttered without animosity or a desire to harm, but really for the sake of public interest. In short, whatever the historians' defense, it will succeed only if the judge is convinced that their statements were made with integrity.[13]

Is *prescription*—the passage of time—a defense for historians? There is always a time lapse between a defamatory statement and the complaint about it. This time lapse may lead to prescription when a defamatory statement is not followed promptly enough by a complaint (a maximum term of one year has been recommended). A late complaint may raise the question of whether the reputation was really harmed. Such a complaint, if allowed to be converted into a formal charge, may complicate a defense when, in the meantime, evidence had been lost or witnesses' memories had become unreliable. In addition, the possibility that a lawsuit can be initiated at any time discourages the historical discussion.

Another aspect is the time lapse between historical events and the defamatory statement that refers to them. When historians invoke the public interest defense, judges must decide whether the controversial historical events still constitute matters of public interest. In the pioneering case *Lehideux & Isorni versus France* of 1998, the judges of the European Court of Human Rights have argued that the passage of time *should* be taken into account in weighing statements about history:

> The Court . . . notes that the events referred to in the publication in issue had occurred more than forty years before. Even though remarks like those the applicants (Lehideux and Isorni, *adb*) made are always likely to reopen the controversy and bring back memories of past sufferings, the lapse of time makes it inappropriate to deal with such remarks, forty years on, with the same severity as ten or twenty years previously. That forms part of the efforts that every country must make to debate its own history openly and dispassionately.[14]

This case was not a defamation case, but the conception of the judges has since played a role in defamation cases as well. Both types of time lapse—between event and statement and between statement and complaint—can certainly give rise to a defense of prescription.

A Worldwide Survey

In November 2000, the Special Rapporteurs on Free Expression of the United Nations, the Organization for Security and Cooperation in Europe, and the Organization of American States issued a joint declaration in which they denounced the abuse of restrictive defamation laws as a major threat to the freedom of expression and added that it had reached crisis proportions in many parts of the world.[15] They also endorsed a July 2000 document, published with UNESCO's support, by the organization Article 19 (Global Campaign for Free Expression), *Defining Defamation: Principles on Freedom of Expression and Protection of Reputation.* This document contains ten principles that function as international guidelines on defamation laws. For historians, the most revealing of these principles is the second, labeled "Legitimate Purpose of Defamation Laws." It holds that only individuals and entities with the right to sue and be sued have reputations and it argues that the harm from an attack on reputation is direct and personal in nature. Consequently, Article 19 identifies three improper uses of defamation laws. First, the reputation of the state or nation as such—if it exists at all—should not be protected by defamation laws; second, these laws should not be used to prevent legitimate criticism of officials or the exposure of official wrongdoing; third, deceased persons do not have reputations, and, therefore, cannot be defamed.

Plenty of examples illustrate the first form of improper use of defamation laws—the protection of the reputation of abstract entities. Indeed, although defamation forms a risk mainly for agency-oriented history (history with an emphasis on the motives, words, and acts of individual human actors), authors of structure-oriented history (history with an emphasis on collective actors and institutions) do not remain aloof from it. Scores of historians in former Communist countries were sued because they had defamed "the nation," "the state," "the Soviet system," "the Communist Party," or its "nationalities policy."[16] Likewise, in the Middle East and North Africa, there is a strong tendency to attack critical historians in the name of concepts such as "Islam" or "justice."[17] The more abstract the public bodies and concepts are, the more arbitrary and fanciful the charges become.

The second improper use of defamation laws is derived from the internationally accepted rule that politicians and civil servants should tolerate more, not less, criticism of their activities than private citizens and, therefore, use defamation laws with restraint or not at all. In practice, the reverse is the case. In Thailand, for example, several historians were charged with *lèse majesté* because their work criticized the monarchy.[18] Worldwide, incumbent heads of state have eagerly used the defamation instrument to repress unwelcome historical statements criticizing their reputation either directly or through comments on their past conduct or ideas. These attacks provide strong evidence for the centrality of reputation, and hence of biography, in the legitimation of power. If rulers cannot do without an acceptable ideology, they surely cannot do without an acceptable biography, that is, a biography with an unblemished reputation.[19]

Unsurprisingly, the third form of improper use—defamation of deceased persons—has been most prominent in cases of former political leaders. For centuries already, rulers have recorded their version of history to secure their posthumous fame and their successors often abide by that version.[20] The Thai legislation on *lèse-majesté*, enacted in 1959, also protects deceased monarchs. And in Turkey, a 1951 law protecting the legacy of Atatürk (modern Turkey's founder, who died in 1938) makes his memory sacrosanct.[21] In Iran, there has been a comparable law to punish insults against the memory of Imam Khomeini since 1995.[22]

There are many examples of attacks of, or on behalf of, present leaders against historians because the reputation or the memory of deceased leaders was deemed offended, *or* because the death of the deceased leader could be connected with the acts of his living successor. The relationship, positive or negative, of leaders in power with their deceased predecessors constitutes a fragile part of the former's official legitimation strategies. This is a fact regardless of whether the latter were immediate predecessors or ruled years before. From all of the leader-related cases listed in the appendices of this chapter, 48 percent (32 out of 67 cases) concern *leaders deceased more than half a century previously*.[23]

Cases of defamation of deceased persons who are not heads of state and government, if less publicized, are not absent. Contrary to Article 19's thesis, I believe that the dead do possess a reputation (see Chapter 4). In any case, judges admit that posthumous reputations as such exist. The evidence for this is considerable. First, many laws contain provisions for "protection of the memory of the dead" and against "defamation of the dead."[24] Second, a legal case, including a defamation case, always stops when defendants die, but it does not necessarily stop when complainants die. Relatives are allowed to continue the case on behalf of the deceased.[25] Third, relatives are not merely allowed to continue such a case, they may also initiate it. Many laws that regulate defamation of the dead aim also (even mainly) at protecting the surviving relatives from the loss of reputation. Fourth, posthumous reputations of genocide victims play a key role in the way judges approach and condemn Holocaust denial (see below). Fifth, the idea of posthumous reputation is a component of the idea of posthumous rehabilitation. Even after the death of a defendant unjustly convicted, the erroneous verdict can be reversed as a symbolic form of reparation. Posthumous restoration of the dignity of deceased victims of serious human rights abuses has been a powerful motive behind the establishment of the International Criminal Court in 2002 (see Chapter 4). All of these reasons show that judges recognize the existence of posthumous reputations.[26]

Even if judges recognize posthumous reputations, I concur with Article 19 that the harm inflicted on the dead is technically not the same as defamation and should preferably not be the court's concern.[27] Be that as it may, defamation does not exist without defamation charges, and defamation charges do not exist without persons who feel harmed to bring suit. Without persons who feel harmed (or their caretakers) to bring suit, careless or dishonest historians cannot be summoned to court. Thus, as judge and historian Jean-Denis Bredin has noted, while contemporary history is monitored rather closely, historians of earlier periods—or future historians of the contemporary period—enjoy broad impunity when writing about the distant past, and they do so because their subjects of study are long dead. Distant relatives and sympathizers who feel defamed by the negative portrayals of these historians are not legally empowered to defend the deceased's reputation. The law does not cope with claims of intellectual or moral harm emerging after long delays or at great distances. When historians specialized in ancient periods lie (for example, by denying certain facts about the remote past), they are morally and scientifically irresponsible, but not legally. Historians of the contemporary period are obligated to tell the truth, not only for moral and scientific reasons, but also for legal reasons. As Bredin distinctively puts this point:

> Undoubtedly, in the course of time [the harm afflicted to the heir] softens. Modern law cherishes the nuclear family and is not interested in distant heirs. Widowers or widows, children, grandchildren, they are allowed to demand before court the price for their honor or suffering when their relative has been wronged. Beyond this, it is doubtful that the heir captures the judge's attention. Collateral distance, the passing of time, and the notoriety of persons or events make his intervention unlikely. Twentieth-century history should be on its guard against the law. The history of the French Revolution is almost without risk. Medieval history opens very quiet horizons. There comes a time when graves are no longer adorned with flowers, when the dead seem really dead. Then the law leaves the historian alone.[28]

So, as a rule, the judge only considers cases brought by close relatives of the recent dead. *As a rule,* because famous people, particularly politicians, as we saw, form an exception to that rule rather often. Judges do not pronounce opinions about whether posthumous reputations fade or last. They do maintain, however, that the need to judicialize conflicts over them gradually extinguishes, in other words, that offending remarks or embarrassing facts about the dead should not be challenged in court for all eternity.

Defamation Cases in Western Europe

In order to study more closely allegedly defamatory statements by historians and the abuse of defamation laws, I shall now focus on a series of 22 cases from nine Western European countries with comparable political and legal regimes, where information is sufficiently available and reliable. The cases involve charges against historians or others who, between 1965 and 2000, made a historical statement considered defamatory by a complaining party. They are listed in Appendix 3.1.

Some preliminary questions of method are noteworthy. The data, extracted from court judgments and other original documents, press articles, and commentaries on the cases, were collected within the context of broader research into the censorship of history (of which the instrument of the defamation suit is often but a form) in the period 1945–2007.[29] Although this broader research was worldwide and systematic, and included, in principle, all of the important lawsuits against historians, it has lacunae, and therefore the selection of countries and the number of cases for each country represented here are partly the result of documentary coincidence. Furthermore, I did not investigate situations where persons who felt offended, *threatened*, orally or by letter, to sue. Plenty of traces of such threats were found, so many even that it is safe to suppose that these tactics have a much higher frequency than the costly and time-consuming trials themselves. Threats alone often suffice to instill self-censorship in historians or to make them retract earlier, plausibly argued statements. They constitute cheaper (and smarter) tactics than lawsuits that are surrounded by publicity about the tarnished reputation, whose effect on public opinion is uncertain, and whose outcome is not necessarily favorable to the complainant. In the third place, trials, for which doubts persisted as to whether they were about defamation, were not included in the sample. On the other hand, I will occasionally refer to cases outside the sample.[30] Finally, one should note that because it is my aim to view defamation from the perspective of Article 19's principles, I shall not discuss the veracity of the historians' allegations so as not to be diverted by the historical controversies themselves.

Profile of Complainants and Defendants

A Council of Europe study showed that defamation was a criminal offense in most of its member states, although many did not apply any criminal sanctions.[31] Therefore, I will use the terms "complainants" and "defendants," which are common in criminal law.

Many complainants were relatively old. This means that, except in cases where factors such as fame and power (and, perhaps, an education emphasizing strongly the individuality of the person) are clearly involved, the importance of reputations grows with age: the older the person, the more sensitive he or she is to the loss of reputation. Part of the explanation is obvious: older persons have longer careers than younger persons. Older persons are targets of attacks more often and they have more to lose. In addition, less time is left to them to repair any reputation damage. Moreover, when complainants are retired, they usually have more time to spot, and react to, statements made about them and they often have more money and patience to sue. They may also feel more acutely the need to come to terms with their past and to make up the balance. Consequently, they may be driven by the fear that letting pass an attack on one episode of their life casts doubt on all episodes, hence their entire reputation, or allows others to repeat the attack left undisputed. In order to prepare a fitting posthumous legacy, they may be anxious to protect their posthumous reputation and fight, while they still can, the prospect that it will be tarnished. Perhaps in so doing, they also want to leave clear indications for their heirs about how to act in the case of posthumous attacks. In one of the 22 cases, the complainants even used their advanced age as an argument for requesting summary proceedings.[32]

Apart from age, other noteworthy elements in the complainants' profiles were the following: one American complainant asked a local sympathizer to sue on his behalf in Belgium;[33] one complainant sued the same defendant in two succeeding cases;[34] another was suing after he himself was convicted of crimes against humanity the same year.[35] Although there were only three cases in which not individuals but groups openly sued a historian,[36] to conclude from this that few groups assumed the role of complainant might be misleading. Some cases initiated by individuals illustrate that these were supported by pressure groups (such as veterans), not least to cover litigation costs.[37] In these circumstances, two options were available: either persons who felt insulted sought solidarity and support from organizations of which they were members, or the organizations themselves felt attacked and appointed a spokesperson who only formally operated in his or her own name.

Switching to the defendants' profiles, 16 out of 21 defendants were full-time or part-time professional historians,[38] while the rest save one had an academic profession or were writers. In the remaining case, the defendant was an institute. As may be expected in cases about history, the defendants were generally younger than the complainants. They often did not take part in the events they described—and although this is beneficial for the necessary scholarly distance, the complainants frequently used this argument against them. Rather often, publishers and employers of the historians were also sued.[39] Among the defendants were three historians not living in the suing country: an Israeli historian was sued in France because his protagonist was French; an American historian was sued in Italy because he had written about the Pope, and an another American historian was sued in Great Britain, a country notorious for its severe defamation laws.[40] One further defendant was sued in two cases with different complainants.[41] Like some of the complainants, some defendants were also supported by associations (obviously made up of historians, in this case) or special interest groups.

It is difficult to assess whether the reputation of the historians played a role in eliciting complaints. The sample of twenty-two cases seems to confirm this possibility, the universe of 160 cases is far less outspoken. Famous and less famous historians are vulnerable in different ways. Famous historians are more visible and therefore more exposed to complaints. It should be noted, however, that some gained their fame, or part of it, precisely because of the (often protracted) defamation trials. Moreover, cases of famous historians tend to be more documented and therefore a documentary bias may have influenced sampling. There is also a tendency in the other direction: lesser-known historians are less protected—in terms of access to media or support of colleagues, for example—and may become targets of complaints for that reason.

Let us now look at Article 19's preoccupations. The sample does not contain examples of trials in the name of abstract entities, such as the nation or the state. Complainants can be divided into two groups: those who sued on their own behalf and those who sued on behalf of others. Among those who felt personally offended, three subcategories are distinguishable: politicians, veterans, and Holocaust deniers. The sample contains some politicians, but not a large number. Except for one case,[42] it does not include heads of state or government, as elsewhere in the world. War veterans are remarkably well represented. Here, we clearly see that they constitute an ambivalent group: they are interesting sources for historians and therefore their natural allies, but, at the same time, as participants or witnesses, some veterans are understandably so emotionally involved in the subject (the waging of war and the defense of freedom) that they may turn into potential adversaries when historians do not (entirely) share their viewpoint. A special type of complainants is the Holocaust deniers, represented by three cases that took place between 1990 and 2000.[43] By suing, deniers double their attacks on *bona fide* historical research: defending defamatory and false views is the first attack, threatening those who expose them, the second.

There are also complainants who sue on behalf of others. In at least five cases, the persons insulted were deceased.[44] In four out of five instances, the case was taken care of by relatives. In the remaining case, two organizations defended the allegedly offended honor of the deceased person.[45]

Context and Content of the Historians' Statements

When were the offending statements made? With only one exception,[46] at least two decades separated the statement from the historical situation to which it referred. At the same time, no statement referred to a historical situation before 1930–40. This confirms an earlier conclusion made, that defamation is clearly an affair of historians of the contemporary period.

Among the channels that historians use to express their opinions, the most common, the classroom lecture, did not lead to cases: this is so because older people—the group from which most complainants are recruited—are underrepresented among students. It is, however, also an indication of the relative immunity of statements uttered in academe. In half the cases, the medium was a book—a classical vehicle for the historian's views. In one case, the draft of a book chapter was leaked by a reviewer (which raises questions about the latter's professional ethics).[47] Five cases concerned a press article or a pamphlet, and remarkably, the five remaining cases were initiated after a written or oral interview. Historians prepared to popularize their views have to be careful.

Surprisingly, statements comparable to those for which some historians were sued, had sometimes been uttered by others before. Unsurprisingly, historians seem often to base their statements on those of others, though this does not necessarily increase the truth value of these statements because untrue statements also may have long lives. In seven of the cases concerned, no trial was initiated at the occasion of the first utterance, which suggests that the perception and timing of the statement is important.[48] Many potential complainants probably never find out about damaging statements uttered about them. Some may do so only when, from a legal point of view, it is too late. Indeed, most cases take place fairly soon after the statement is uttered; in the one case where it took the complainants a decade (and two failed attempts) to sue, this became a strong argument against them.[49] Some complainants may notice the statement in time, but may not be in a position at that time to start a case or may not be aware of that possibility. Repeating statements formerly declared defamatory by a judge remains risky (if this occurs without the defense of privilege). Indeed, the sample contains two examples of complainants who, reassured by their success in a preceding case, initiated a trial concerning the same defamatory statement for the second time: one won again, the other lost.[50] The reverse is also true: statements of acquitted historians repeated by others normally go unpunished.[51] And when the rulings of judges were challenged on appeal, they were, with one exception, all confirmed by the higher courts.[52] Another intriguing observation is the following: statements central to defamation cases, however important they may intrinsically be, were not necessarily central to the argument of the historian who uttered them. Book passages objected to, for example, were sometimes digressions, sometimes details, with no essential impact on the core of the argument—they could have been omitted.

What were the statements about? Even if we keep in mind the partly accidental nature of our data collection, it is easy to see that the large majority of statements were about the complainants' acts during World War II, particularly war crimes and acts of collaboration or resistance. A second theme—the behavior of colonial armies during decolonization—is probably significant as well, especially in the Netherlands (Indonesia), and, to some extent and indirectly in France (Algeria). People who once risked their life are not quickly deterred from attacking critical stories about their experience. Reputations count in matters of life and death.

The conclusion about World War II and decolonization leads to new questions about the relationship between reputation and chronology and between reputation and geography. The first is whether the trend to sue for defamation over historical issues is accelerating.[53] When one observes the universe of cases under review (22 in the sample, more than 160 worldwide), one is inclined to confirm this. Nevertheless, as I said earlier, the total documentation is unpredictably uneven and partly the product of coincidence: many countries are not represented in the appendices and the list of cases of those that are present often seems capricious. In addition, collection is easier for recent cases than for cases of the more remote past. Does such a trend of increasing lawsuits fit into a larger trend of judicialization of history? Some French historians noted a tendency to settle historical disputes by law or in court in their country.[54] This trend is indeed clearly discernible in France and—if one thinks of the increasing number of laws against denial of the Holocaust or the Armenian genocide—in some other European countries as well. But it is not a universal trend.

The second question is: why are there so many French and Dutch cases? In the sample alone, there were eight French and five Dutch cases. If we add cases from outside the sample for the same period 1965–2000, the total amounts to fifteen and eight respectively.[55] Four French cases were eventually decided before the European Court of Human Rights, another record among the countries mentioned in the appendices.[56] There may be more at stake here than documentary coincidence. For France, the explanation is partly legal. French law forbids the truth defense for facts older than ten years—a rule affecting most cases against historians.[57] This legal rule may encourage potential complainants to sue. We just observed, however, that the judicialization of history, although far from universal, is a trend extending beyond France to other countries. Hence, this factor may not be sufficiently discriminating.

As for the Netherlands, the reason for the higher frequency may be my myopia: I work in that country, albeit as a Dutch-speaking Belgian, and therefore I am in a better position to monitor the local situation. In the four months during which the bulk of this chapter was written, however, I counted no less than three public threats to sue for defamation in which historians were involved, including one directed by a historian to a colleague who had made a disparaging remark. (The latter had declared that a historical opinion of the former concurred with a National-Socialist thesis; he apologized later.) Other reasons than my *Standortgebundenheit* may be at work. It is certainly true that Indonesia is a sensitive topic in the Netherlands because it is a former colony. It is equally true, however, that censorship attempts and taboos in almost all formerly colonizing countries—not only in the Netherlands—frequently revolve around their colonial role.[58]

Looking at both France and the Netherlands, we see that World War II is a central focus of French and Dutch collective memory with a proven ability to stir collective passions. The complicity of the Vichy régime with the Germans in France and the high incidence of Jewish Holocaust victims in the Netherlands are largely responsible for this collective sensibility. Even so, in Germany and other countries too, World War II is a highly sensitive topic, but this is not matched there—as far as I could document—by a comparably high incidence of defamation cases.

If legal and historical factors do not seem decisive, do cultural factors? I see three of such factors, the first of which is improbable. The cultural prejudice that egos are more inflammable in southern European countries than in northern ones, if it has any factual basis at all, is not supported by our findings. The high frequency of defamation cases for France is not parallelled by a comparable frequency for countries south of France. And, likewise, if northern countries, including the Netherlands, are really known for their levelheaded inhabitants, how can we explain the high incidence of defamation cases for the latter country, but not for its neighbors? Essentialistic explanations such as geographically determined personal pride are improbable. A second possibility is statistical: if we suppose that French and Dutch citizens are more concerned with their past and display greater historical awareness than their counterparts in neighboring countries, then higher historical awareness and broader historical culture would, in these highly developed societies, translate themselves into higher production and consumption of historical works and, logically, into more conflicts and lawsuits. Perhaps parts of this thesis could be tested with international comparative research. When I think, however, of the elaborate historical infrastructure that also exists in other European countries, I doubt that the thesis passes the test. On the other hand, it is also true that countries with comparable levels of historical culture and historical awareness (if these are measurable at all) may treat their historians—and the visibility of professional historical writing for third parties and the latter's place in the public debate—very differently. A third factor, the attention given to the expression of individual emotions in education, could also play a role. The geographical question remains puzzling. After all, specific provisions of defamation legislation in the various countries may count for the most substantial part of the explanation.

The Verdict of the Judges

Many defamation cases took place in a stormy, often intimidating, atmosphere. In two instances, complainants published their objections in a book during the trial period, in three they did so afterward. Four of these rebuttals came from Dutch complainants—interesting in the light of the preceding discussion about geography—the fifth was written by a Flemish (Dutch-speaking) complainant.[59] In other cases, the defendants were threatened, sometimes with death, or harassed.[60] From time to time, historians had to meet additional challenges. In one case, a historian was sued for defamation while two other procedures against him (indirectly related to the case) were running: a lawsuit to rectify statements close to defamation and a freedom of information procedure with the aim of gaining access to the reading reports of the reviewers of his manuscript.[61] Another case was followed after the trial by no less than fifteen applications to the court.[62] In at least one case, the judge's independence was questioned,[63] in two others the independence of the complainant's lawyer was questioned.[64] Three cases were suspended,[65] but no less than seven became appeals and supreme court cases, and two of them were eventually sent to the European Court of Human Rights.[66]

The legal reasoning according to which the courts pronounced their judgment was at the core of my research. If we know how judges think and decide, we can infer from this some rules and clues for historians. The Article 19 *Principles on Freedom of Expression and Protection of Reputation* emphatically endorse the truth defense and the joint Special Rapporteurs recommend that complainants, not defendants, should bear the burden of proving the falsity of any facts. Reality is different. In some countries (France was mentioned as an example), it is not legally possible to prove the truth of statements about facts from the distant past. The idea behind this regulation is that it is not desirable to keep dragging up the past. One of the main purposes of the law is to restore and maintain social peace, which implies that it should be made legally impossible to reevaluate all of the past all of the time. This is a wise idea, but it amputates the defense of historians. One French case convincingly illustrates this: the argument of the defending historian—that some of the archives proving the truth of his statement had disappeared or were destroyed after he consulted them—was to no avail. Even archivists confirming his version in the courtroom risked being charged with complicity in defamation. In addition, the archivists were reprimanded by the French Archives Directorate and the French Association of Archivists, because they had violated the existing restrictions on freedom of information.[67]

There is, however, another—in many respects more important—reason why judges, not only in France but elsewhere also, usually avoid considering the crux of the problem itself (the truth value of allegedly offending facts). They appear to be particularly sensitive to the argument that historical truth should be settled by historians in academe and not by the courts. Following this principle, judges themselves do not initiate research on the cases, but instead form their judgment exclusively on the basis of the information provided by the two parties, sometimes after hearing expert witnesses. Often, too, they have an uneasy relationship with historical truth: proof of the truth is far from simple, because many historical facts and opinions have to be extracted from specialist knowledge which judges do not possess. Frequently, they are not capable of deciding on the quality of the facts and opinions brought by the parties. In addition, historical truth is susceptible to change and adaptation—to a limited degree in the case of facts, to a large degree in the case of opinions.[68] This explains why many judges are uncomfortable with truth defenses in historical issues and will attempt to avoid the question of *content.*

If, then, judges avoid considering the truth value of historical facts and if, logically, they cannot consider the truth value of opinions, on what grounds *do* they rule? They take their decisions after having inspected the historians' method and ethics (judges often succinctly refer to these as "procedural aspects"). When reasoning a decision for an acquittal, judges usually do not say that the historians told the truth; instead, they endorse the defenses of prudence, fair comment, public interest, and good faith. They typically say that the historians acted in good faith and that their statements were part of a serious historical debate. They also say that the historians applied professional methods carefully and objectively, notably the use of, and balanced and critical approach to, all available sources, the elimination or correction of falsehoods, and the equitable reporting on all historical protagonists. Again, Bredin is more eloquent: "In the judge's view, the image of the "good" historian [is]: meticulous, scrupulous, always moderate in opinion and tone, apparently neutral, without avowed passion or irritating nerve. He resembles the good judge like a brother."[69] Convicted historians are censured because they did not interview eyewitnesses, overestimated the value of certain texts or acts of the complainant,[70] did not consult original sources but literature only,[71] or attached excessive importance to a single source.[72] One French defendant—the historian already cited who was not given the opportunity to prove the truth of his allegations—was eventually found guilty of defamation; but although the judge meted out a symbolic penalty, damages were not awarded because of the defendant's careful method.[73] Likewise, another French defendant was found guilty of defamation and was still acquitted, because he had acted in good faith and within the context of a legitimate debate.[74]

The British situation is a partial exception. British libel law puts the burden of proof on the defendant and in contrast to France, the truth defense is allowed. In one such case, the defendant and her publishers employed a group of experts; for two years, three of them combed through all of the publications of the complainant to prove the truth of the allegations of the defendant. The judge agreed with the defendant; in his judgment, he exposed the methods utilized by the complainant, a writer, in his works.[75]

Judges allow a broad margin of freedom to historians, which enables the latter to examine, to doubt, to formulate facts and hypotheses based on them, and to present opinions. At the same time, they demand that historians proceed methodically and prudently when they do research and present findings, and follow an ethic in which the values of scholarship are expressed. But it remains to be seen if in judging historians, judges succeed in avoiding judging the past itself. Numerous rulings prove that, in the process of judging the method and ethic of historians, judges unavoidably also fix, and sometimes freeze, parts of the historical truth—especially in cases where statements of fact and description rather than statements of opinion and analysis are disputed.[76]

A subject causing problems in some defamation cases is the amnestied crime. The question here is whether historians are allowed to mention a crime that has been amnestied later, and if not, whether mention of it equals defamation or an invasion of privacy. According to the public interest defense, the mention in historical research of amnestied crimes and spent convictions, in view of their detrimental effect upon reputation and privacy, is only allowed on the condition that it serves the public interest.[77] One of our cases concerned such an amnestied crime: the judge allowed its mention not only in the courtroom, but also in the defendant's work itself, on the grounds that solid historical research would otherwise become impossible.[78] Similar problems could arise with other sensitive statements, such as naming the names of murderers, torturers, spies, traitors, and collaborators with the enemy; accusing others of dishonesty, corruption, cowardice, plagiarism, incompetence, or sexual misbehavior; and mentioning the names of persons who made confessions under torture or were the subject of sexual violence.

Finally, which sanctions were pronounced? In one third of all cases, damages were awarded or punishment was meted out. If we leave aside the dismissal of three cases, historians were acquitted in ten cases and convicted in five. In the remaining four cases, the judgment was (eventually) qualified.[79] Two convicted historians went to prison (one of them was released on bail).[80] In six or seven cases, the complainant was awarded damages. In one British case, the damages were disproportionately high—the highest in the nation's history. The damages were eventually successfully challenged before the European Court of Human Rights, but in the meantime, five years had elapsed.[81] In some cases, publication of the court's judgment was ordered.

To complete our analysis, it is interesting to compare defamation trials of *bona fide* historians with applications of Holocaust deniers before international courts. We are dealing here not with Holocaust deniers in their capacity of complainants in national defamation cases against historians (such as in the three cases referred to above), but with Holocaust deniers whose judicial concerns were declined at the national level and who sought a remedy at the international level. Fifteen Holocaust deniers, who were convicted before national courts, protested these convictions before the European Court of Human Rights in Strasbourg (a sixteenth did so before the United Nations Human Rights Committee). Without exception, the applications were turned down in Strasbourg on several grounds, which included defamation. The reasoning of the European judges in Holocaust denial cases is as follows. The Holocaust, they maintain, is a clearly established historical fact and its conscious denial or minimization is *not* a quest for truth *nor* part of a public debate about history, but a lie and a threat to truth. According to the court, this has three consequences: (1) the denial implies that genocide victims themselves lie and falsify history and, therefore, it is racially defamatory and harms the individual and collective dignity and reputation of those genocide victims (the dead as well as the survivors) and their descendants; (2) the denial incites hatred, discrimination, and violence, either directly and publicly or indirectly as a catalyst, and, therefore, it constitutes a serious and immediate threat to the rights of others and to public order; (3) the denial is an abuse of the right to free expression from the perspective of society; it undermines fundamental democratic values (such as equality, antiracism, justice, and peace) with the purpose of rehabilitating the Fascist regimes of World War II.[82] In sum, the protection of the reputation and rights of Holocaust victims and the public interest in the prevention of the crime of disorder outweigh, in a democratic society, the deniers' freedom of expression. These three consequences usually come together, but the first in particular suffices as evidence of culpability. Even if Holocaust deniers plead that they do not intend to incite hatred or violence and that no serious threat to public order (and therefore no need to prevent disorder) exists, Holocaust denial always constitutes racial defamation.[83]

The difference, in short, amounts to this: a defamatory statement jeopardizes reputation and therefore it may be restricted in precise conditions; denial of the Holocaust jeopardizes the entire system of freedoms and it is therefore forbidden. That is the way the European judges look at the denial of the Holocaust.[84] In addition, these judges never asked the Council of Europe member states with laws specifically prohibiting genocide denial to repeal them.[85] A ruling by the United Nations Human Rights Committee on a complaint by a French Holocaust denier followed analogous reasoning.[86] It is not the place here to comment on the Holocaust denial issue, although the views of the Court and the Committee elicit questions. After conversations with many colleagues, I conclude that most professional historians support the vision of the international courts about genocide denial as expounded above, but reject national laws that specifically prohibit genocide denial.

Conclusion

Both the worldwide survey and the empirical analysis of defamation cases inevitably turn our attention to the use of defamation laws and cases as instruments that discourage historical research. Defamation cases may have an effect in three directions. If the judge confirms the position of historians, the historians may perceive this as confirmation of the professional character of their work.[87] If the judge disagrees with their position, and if that position is indeed untenable, either because the fact was untrue, the opinion unfair, or the statement malicious, historians should, at the very least, conduct better and more responsible research in the future. But if the judge disagrees with their position (especially in cases where the truth defense is not allowed), and if that position could be shown to be plausible, the lesson is bitter and may make historians muse on the differences between legal and historical judgment and the distance between legal and historical truth. They may reflect on the limits of expressing historical truth. Knowing and expressing the historical truth are two different things indeed.

The example of mentioning amnestied crimes, among others, shows that even true statements may be privacy-sensitive and offensive. Therefore, such true but sensitive or controversial statements should be made only when the public interest is served. Where this is not the case, historians should, following Schauer's reasoning quoted at the beginning of this chapter, have a right *not* to express opinions or true facts about private lives and reputations.[88] In Chapter 4, I will develop a procedure to apply this rule. The plea for a strictly delineated right to silence should, however, not eclipse another conclusion, which is more important here: the analysis of this chapter, based on more than 160 cases (including 22 cases studied in detail), proves that, worldwide, defamation laws have a chilling effect on the expression and exchange of historical information and ideas, are often but barely veiled attempts at censorship, encourage self-censorship, and hamper discussion on historical subjects.

Afterword: Should History be Understood or Judged?

What has been said about the right to silence in the conclusion of this chapter gives us the key to solve a centuries-old problem. At least since the days of Kant, there is a debate of whether historians should limit themselves to understanding history or whether, *in addition,* they should enunciate a moral judgment about it. Of course, we are speaking here not about implicit moral judgments, which are difficult to avoid, but explicit moral judgments, made after a careful study of given historical problems. Both sides of the debate ("understanding" and "judgment") bring together historians who otherwise have often little in common.[89] In the solution that I offer below, neither side is entirely right nor entirely wrong. My reasoning is as follows.

According to Article 19 of the *Universal Declaration of Human Rights*, we have freedom of opinion and expression. Freedom of expression includes its counterpart, the freedom *not* to express opinions. The rationale behind this is that the right to free speech would be seriously undermined by any requirement to express opinions not honestly held by an individual,[90] and, in the case of scholars, also by the requirement to express opinions which are premature and not based on sufficient research. I call this freedom *not* to express opinions the right to silence (or the right not to speak). This right to silence is an integral part of the core right of free expression. Therefore, it is firmly rooted in the doctrine of human rights. We will encounter it under another guise in Chapter 5 also (namely as the right not to be compelled to remember certain historical events.)

Let us now look again at the basic distinction between facts and opinions. The right to silence is applicable to facts from time to time, that is, when a balancing test indicates that the interest in privacy and reputation outweighs the public interest in disclosure of those facts. This is what I have argued in the conclusion above. In contrast to facts, however, opinions may *always* fall within the ambit of the right of silence. By opinions, I mean thoughts, ideas, beliefs, comments, views, or value judgments. Moral judgments, including moral judgments about the past, are forms of opinions. Therefore, making moral judgments is a right, not a duty. Historians defending the position that history should be understood, not judged, and historians defending the contrary position, that history should be judged, not solely understood, are both right. But they are only right to the extent that their position does not harbor a necessary reason for others to adopt it. Both viewpoints have to be stripped of their absolute character.

However, the symmetry is not perfect. Whereas the right to silence for *holding* opinions is absolute, the right to *express* them in public is subject to some strictly defined requirements, such as, among other things, respect for the reputations of others. Hence, historians wanting to enunciate moral judgments about persons of the past should reconcile themselves with these requirements, even when it is true that judges are more tolerant of opinions, including moral judgments, than of statements of fact, and even when it is true that they will not be interested in statements about the more remote past. Codes of ethics for historians should contain a rule that making moral judgments about the past is a right, not a duty, and that this right should be exercised prudently.

APPENDIX 3.1

Defamation Cases against Historians Studied in Detail (1965–2000)

General notes

The universe of cases for the years 1945–2007 given in the Appendices 3.1 to 3.5 is not complete. Dates indicate the estimated time span of an entire affair, including, if any, attacks and/or trials. The annotation of the affairs is always "complainant(s)" *versus* "defendant(s)." Those complaining can be anyone, including historians; unknown complainants are named "X." Defendants are always *bona fide* historians, defined here as either professional historians *or* others studying the past. I do not necessarily share the views and beliefs of the historians or others mentioned in the affairs. Holocaust deniers are *not* considered historians (even if some of them studied history or obtained a history degree).[91] Where known, decisions of the European Commission of Human Rights and judgments of the European Court of Human Rights related to the affairs are given. Historians who were "defendants" at the national level become "applicants" at the European level. Cases about privacy, blasphemy, hate speech, and group defamation are included when there is a clear connection with reputation issues. Cases marked with (*) deal with posthumous reputation or posthumous privacy; cases marked with (**) deal with political leaders deceased more than half a century previously (see text for further explanation).

Not included in the appendices are: reports about *threats* to sue for defamation if they were isolated and not part of a larger affair; cases in which historians sued for access to information; cases in which historians were sued for plagiarism; and cases in which Holocaust deniers were sued (see for the latter, however, Appendix 3.6).

Sources for the appendices: for many of the pre–2000 cases listed, see Antoon De Baets, *Censorship of Historical Thought: A World Guide 1945–2000* (Westport, CT, and London: Greenwood, 2002); for many of the post–1995 cases listed, see the website of the *Network of Concerned Historians* (<http://www.concernedhistorians.org>).

Note for Appendix 3.1

After each case, the allegedly defamatory statement or act is given.

Austria

1. (1999–2000) Jörg Haider *versus* Anton Pelinka (Pelinka compared Haider's linking of Austria's level of unemployment with the number of foreigners to the way the Nazis linked high unemployment rates to the size of the Jewish population.)
2. (1999–2001) Jörg Haider *versus* Anton Pelinka (Haider trivialized Nazism.)

Belgium

3. (1992–96) Siegfried Verbeke (on behalf of [American] Fred Leuchter) *versus* Gie van den Berghe (Leuchter, author of a 1989 report denying the use of Nazi gas chambers for murder, was not an engineer; his report was deceptive.)

France

4. (1964–65) Jean Lousteau *versus* Michèle Cotta (Lousteau was found guilty of betrayal for his collaboration with the Germans in 1940–44; he was amnestied later.)
5. (1983–84) Bertrand de Jouvenel *versus* (Israeli) Zeev Sternhell (Sternhell's book *Ni droite ni gauche: l'idéologie fasciste en France* contains eight passages in which de Jouvenel is presented as a theorist of French Fascism with pro-Nazi sympathies.)
6. (1983–85) Two organizations of former deportees (on behalf of the late Marcel Paul) *versus* Laurent Wetzel (& Philippe Meaulle) (Communist and former minister Paul displayed cruel behavior as a deportee in the Buchenwald concentration camp)(*).
7. (1984) Henri Frenay *versus* Institut national de l'audiovisuel (INA broadcast part of Frenay's testimony on his resistance during World War II only and juxtaposed his view with those of others.)
8. (1990) Robert Faurisson *versus* Georges Wellers (Faurisson falsified the history of the Jews during the Nazi period.)
9. (1997–2004) Raymond & Lucie Aubrac *versus* Gérard Chauvy (& Albin Michel) (The Aubracs betrayed resistance leader Jean Moulin in 1943.) [*European Court of Human Rights,* 2004: Chauvy's freedom of expression was not violated.]
10. (1997–98) Maurice Papon *versus* Jean-Luc Einaudi (Papon ordered the police to organize a razzia against Algerians in Paris—leading to a massacre with at least 200 deaths in October 1961.)
11. (1998–99) Jean-Marie Le Pen *versus* Pierre Vidal-Naquet (Le Pen was a torturer during the war in Algeria [1954-62].)

Germany

12. (1983–[90]) Erwin Janik (on behalf of the late Emil Janik, his brother) *versus* Anja Rosmus-Wenniger (Emil Janik sympathized with the Nazis)(*).

Italy

13. (1967–84) Countess Elena Pacelli Rossignani, niece of the late Pope Pius XII (on his behalf) *versus* (American) Robert Katz (& Carlo Ponti & George Cosmatos) (Although informed about Nazi plans to retaliate against Italian partisans for the killing of SS soldiers, Pope Pius XII did nothing)(*).

Netherlands

14. (1969–73) Hendrik Willem van der Vaart Smit *versus* Loe de Jong (In his work about World War II, De Jong mentioned that in 1963, another author had called Van der Vaart Smit a liar.)

15. (1987–88) Hans Düster *versus* Loe de Jong (De Jong's leaked draft on Dutch-Indonesian relations in 1945–49 contained a section entitled "War Crimes," which was defamatory to the Dutch army in Indonesia.)

16. (1992–95) Lodewijk Buma *versus* Graa Boomsma (& Eddy Schaafsma) (The behavior of the Dutch military in Indonesia in 1945–49 was sometimes comparable to the behavior of SS soldiers during World War II.)

17. (1998–99) Ten family members of the late W. van de Langemheen (on his behalf) *versus* Madelon de Keizer (Van de Langemheen was a traitor; in October 1944, he gave away the whereabouts of the resistance to the police and the German occupier)(*).

18. (1990–2005) 25 World War II veterans & relatives of soldiers killed in action and of deceased veterans (led by Wim Jagtenberg), two veterans' associations, & a military personnel trade union *versus* Herman Amersfoort & Piet Kamphuis (& defense ministry) [The trial of 2000 was preceded by two inadmissible complaints (Jagtenberg *versus* Amersfoort & Kamphuis) in 1994 and 1996.] (During the May 1940 German invasion of the Netherlands, both Dutch military and German units committed war crimes on an incidental basis; one example concerned a Dutch soldier who allegedly continued shooting after his capture by the Germans on the Grebbeberg)(*).

Spain

19. (1981) X *versus* Francisco Carballo (A wave of terror in Galicia in August 1975 led to the killing of a political leader, which was attributable to the police.)

Switzerland

20. (1983–99) Son of the late lawyer Wilhelm Frick (on his behalf) *versus* Walther Hofer, and (1987–90) son of the late lawyer Wilhelm Frick (on his behalf) *versus* Walther Hofer and 74 other historians, including Georges-André Chevallaz (Frick was a Gestapo confidant)(*).

United Kingdom

21. (1987–95) Lord Aldington *versus* Nikolai Tolstoy Miloslavsky (& Nigel Watts) (Aldington, in May 1945 a brigadier in Carinthia, Austria, was co-responsible for

the slaughter of 70,000 prisoners-of-war and refugees handed over by the British to Soviet and Titoist forces; therefore, he was a war criminal.) [European Court of Human Rights, 1995: Tolstoy's freedom of expression was violated because the damages awarded were disproportionate.]

22. (1993–2000) David Irving *versus* (American) Deborah Lipstadt (& Penguin Books) (Irving was a Holocaust denier.)

APPENDIX 3.2

Other Defamation Cases Against Historians Studied (1945–2007)

Note

See general notes of Appendix 3.1.

Algeria

(2004) X *versus* Hafnaoui Ghoul.
See also Appendix 3.2 under France (Souaïdia case).

Argentina

(1995–2002) Miguel Brevetta Rodríguez *versus* Raúl Dargoltz.
(2005–) A retired military officer and a former policeman *versus* Mariano Saravia.

Armenia

See Appendix 3.2 under France and Turkey.

Australia

(1984) Joh Bjelke-Petersen *versus* Ross Fitzgerald.
(1996–97) (New Zealandian) David Lange *versus* Australian Broadcasting Corporation.
See also Appendix 3.2 under New Zealand.

Austria

(1997–2003) Salzburger Nachrichten *versus* "Cato" & Neue Kronen Zeitung [European Court of Human Rights, 2003: the injunction was not disproportionate.]
See also Appendix 3.1 (cases 1, 2); Appendix 3.2 under France (Giniewski case) and Germany (Schafranek case).[92]

Bahrain

(2007–) X *versus* Abdulla Khalifa.

Belgium

(1952) Henry de la Lindi *versus* Georges Moulaert.
(1975) Bufquin des Essarts *versus* René Campé, Marthe Dumon & Jean-Jacques Jespers.
(1977) Leo Delwaide *versus* Marcel Liebman.
See also Appendix 3.1 (case 3).

Bulgaria

(1991–97) P. *versus* Sevdelin Panev [*European Commission of Human Rights,* 1997: Panev's application was inadmissible.]

Canada

(1961–73) Anne, Marie, Jeanne & Jean Bourassa *versus* Fernand Ouellet (& Presses de l'Université Laval).
(1992) Canadian World War II veterans *versus* Brian & Terrence McKenna.
(1993–2003) Pierre & Claude Michaud *versus* Pierre Turgeon (& Lanctôt Éditeur).

Chile

(2000) Mapuche indigenous organizations *versus* Sergio Villalobos Ribera.

Djibouti

(2007–) X *versus* Jean-Paul Noël Abdi.

Egypt

(2007–) Aziz Al-Fiki family *versus* Sherin Abu El Naga & Shahenda Mekled (& Dar Merit Publishing House).

France

(1951) Édouard Branly *versus* Albert Turpain.
(1963–64) Paul Rassinier *versus* Bernard Lecache.
(1964–68) Jacques Soustelle *versus* Morland, Barangé & Martinez (& Éditions René Julliard).
(1984) Jean-Marie Balestre *versus* Jean-Pierre Dubreuil (& Éditions Lieu commun).

(1993–95) Forum des Associations Arméniennes de France & Ligue contre le Racisme et l'Antisémitisme *versus* (British-American) Bernard Lewis.

(1994) Family of the late Antoine de Saint-Exupéry (on his behalf) *versus* Emmanuel Chadeau (*).

(1994–2006) Alliance générale contre le racisme et pour le respect de l'identité française et chrétienne *versus* (Austrian) Paul Giniewski (& *Le quotidien de Paris* & P. Tesson). [European Court of Human Rights, 2006: Giniewski's freedom of expression was violated.]

(1995–2004) Widow and children of former President François Mitterand (on his behalf) *versus* Éditions Plon (& Claude Gubler, Michel Gonod). [European Court of Human Rights, 2004: Plon's freedom of expression was partially violated](*).

(1997–2004) Michel Junot *versus* Radio France (Michel Boyon & Bertrand Gallicher). [European Court of Human Rights, 2004: Radio France's freedom of expression was not violated.]

(2001–2) (Algerian) Khaled Nezzar *versus* (Algerian) Habib Souaïdia (& Marc Tessier).

(2005–6) Collectif DOM des Antillais, Guyanais et Réunionnais *versus* Olivier Pétré-Grenouillau.

See also Appendix 3.1 (cases 4–11).

Germany

(1963–71) Peter Gorski, adopted son of the late Gustaf Gründgens (on his behalf) *versus* Nymphenburger Verlagshandlung [Mefisto case](*).

(1987–1990) (The late) Franz Josef Strauss and heirs (on his behalf) *versus* Stern Magazine and G. (*).

(1990–94) Emil Carlebach *versus* (Austrian) Hans Schafranek (& ISP publishers).

See also Appendix 3.1 (case 12); Appendix 3.2 under United Kingdom (Plato Films case).

Greece

(2003) X *versus* Ioannis Malakassis.

(2003–) X *versus* Athanasios Flitouris.

(2007–8) Kostas Plevris *versus* Panayote Dimitras (& Greek Helsinki Monitor, Central Board of Jewish Communities in Greece).

See also Appendix 3.2 under United Kingdom (Packard case).

Hungary

(1953–57) Rezsó (= Rudolph) Kasztner *versus* Hungarian-Jewish journalist.

(2004) Imre Mecs *versus* Andras Bencsik & Laszlo Attila Bertok.

India

(1984–98) Jagjit Singh Chohan *versus* Khushwant Singh.

Ireland

See Appendix 3.2 under United Kingdom (Reynolds case).

Israel

(2000–3) Organization of Veterans of the Alexandroni Brigade *versus* Teddy Katz.
(2002–3) X *versus* Ilan Pappé.
See also Appendix 3.1 (case 5).

Italy

See Appendix 3.1 (case 13).

Kazakhstan

(2007–) Almaz Dzhambulov, Zhenis Zhambylov, Katshibek Abdykalykova *versus Svoboda slova* & Yerbol Kurmabayev (*).

Mongolia

(2005–) Purevbat *versus* G. Dashrentsen.

Netherlands

(1984–90) Comité Geschiedkundig Eerherstel Nederlands-Indië [Committee for the Historical Rehabilitation of the Dutch East-Indies], led by Ralph Boekholt & Gerard Jonker *versus* Loe de Jong [two cases: one for rectification of allegedly defamatory manuscript contents; one for access to reading reports.]
(1990–98) X *versus* Bart Middelburg & Sytze van der Zee (& *Het Parool*). [European Commission of Human Rights, 1998: application by Middelburg & Van der Zee & *Het Parool* was inadmissible.]
(1993) Son of the late J. R. Müller (on his behalf) *versus* Marga Coesèl (*).
(2003) X (Rosalie Bresser-Dukker) *versus* Foundation Digital Monument to the Jewish Community in the Netherlands & Isaac Lipschits.
See also Appendix 3.1 (cases 14–18).

New Zealand

(1995–2000) David Lange *versus* Joe Atkinson (& Australian Consolidated Press, publisher of *North and South*).[93]
See also Appendix 3.2 under Australia (Lange case).

Peru

(2005–) Rafael Rey *versus* Nelson Manrique.

Poland

(1992–96) Jerzy Urban *versus* Ryszard Bender.

Romania

(2002) Ristea Priboi *versus* Marius Oprea.

Slovakia

(1992–2001) Dušan Slobodník *versus* Ľubomír Feldek. [European Court of Human Rights, 2001: Feldek's freedom of expression was violated.] (1994–2004) Š. [a Supreme Court judge] *versus* Andrej Hrico. [European Court of Human Rights, 2004: Hrico's freedom of expression was violated.]

South Africa

(1979) Afrikaner Resistance Movement *versus* Floris van Jaarsveld.

Spain

(1982) Sons of Andalusian landowner *versus* Fernando Ruiz.
(2007) Family of the late Manuel Gutiérrez Torres (on his behalf) *versus* Dionisio Pereira González. (*)
See also Appendix 3.1 (case 19).

Sweden[94]

Switzerland

(1979–85) Robert Eibel *versus* Jürg Frischknecht, Peter Haffner, Ueli Haldimann, Peter Nigli.
(2002) X *versus* Christoph Schlatter (*).
See also Appendix 3.1 (case 20).[95]

Turkey[96]

(2000) X *versus* Akin Birdal.
(2004–) X *versus* Hrant Dink (& Arat Dink, Serkis Serkopyan, Aydin Engin, Aris Nalci).
(2004–) X *versus* Zülküf Kişanak.
(2005–7) X *versus* Eren Keskin.
(2005–6) X *versus* Orhan Pamuk.
(2005–6) X *versus* Murat Belge, İsmet Berkan, Erol Katircioğlu, Haluk Şahin, Hasan Cemal.

(2005–) X *versus* Erkan Akay.
(2006–) X *versus* Abdullah Yildiz (& Mara Meimaridi).
(2006–) X *versus* Elif Shafak.
(2006–) X *versus* Taner Akçam.
(2006–) X *versus* Muazzez Ilmiye Cig (& İsmet Ogutcu).
(2006–) Sükrü Elekdag *versus* *Agos* weekly & Taner Akçam (& Muzaffer Erdogdu, Ahmet Güner).
(2006–) X *versus* Ali Riza Vural, Ahmet Zeki Okçuoglu, Vahdettin Ince, Bedri Vatansever.
(2007–) X *versus* Temel Demirer.
(2007–) X *versus* Osman Tiftikci (& Sýrrý Öztürk).
(2007–) X *versus* Hasan Çakalkurt (& British Robert Fisk).
(2007–) X *versus* Haci Bogatekin.

United Kingdom

(1961) (German) Hans Speidel *versus* Plato Films.
(1987) Martin Packard *versus* (Greek newspaper) *Eleftherotypia*.
(1988–92) Joan Austoker & Charles Webster *versus* David Cantor & *Social History of Medicine*.
(1994–99) (Irish) Albert Reynolds *versus* *Times Newspapers* (& others).
(1996) David Irving *versus* Gitta Sereny (& *The Observer*).
See also Appendix 3.1 (cases 21–22); Appendix 3.2 under France (Lewis case) and Turkey (Fisk case).

United States

(1978–79) Sam Krieger *versus* Allan Weinstein (& Knopf & *New Republic*).
(2003–7) Alan Dershowitz *versus* Norman Finkelstein (& University of California Press).
See also Appendix 3.1 (cases 3, 13, 22); Appendix 3.2 under France (Lewis case).

APPENDIX 3.3

Attacks of Leaders on Historians Who Defamed Them (1945–2007)

Notes

See general notes of Appendix 3.1. *Leaders* (or *rulers*) are heads of state and government or their functional equivalents (e.g., dominant Communist

Party leaders or theocratic leaders). Excluded are lower ranking politicians or future heads of state and government (such as independence leaders or presidential candidates). *Attacks* are public statements or acts (for example, lawsuits) by leaders personally or in their name, directed against historians and concerning a historical topic.

Azerbaijan

(1994–95) President Heidar Aliyev *versus* Movsum Aliyev.

China

(1965–69) Communist Party chairman Mao Zedong *versus* Wu Han (for comparison with Ming Dynasty Emperors Hongwu [Zhu Yuanzhang] & Jiajing [Zhu Houcong])(**).

Croatia

(1996–98) President (and historian) Franjo Tudjman *versus* Viktor Ivančić, Marinko Čulić & *Feral Tribune*.

France[97]

Germany[98]

See Appendix 3.3 under Namibia (Groth case).

Greece

(1981) President Constantinos Karamanlis *versus* Theodosis Theodosopoulos. See also Appendix 3.5 under Greece.

India

(1981–84) Prime Minister Indira Gandhi *versus* (British) Salman Rushdie (& Jonathan Cape).

Indonesia

(1994) X (on behalf of President Suharto) *versus* Wimanjaya Liotohe.
(1997) Arrest (on behalf of President Suharto) of Wimanjaya Liotohe.

Iran

(1945) Prime Minister Mohammad Sadr *versus* Ahmad Kasravi.

(1979) Ayatollah Ruhollah Khomeini *versus* Ahmad Kasravi (posthumously attacked).
(1989–) Ayatollah Ruhollah Khomeini *versus* (British) Salman Rushdie.

Japan[99]

Kazakhstan

(1992–93) President Nursultan Nazarbayev *versus* Karishal Asanov.
(2000–2001) President Nursultan Nazarbayev *versus* Karishal Asanov.

Malawi

(1974–) President Hastings Banda *versus* (British) Philip Short.

Mexico

[1990] President Carlos Salinas *versus* Lorenzo Meyer.

Namibia

(1996) President Sam Nujoma *versus* (German) Siegfried Groth & Christo Lombard.

Palestinian Authority

(1995) President Yasser Arafat *versus* Maher al-Alami.

Romania

(1995–2002) President Ion Iliescu *versus* Sorin Roşca Stănescu & Cristina Ardeleanu. [European Court of Human Rights, 2002: application by Roşca Stănescu & Ardeleanu was inadmissible.]

Saudi Arabia

(1984) King Fahd (on his behalf) *versus* Ghazi al-Ghusseibi.

Sierra Leone

(2004–5) President Ahmad Tejan Kabbah (on his behalf) *versus* Paul Kamara.

Thailand

(1957–[62])King Bhumibol Adulyadej Rama IX (on his behalf) *versus* Kosai Mungjaroen(*lèse majesté*).

(1976–78) King Bhumibol Adulyadej Rama IX (on his behalf) *versus* Thong-chai Winichakul (*lèse majesté*).
(1983–86) King Bhumibol Adulyadej Rama IX (on his behalf) *versus* Saman Kongsuphol & others (*lèse majesté*).
(1991–95) Prime Minister Suchinda Kraprayoon & King Bhumibol Adulyadej Rama IX (on his behalf) *versus* Sulak Sivaraksa (*lèse majesté*, among other things).

United Kingdom

See Appendix 3.3 under India and Iran (Rushdie cases) and under Malawi (Short case).

APPENDIX 3.4

Attacks of Leaders on Historians Who Defamed Dead Leaders (1945–2007)

Note

See general notes of Appendix 3.1 and notes of Appendix 3.3.

Egypt[100]

(1998) President Hosni Mubarak *versus* (French) Didier Monciaud (& [French] Maxime Rodinson) (*re* Prophet Mohammed)(*)(**).

France

See Appendix 3.4 under Egypt (Monciaud case).

India

(2003–2004) Prime Minister of India Atal Vajpayee, Maharashtra Government, & others *versus* (American) James Laine (*re* founder of Maratha state Shivaji)(*)(**).

Pakistan

(1984) President Zia ul Haq *versus* (American) Stanley Wolpert (*re Quaid* Ali Jinnah).

Soviet Union[101]

United States

See Appendix 3.4 under India (Laine case) and Pakistan (Wolpert case).

APPENDIX 3.5

Attacks of Others on Historians Who Defamed Dead Leaders (1945–2007)

Note

See general notes of Appendix 3.1 and notes of Appendix 3.3.

Armenia

See Appendix 3.5 under Turkey (Zarakolu case).

Belgium

(1986) Patriotic movement Pro Belgica *versus* Daniel Vangroenweghe (*re* King Leopold II)(*)(**).
(1995) Lilian Baels (widow of King Leopold III) & Prince Alexander *versus* Pierre Mertens (& Le Seuil) (*re* King Baudouin)(*).

Egypt[102]

Greece

(1992) X *versus* Michalis Papadakis (*re* Emperor Alexander the Great) (*)(**).
(1993) X *versus* Tákis Michas (*re* Emperor Alexander the Great)(*)(**).

India

(2001) Maneka Gandhi (on behalf of the late Prime Minister Indira Gandhi, the late Sanjay Gandhi, & herself) *versus* (American-British) Katherine Frank (& HarperCollins)(*).
See also Appendix 3.4 under India.

Indonesia

(1981–82) X *versus* Sunardi (*re* President Sukarno)(*).

Iran

(1992–94) Ministry of Islamic Culture and Guidance *versus* Manouchehr Karimzadeh (*re* Ayatollah Khomeini)(*).
(1998) X *versus* Mohammed Reza-Zaeri (*re* Ayatollah Khomeini)(*).
(2003) X *versus* Alireza Eshraghi (*re* Ayatollah Khomeini)(*).

Italy

See Appendix 3.1 (case 13).

Japan

(1989) Attack of foreign ministry against BBC television documentary (*re* Emperor Hirohito)(*).
(1989) Attack against (British) Edward Behr (& his Japanese publisher) (*re* Emperor Hirohito)(*).

Kuwait

(2003–) X *versus* Yasser al-Habib (*re* Prophet Mohammed)(*)(**).

Paraguay

(1989) X *versus* Alcibíades González Delvalle (*re* President Francisco Solano López)(*)(**).

Spain

(1998) State Memorial Society for the Philip II and Charles V Anniversaries *versus* public television channel (*re* King Philip II)(*)(**).

Sudan

(2005–6) X *versus* Mohamed Taha Mohamed Ahmed (*re* Prophet Mohammed)(*)(**).

Thailand

(1956) King Bhumibol Adulyadej Rama IX (on his behalf) *versus* (American) Walter Lang (*lèse majesté; re* King Mongkut Rama IV)(*)(**).
(1967) King Bhumibol Adulyadej Rama IX (on his behalf) *versus* Sulak Sivaraksa (*lèse majesté; re* Ayutthaya's last two kings)(*)(**).
(1984) King Bhumibol Adulyadej Rama IX (on his behalf) *versus* Sulak Sivaraksa (*lèse majesté; re* kings and princes of last two centuries) (*)(**).

(1998) King Bhumibol Adulyadej Rama IX (on his behalf) *versus* (American) Andy Tennant (*lèse majesté; re* King Mongkut Rama IV)(*)(**).

Turkey

(1979–81) X *versus* Ismail Beşikçi (*re* President Mustafa Kemal Atatürk)(*)(**).

(1988) X *versus Encyclopedia of Modern Times* (*re* President Mustafa Kemal Atatürk)(*)(**).

(1991) X *versus* Ismail Beşikçi (*re* President Mustafa Kemal Atatürk)(*)(**).

(1991) X *versus* Sinami Orhan (*re* President Mustafa Kemal Atatürk)(*)(**).

(1997) Attack against Abdurrahman Dilipak (*re* President Mustafa Kemal Atatürk)(*)(**).

(1999–2000) X *versus* B. [historian interviewed by Human Rights Watch] (*re* President Mustafa Kemal Atatürk)(*)(**).

(2001–2) X *versus* Ömer Asan (*re* President Mustafa Kemal Atatürk) (*)(**).

(2001–7) X *versus* Ahmet Önal (& Aydar Çiçek, Munzur Cem, Huseyin Baysulun) (*re* President Mustafa Kemal Atatürk)(*)(**).

(2003–) X *versus* Damla Demirözü (*re* President Mustafa Kemal Atatürk)(*) (**).

(2003–) X *versus* Mehmet Ali Varis (*re* President Mustafa Kemal Atatürk)(*) (**).

(2004) X *versus* Hakan Albayrak (*re* President Mustafa Kemal Atatürk)(*)(**).

(2004–) X *versus* Ragip Zarakolu (& Atilla Tuygan & Armenian George Jerjian) (*re* President Mustafa Kemal Atatürk)(*)(**).

(2005–6) X *versus* Fatih Tas (& American John Tirman) (*re* President Mustafa Kemal Atatürk)(*)(**).

(2006) X *versus* Ipek Çalislar & Necdet Tatlican (*re* President Mustafa Kemal Atatürk)(*)(**).

(2006–) Izmir Bar Assocation & Atatürk Foundation *versus* Attila Yayla (*re* President Mustafa Kemal Atatürk)(*)(**).

(2007–) X *versus* Berkant Coskun& Yasin Yetisgen (*re* President Mustafa Kemal Atatürk)(*) (**).

United Kingdom

See Appendix 3.5 under India (Frank case) and Japan (BBC and Behr cases).

United States

(1963–71) Heirs of the late President Warren Harding (on his behalf) *versus* Francis Russell (& Kenneth Duckett, McGraw-Hill, *American Heritage*) (*re* President Warren Harding)(*)(**).

See also Appendix 3.4 under India (Laine case) and Pakistan (Wolpert case) and Appendix 3.5 under India (Frank case), Thailand (Lang and Tennant cases), and Turkey (Tas case).

Venezuela

(1983) X *versus* Jorge Olavarría (*re* Liberator of Latin America Simón Bolívar) (*)(**).

Vietnam

[1993] X *versus* *Tuoi Tre* magazine & chief editor Vu Kim Hanh (*re* President Ho Chi Minh)(*).
(2002) X *versus* magazine *Far Eastern Economic Review* (*re* President Ho Chi Minh)(*).

Yugoslavia

(1980–84) Defense ministry and others *versus* Vladimir Dedijer (*re* President Josip Tito)(*).

APPENDIX 3.6

International Decisions against Holocaust Deniers

Note: See general notes of Appendix 3.1. The following are *international* cases in which genocide deniers were *applicants*. For *national* cases in which Holocaust deniers were *complainants*, see Appendix 3.1 (cases 3, 8, 22), and Appendix 3.2 under France (Lecache case) and United Kingdom (Sereny case).[103]

European Commission of Human Rights and European Court of Human Rights (http://www.echr.coe.int)

Austria

(1989) B.H., M.W., H.P., G.K. *versus* Austria.
(1994) Walter Ochensberger *versus* Austria.
(1996) Friedrich Rebhandl *versus* Austria.
(1997) Gerd Honsik *versus* Austria.
(1998) Herwig Nachtmann *versus* Austria.

Belgium

(1983) T. *versus* Belgium.

France

(1996) Pierre Marais *versus* France.
(2003) Roger Garaudy *versus* France.

Germany

(1982) X. *versus* Germany.
(1993) F.P. *versus* Germany.
(1995) Nationaldemokratische Partei Deutschlands *versus* Germany.
(1995) Otto Remer *versus* Germany.
(1995) Udo Walendy *versus* Germany.
(1996) D.I. [David Irving] *versus* Germany.
(1999) Hans-Jürgen Witzsch *versus* Germany.

United Kingdom[104]

United Nations Human Rights Committee (http://www.ohchr.org)

France

(1996) Robert Faurisson *versus* France.[105]

❦ II

RESPONSIBLE HISTORY

4

Duties of the Living to the Dead

Those who are dead have never gone
They are in the shadow that fades away
And in the shadow that darkens
The dead are not under the earth
The dead are not dead.

— *Souffles*, Birago Diop.[1]

In a recent essay, demographer Carl Haub "guesstimates" that the total number of people who have ever been born since the dawn of the human race is 106 billion. Of these, six billion are alive and 100 billion are dead.[2] This chapter is about these two very large and very unequal groups: the living and the dead. Members of both groups are actual or potential subjects of historical study. The *rights* of the subjects studied by historians dominate the latter's professional ethics, as is the case in any profession.[3] Consequently, knowledge of the rights of the living and the dead may provide historians with a solid infrastructure for formulating their duties.[4] The first question—what are the rights of the living?—will be tackled in Chapter 5. The other question—if the dead have rights, what are these?—is treated here. This question found its origin in an address to the nineteenth International Congress of Historical Sciences in 2000 as part of a session on the use and abuse of history. The session was meant to look back at the fate of history and historians in the twentieth century. At a given moment, I said:

> Today, few historians believe that they are judges before the tribunal of history charged with the vengeance of peoples, as René de Chateaubriand did in the early nineteenth century; they nevertheless possess the power to reopen cases and challenge rulers' amnesia and falsification of history. It is never too late for the historical truth, because truth is able to transcend its particular roots and context. Even when sources of information are disappearing, research on past crimes may always begin. It is a task with many risks. Without the passion of the survivors, historians

may "normalize" the cruel abuses of the past by inserting them into the stream of history. They may omit crucial findings for fear of breathing new divisive fever into the collective memory. It is, however, the historians' professional obligation to see that the dead do not die twice; for it is the first human right of deceased persons to be treated with dignity.[5]

In a different context, I made a similar remark:

[D]o past and future generations have human rights? As to past generations, one could think of the right to a decent burial or the right to be treated with respect in historical works. As to future generations, the preservation of the cultural heritage of humanity and of the natural environment are chief concerns as is the relationship between human rights and the human genome. As to future generations in relation to past generations, the accountability of successor governments for human rights abuses committed by their precursors and the obligation to investigate them are matters of legitimate debate.[6]

In retrospect, ascribing rights to the dead, as I did in those quotations, was much too hasty. But such raw thoughts about past generations kept haunting my mind. They crystallized into fertile research only when I finally formulated the problem as two simple but intriguing questions.

Temporal Asymmetry

Why, I first asked, do we have a *Universal Declaration of Human Rights* for the living, but do not have a comparable document for the dead? And which rights would find a place in a *Universal Declaration of Rights of the Dead*, if such a document existed? In trying to answer these questions, I stumbled over two asymmetries. The first was that the living and the dead, although both clearly part of something like a *historical* community, were marked by essential differences—differences that will be explored in detail in this chapter. This asymmetry meant that talking about a *Universal Declaration of Rights of the Dead*, however appealing the phrase, was not correct, whereas talking about a *Universal Declaration of Duties of the Living to the Dead*, for reasons also explained below, does make sense.

A second asymmetry emerged when I compared past generations with future generations. In my quest for clues to make such a comparison, I came across the existence of the 1997 UNESCO *Declaration on the Responsibilities of the Present Generations towards Future Generations*. This declaration spoke about "intergenerational solidarity" and even about "the needs and interests of future generations." How could people who were not yet born, I asked myself, have needs and interests? And if they have needs and interests, do those who have died have needs and interests also? How is solidarity with future people to take shape? And how should we characterize our relationship with the dead? These are puzzling but important questions which turned the UNESCO *Declaration* into a major source of inspiration for my research about the dead.[7] Indeed, in some respects, the problems of past generations looked similar to those of future generations. To give two striking similarities, both generations do not exist in the same sense as the living and both are unable to represent themselves—they need caretakers.

But the differences are far larger, as became already apparent from the second quotation above. A *Declaration of the Duties of the Living to the Dead* could not, I quickly saw, possibly be a simple mirror of the UNESCO *Declaration*. Even a superficial comparison of the UNESCO document about future generations with the *Declaration* about the dead that I wrote myself (in Table 4.1) shows how utterly different they are. Consider the headings of the eleven articles of the UNESCO *Declaration:*

"needs and interests of future generations"
"freedom of choice"
"maintenance and perpetuation of humankind"
"preservation of life on earth"
"protection of the environment"
"human genome and biodiversity"
"cultural diversity and cultural heritage"
"common heritage of humankind"
"peace"
"development and education"
"nondiscrimination"

Compare these now with the eight headings of my *Declaration:*

"body"
"funeral"
"burial"
" will"
"identity"
"image"
"speech"
"heritage"

The only characteristic that the two declarations share is "heritage."[8] The declaration about the future is cast in collective and abstract terms, while the one about the past is cast in individual terms. This is natural: each of those who died was a living individual once, with a personality that is still lacking for those yet to be born.[9]

It is strange that the individuality of the dead and the ensuing personal ties with surviving relatives and friends seemed not to have been a sufficient reason to draft a declaration in their honor, whereas the anonymous collectivity of future generations did provoke such a declaration. Surely, the puzzle could be answered partly. It is possible to argue that time's passage is an illusion and that there is no essential difference between past, present, and future persons. We can claim that future people are just as individual as past or present people.[10] On this view, the fact that we do not know anything about future people to refer to them as individuals is not decisive: we do not have sufficient knowledge about future individuals, but neither have we sufficient knowledge about the countless anonymous dead of history who left no recognizable traces. But even if this would make past and future generations more look alike, my basic question remains the same: if there was a declaration on our duties to future generations, why, then, is there not a declaration on our duties to past generations? How could this astonishing asymmetry be explained?

The obvious answer, I thought, is this. The consensus about what constitutes our duties to the dead is so overwhelming that there is no need to draft a declaration. As we shall see, the consensus is important indeed, but not to such extent that it would be safe to assume that everybody would always behave with spontaneous respect toward the dead. There surely is a need for a *Declaration*. The obvious explanation is not a good explanation. Other factors, as demonstrated by Derek Parfit, were at work.[11] First among them is the irreversibility of the past: in contrast to the present in which we act, or the unknown but open-ended future for which we can make plans to influence it, the past is unalterable and cannot be affected. In particular, we have the capacity to harm or benefit future people, while our capacity to harm or benefit the dead is, as I will make plausible below, nonexistent or at most very limited.[12] Therefore, one can afford to be less concerned about the past than about the future. It follows that the moral questions the past and its dead entail, may look less urgent. But this is not a sufficient explanation, since the future, especially the further future, is at least partly symmetric to the more remote past in this respect.

An additional reason to explain the asymmetry is that most human beings have a bias toward the future. Epicurus and Lucretius already pointed to our different attitude toward our past (prenatal) nonexistence, which we view with great equanimity, and our future (posthumous) nonexistence, which creates existential anguish in most of us. They emphasized that this difference was not logical. In a letter to Menoeceus, Epicurus wrote: "So death, the most terrifying of ills, is nothing to us, since so long as we exist, death is not with us; but when death comes, then we do not exist. It does not concern either the living or the dead, since for the former it is not, and the latter are no more."[13] The bias toward the future can explain why people adopt different attitudes toward their own past and future.[14] This bias, as described by Parfit, regards *personal experiences*. A very important precaution is that the bias toward the future does not apply to events that give us pride or shame.[15] Furthermore, it is unknown whether the bias toward the future is truly universal across all time and cultures. Although the first recognition of the bias stems from Epicurus, hence from antiquity, it is a bias that seems to connect more easily with a linear than a cyclical time conception and more with modernity than tradition.[16] Despite all precautions, however, the personal bias toward the future appears to be a psychological feature so deeply rooted in each of us, that it may affect our global attitude toward the nonpersonal past as well, and thus constitute a chief factor in causing the all-pervading asymmetry between past and future generations.

The irreversibility of the past and the bias toward the future work together and lead to a *relative* underestimation of the past and its problems. And this may be so, even if it has a paradoxical tinge, notwithstanding the huge numbers of deceased people and notwithstanding the consensus that the dead possess dignity. This relative underestimation implied that I could not count too much on intergenerational symmetry and that answering my question—what are the rights of the dead, or, more precisely, what are the duties of the living to the dead?—would take me along longer roads than I expected. The first stage of the trajectory was to define the dead and the second to find out whether they had any rights. I shall come to the conclusion that the dead do *not* possess rights, but that the living nevertheless have some definable core duties to them. I shall then attempt to determine these duties and explore the many aspects related to them, including the modalities of noncompliance.

Who or What Are the Dead?

The dead—do they belong to the realm of things or the realm of beings?[17] Should the question of definition be formulated with a "who" or a "what"? Let us try both possibilities.

Are the dead bodies? The dead are bodies indeed, but there is little doubt that a dead body is qualitatively different from other things.[18] It is a *res nullius*, or thing of nobody (not in the sense that everybody can own it, but in the sense that nobody can own it). This means that the dead body (or its parts) is not property as such and, therefore, that it has no price. It cannot be sold or otherwise commercialized.[19] Even if the dead are bodies, they are always less and more. On the one hand, they are *less* because the bodily status of the dead is temporary: cremation or the passage of time changes bodies into remains. The status of remains is less clear than the status of dead bodies, but most of us would say that while relatives can have *custody* of the remains, they cannot *own* them. On the other hand, the dead are—or appear to be—*more* than bodies, for lingering human characteristics play an essential role in the discussions about them, as we shall see time and again. This also perhaps suggests that the question "who are the dead" is a better question than "what are the dead." I conclude that the term "bodies" is too ambiguous.

Are the dead persons? The literature on the concept of "person" shows two things. First, that many perceive persons as human beings with certain characteristics. Persons are variously defined as *conscious* or *self-conscious* human beings, *rational* human beings, human beings *with interests, free* human beings, or *moral* human beings. Second, some exclude certain categories of human beings from the definition of person, depending on how exactly the terms conscious, self-conscious, rational, with interests, free, or moral are defined. The categories usually excluded are young children (according to many, human beings who are potential or developing persons), the mentally ill (according to some, human beings who, temporarily or permanently, are not persons), and the irreversibly comatose (according to some, human beings who are no longer persons).[20] This exclusion is controversial, but even those who accept it, would certainly not agree to exclude these groups, when deceased, from the community of the dead. Because it is *potentially* discriminatory, I am inclined to reject the term "persons" in my definition. By implication, I should reject the term "postpersons"— sometimes used as a name for the recently deceased. My decision not to allow terms such as persons seems to diverge from the practice of the *Geneva Conventions* and the International Criminal Court, both of which speak of "dead persons."[21] But it coincides with that practice if I reject the interpretation of the term "persons" as "human beings with certain characteristics," and treat both, human beings and persons, as synonyms.[22] From the duties to the dead mentioned in Table 4.1, one group of duties refers to what is left of the *human being* after death, while another refers to what is left of the *person* after death; but all duties form a coherent and integrated whole. This prepares the ground for the cardinal question, which follows.

Are the dead human beings? Although "human beings" seems to be a better term than either bodies or persons, to call the dead human beings is utterly problematic. In the usual sense, human beings have interests, claims, needs, duties, choices, and entitlements—things that the dead obviously do not possess. Without exception, however, *all* of the dead have *been* human beings. This simple fact enables me to test three rival definitions.

The dead are human beings who no longer live. This definition is confusing because it appears to refer to two classes of human beings (those who live and those who do not), the second of which has been excluded above. We come no farther with "the dead are nonliving human beings." This definition raises a controversial problem: until which moment can we appropriately speak of human beings?[23] Regardless of whether the criterion for death is brain death or heart/lung death, it is obvious that some body parts live on for a brief time after death. Death is a process rather than a moment.[24] I reject this definition.

The dead are human beings who no longer exist. The reasons to refute this definition are similar to the ones just presented. There are not two categories of human beings: those who exist and those who do not. Nor is "the dead are nonexistent human beings" a foolproof definition; the body continues to exist after death as a corpse, as bones, as ashes.[25] Neglecting physical postmortem existence is to miss an entire area of duties that rightfully may be assigned to the living.[26] Another consideration, less important in our search for a definition but worth mentioning, is that the dead continue to exist metaphorically as well: as memories in the minds of some of those surviving them and as symbols in masks, effigies, and so on. I reject this definition too.

The battle of terms and definitions leaves us with only one possible definition, helpless and modest, but meaningful: *the dead are past human beings.* Given that I take "past" as synonymous for "former" and reject the Lockean difference between "human being" and "person," four variations of the definition are correct: the dead are past human beings, former human beings, past persons, or former persons.

A last objection is this. Can we accept a definition with a negative description—implicit in the words "past" or "former" (or in the string "no longer" in the rejected definitions)? Two classical definition rules are that a definition should state the *essential* attributes of the species, and that it should not be negative where it can be affirmative. That it should not be negative where it can be affirmative, however, does not mean that there exist no definitions in which negative forms are appropriate for specifying essential attributes.[27] That is exactly the case here. And although it is notoriously difficult to grasp the essence of the dead, part of it *must* be the connection and contrast with the living.

The definition clearly reflects the paradoxes at stake. The dead are no longer human beings (or persons), but are still *reminiscent* of them. They are less than human beings, but more than bodies. However modest, my definition has one important consequence.

Do the Dead Have Rights?

The consequence of the definition is this: *since the dead are not human beings, they do not have human rights.* Since they are no longer living, they do not constitute a category of rights-holders. Unlike living persons (and perhaps other living creatures), they are incapable of having needs, interests or duties, or of making choices or claims, either now or in the future. The mistaken idea that the dead nevertheless possess rights has an interesting linguistic side, recognized not only by the few who defend it,[28] but also by many who reject it. Speaking of the "rights of the dead" may sometimes further our understanding.[29] Only the living have rights and duties, however. The dead, while still alive, had rights and duties by virtue of the fact that they were human beings; once deceased, they lose the (potential) autonomy of human beings and therefore the latter's rights and duties.

Do the Living Have Duties to the Dead?

That the dead have neither rights nor duties does not imply, however, that the living have no duties to them. Moral principles do not only cover people who can reciprocate, or can harm and benefit each other.[30] Moral philosopher Alan White emphasized this point:

> Moral and religious codes, such as the *Decalogue*, commonly lay down duties without conferring any corresponding rights . . . [E]ven where one person has . . . a duty *to* someone, the one to whom he has such a duty does not necessarily thereby acquire any corresponding right. . . . If we have duties to the dead, for example to tend their graves or not to slander their memory, it does not follow that they have a corresponding right.[31]

Why do the living have duties *toward*—or more accurately *regarding*—the dead? I argue that this is so because the dead deserve respect,[32] and they deserve respect because they possess dignity.[33] The basis for assigning duties to the living is thus to show that the dead possess dignity. Given that the dead are *past* human beings, *posthumous dignity* is not the same as the *human dignity* (or *personal dignity*) of the living, though both are closely related. Human dignity implies an appeal to respect the actual humanity of the living and constitutes the foundation of their human rights;[34] *posthumous dignity* implies an appeal to respect the past humanity of the dead and constitutes the foundation for the duties of the living.

Is There Evidence for Posthumous Dignity?

The claim that the dead possess posthumous dignity and therefore deserve respect rests on indirect but firm evidence. It consists of one set of coherent facts.

One of the most corroborated facts within anthropological research is that the living almost universally *do* respect the dead and believe that the latter have dignity. In 1955, Claude Lévi-Strauss wrote: "There is probably no society that does not treat its dead with dignity. At the borders of the human species, even Neanderthal man buried his dead in summarily arranged tombs."[35]

Archaeologists consider traces of funerary rites in a certain territory as very powerful proof of the presence of human activity there. The Latin word for humanity, "humanitas," is reportedly derived from "humando," which means, "burying."[36] Even if mourning seems to be a feature of some other living creatures also, only human beings developed a sustained and deeply ritual relationship with their dead.

In various provisions, the universally ratified *Geneva Conventions* stress that human remains should be respected.[37] International regulations and conventions have emphasized this at least since the nineteenth century. In addition, all countries have elaborated burial and cemetery regulations to secure the decent treatment of human remains. Moreover, the costly and time-consuming search for remains of fallen soldiers or victims of disasters is explainable only by the importance of posthumous dignity. Not surprisingly, posthumous restoration of the dignity of deceased victims of serious human rights abuses was a powerful motive behind the establishment of the International Criminal Court in 2002. One of the crimes within the court's jurisdiction is the war crime of outrages upon personal dignity, which officially includes "outrages upon the dignity of dead persons."[38] Paradoxically, even these outrages upon the dignity of the dead (mutilation of dead bodies and refusal of decent burial) are proof *a contrario* for the existence of posthumous dignity: those who desecrate corpses and graves often perceive dead bodies as more than things. Likewise, the fact that most people feel offended by such desecration suggests that human remains possess value.

The evidence provided by this set of facts is strengthened by five assumptions.[39] The first two concern the dead themselves. I have already expounded my first assumption, that the dead body as a *res nullius* has a special status between human beings and things. My second and related assumption is that human beings retain symbolic traces of their humanity and personality after they die. Philosopher Joel Feinberg formulated this insight as follows:

> [P]ostpersons . . . are naturally associated with actual persons, and thus become natural repositories for the sentiments real persons evoke in us. . . .
> [T]he neomort . . . is not only a symbol of human beings generally, but . . .
> it is the symbolic remains of a particular person and his specific traits and history. . . . One cannot murder a corpse . . . but one can violate it symbolically, and few societies are prepared to tolerate its public mutilation.[40]

In his four-volume work on the moral limits of criminal law, Feinberg does not treat the mutilation of corpses in the first volume, *Harm to Others*, but in the second, *Offense to Others*. And of course, by "others" are meant the living here. The dead themselves are defenseless and vulnerable, and arouse the need for protection in the living. In the quotation, Feinberg spoke only about the recently deceased, but I do not believe that the passage of time entirely erodes these feelings of respect and compassion. When we observe how the living treat those long dead, how skulls, relics, effigies, and masks inspire awe, we can say that the symbolic value of the dead never disappears completely.[41]

The third assumption affects the dead when still alive. Concerns can extend beyond the limits of one's lifetime. Some interests and claims survive, as it were, their owner's death, although the posthumous status of these interests and claims probably requires another name than "interests" or "claims." The wishes of the living about what will happen to their body, wealth, or reputation after their deaths are often expressed as promises, contracts, life insurance policies, testaments, and deathbed wishes. Nobody would ever go to that much trouble if no social practice of respect existed and if it were known that these wishes would not be honored posthumously. In short, the prospect that, once dead, we ourselves will be treated with respect and that our wishes will not be neglected, powerfully contributes to a generalized attitude of respect.[42]

The last two assumptions concern the relationship between the dead and the living.[43] The fourth assumption is that, for most of us, the web of rights and duties does not seem to stop at the death of our loved ones. We pity the dead because we knew them before they died and experience their death as a loss. "We *think of* the dead as the persons they were antemortem."[44] If, in my second assumption, I defended the view that the dead themselves retain traces of humanity, I now add that the dead continue their life, as it were, in the resemblance of their children (if they had children) and in memories that capture the mind of surviving families, friends, and, perhaps, of wider circles. Moreover, their former life leaves traces in the objects, projects, and works on which they left their mark. All of this constitutes a personal legacy and continues the relationship beyond death.[45] The fifth assumption repeats this idea at the level of humanity as a whole. The living and the dead are two groups of sufficient similarity to speak of them as members of one historical community. In its 1997 *Universal Declaration on the Human Genome and Human Rights,* UNESCO stated that the human genome underlies the unity of all members of the human family and can be called, in a symbolic sense, the heritage of humanity.[46] At the same time, the living and the dead are sufficiently different to assign each group its own moral status, entailing rights and duties for the living and protection for the dead.

From the preceding discussion, I conclude that the dead possess dignity and therefore deserve respect and protection. This, in turn, constitutes a credible basis for assigning duties to the living. I do not need concepts with such metaphysical echo as "afterlife," "immortality," "spirits," "souls," or even "ancestors," to justify such duties, but I cannot imagine them without the twin concepts of posthumous dignity and posthumous respect.

Why does posthumous dignity exist? This question is as difficult as the one about the reasons for the existence of human dignity.[47] Some may believe that posthumous dignity is attributed to the dead by the living, others that it is intrinsic—and recognized as such by the living. Perhaps both are true, in that the dead possess *potential* dignity, which is aroused and becomes manifest each time the living come into contact with them.

Which Duties Do the Living Have to the Dead?

The duties to the dead are:[48]

1. partly *passive* or *negative,* partly *active* or *positive:* many favoring abstention, others favoring intervention;

2. wholly *moral* and partly *legal:* all are addressed to the conscience, but some are also enforceable by law; in general, the more remote the dead, the more duties are moral;
3. *universal, not specific.*

I will implicitly show the validity of the first and second characteristic by presenting a list of duties. Later, I shall return to the issue of universality.

The list in Table 4.1 was compiled as follows. Some United Nations instruments mention the dead explicitly or contain articles partly applicable to them. Other texts about victims of armed conflicts describe the treatment of the dead directly. Finally, still other codes tell museums, archaeologists, physicians, and copyright holders how to behave responsibly toward the dead. Relevant passages of these texts are quoted in Appendix 5.1.

On the basis of these documents, I identify eight duties in what I call a *Declaration of Duties of the Living to the Dead:* four body- and property-related duties, three personality-related duties, and one general duty. In order to fulfill these duties, two rights in particular are necessary; they will be discussed in Chapter 5. Let us now look at the *Declaration.* The formulation of the structure and content of this *Declaration* took shape after much trial and error. In early drafts, I looked at what are now the second and third duties (funeral and burial) as a single duty; only when I separated the ritual of departure from the pure act of burial, did many data about the dead fall into their right place. Originally, I underestimated the property-related aspects of the fourth duty (will)—although they are so obvious. My first wording of the fifth duty (identity) was incomplete. And it took a long time before I added "heritage"(the eighth duty) to the list. While gradually refining the group of duties, very early in the process I developed the idea of two facilitating rights that the living needed to execute their duties to the dead (see Chapter 5).[50]

In an advanced version of the *Declaration,* a preamble should be inserted to refer to the posthumous dignity of the dead and to the respect owed to them. Perhaps it should also state one general clause: when the duties of the living to the dead conflict with the rights of the living, the latter take precedence (because, as mentioned, the living have a higher moral status than the dead), but only after the performance of a test in which those rights and duties of the living are carefully assessed. Such a balancing process should be based on principles of accountability (of those taking action) and free, prior, and informed consent (of the dead when still alive or of their representatives). The

TABLE 4.1 *Universal Declaration of Duties of the Living to the Dead*
(outline)

Source of duties:
The dead possess posthumous dignity and therefore deserve respect and protection.

Class		Duties
Body- and property-related duties	Art. 1	**Body** The duty to protect the physical integrity of the dead.
	Art. 2	**Funeral** The duty to honor the dead with last rites.
	Art. 3	**Burial** The duty to bury or cremate the dead decently and not to disturb their rest.
	Art. 4	**Will** The duty to respect the will of the dead concerning their body and property.
Personality-related duties	Art. 5	**Identity** The duty to search for and identify the dead; to record their death and its cause, their name, date of birth and death, and (if applicable) their nationality.
	Art. 6	**Image** The duty to weigh the privacy and reputation of the dead against the public interest when depicting them.
	Art. 7	**Speech** The duty to weigh the privacy and reputation of the dead against the public interest when disclosing facts about them.
General duties	Art. 8	**Heritage** The duty to identify and safeguard the heritage of the dead.
Consequential rights (see Table 5.1)	Art. 9	**Memory** The right to mourn, to bury and cremate, and to commemorate.
	Art. 10	**History** The right to know the truth about past human rights abuses.

Sources:[40] *Basic Principles and Guidelines on the Right to a Remedy and Reparation* (2005); *Berne Convention for the Protection of Literary and Artistic Works* (1979); *Code of Ethics for Museums* (2004); *Declaration on the Responsibilities of the Present Generations towards Future Generations* (1997); *Guiding Principles on Human Organ Transplantation* (1991); *International Convention for the Protection of All Persons from Enforced Disappearance* (2006); *International Covenant on Civil and Political Rights* (1966); *International Criminal Court Statute* (1998) and *Elements of Crimes* (2002); *Pre-Draft Declaration on Human Social Responsibilities* (2003); *Protocols Additional to the Geneva Conventions* (1977); *Third Geneva Convention* (1949); *Universal Declaration of Human Rights* (1948); *Universal Declaration on Democracy* (1997); *Universal Declaration on the Human Genome and Human Rights* (1997); *Updated Set of Principles To Combat Impunity* (2005); *Vermillion Accord on Human Remains* (1989).

balancing, however, is not between two interests of equal importance; it should be carried out with a presumption in favor of the living.[51]

On Posthumous Privacy and Posthumous Reputation

Before looking at the *Declaration* step by step, a broader problem encompassing more than just single duties has to be addressed. Some maintain that privacy and reputation do not extend beyond death. This thesis is only tenable when privacy and reputation are perceived as rights; it is not when the latter are seen as characteristics. Hence, posthumous privacy and reputation do exist: they are *characteristics* of the dead, not rights.

William Prosser has made a famous classification of invasions of privacy (of living persons), which can be applied, *mutatis mutandis*, to the dead. He distinguished four torts:

(1) "intrusion": intrusion upon the victim's seclusion or solitude, or into his private affairs; (2) "disclosure": public disclosure of embarrassing private facts about the victim; (3) "false light": publicity which places the victim in a false light in the public eye; and (4) "appropriation": appropriation, for own advantage, of the victim's name or likeness.[52]

How does Prosser's list apply to the dead? "Intrusion" is applicable to the body- and burial-related Articles 1, 2 and 3; from this angle, the privacy of the dead is understood as the duty not to handle the body indecently, not to show it disrespectfully during the funeral, and not to disturb the grave. This is well summarized in the phrase "rest in peace." Both body- and burial-related invasions of the privacy of the dead are regulated by law; the mutilation of corpses and the desecration of graves are prohibited everywhere. As already mentioned, the International Criminal Court is empowered to punish such "outrages upon the dignity of dead persons" when they occur during armed conflicts. This area is rightly judicialized. But perhaps one exception can be made for scientific concerns. In recent decades, there has been a heated debate between indigenous peoples and archaeologists about the question of whether the latter are allowed to excavate and study the dead bodies, graves, and grave goods of the ancestors of indigenous peoples without the latter's approval. As a result of this debate, archaeologists codified responsible conduct in this area.[53] A solution for the tension between the privacy of the dead and the need of scholars to gather knowledge about the past and the dead is better served by a code of ethics than by law.

The duty to respect the last will of the deceased (Article 4) is also privacy-related. In a case about a German citizen who wished to scatter his ashes in his garden, the European Commission of Human Rights, while declaring the application inadmissible, stated about Article 8 of the European Convention of Human Rights (the right to privacy):

> It may be doubted whether or not this right [to privacy, *adb*] includes the right of a person to choose the place and determine the modalities of his burial. Whilst those arrangements are made for a time after life has come to an end, this does not mean that no issue concerning such arrangements may arise under Article 8 since persons may feel the need to express their personality by the way they arrange how they are buried. The Commission therefore accepts that the refusal of the German authorities to allow the applicant to have his ashes scattered in his garden on his death is so closely related to private life that it comes within the sphere of Article 8 of the Convention.[54]

Although the scattering of ashes was *covered* by the right to privacy, in this specific instance, it was not *protected* by it.[55] On the other hand, in this case, the body- and personality-related aspects of the dead came together.

The next two invasions, disclosure of private information of the dead (if it is arbitrary or unlawful) and putting them in a false light, are obviously relevant for the image- and speech-related duties of Articles 6 and 7 of my *Declaration*. Judges, for example, have called the publication of photographs of a mutilated body shortly after an assassination an attack on the dignity and privacy of the deceased person (Article 6).[56] Clearly, arbitrary or unlawful disclosure and false light are not only invasions of privacy, but often also attacks on reputation.[57] Articles 6 and 7 presuppose that journalists and researchers treat sensitive personal data with care, and, in exceptional cases, with confidentiality.[58] The scope of Articles 6 and 7 is best served with dejudicialization. This is so because the use of laws leads all too often to glaring abuses in this domain (see Chapter 3).[59] When I discuss Articles 6 and 7 in detail, I shall propose a strategy to cope with the tension between the privacy and reputation of the dead and the right to historical research.

Prosser's fourth tort, appropriation of name or likeness, is connected with the identity- and image-related duties of Articles 5 and 6. In a sense, this is probably the most frequent invasion of the privacy of the (famous) dead, because there are always people who want to reap the benefits of their fame. Transferability of fame after death and descent of the right of publicity are relevant questions here, but they touch on property rights rather than privacy rights.[60]

In sum, seven of the eight duties to the dead have privacy and (to a lesser extent) reputation aspects. The question whether the eighth duty (Article 8: "heritage") has privacy- and reputation-related aspects is more complex. This is so because in this article, the perspective is switched from individuals (the level at which Articles 1–7 are best understood) to communities.[61] It follows that privacy- and reputation-related aspects seem to be less obvious here and that Prosser's scheme should be dropped. And still, even heritage has a clear privacy- and reputation-related dimension. To the extent that heritage, either material or immaterial, is the work of individual authors, certain copyright regulations are at stake. The crucial idea here is that, in principle, authors have a so-called *moral right*, that is, a right to be recognized as author and to object (personally or otherwise) to any defamatory distortion or mutilation of their work (see also Chapter 1). That the moral right of authors extinguishes fifty years after their death, that heritage is commonly older that fifty years, that many authors of works of heritage are unknown, and that in many cultures and times, copyright did either not exist or was collective—all of these are circumstances that are not relevant in the present discussion. The idea of a moral right of authors proves that heritage has a privacy- and reputation-related element. Therefore, all eight duties of the living to the dead have a privacy dimension. They express the idea that posthumous privacy and posthumous reputation are nothing else than empirical dimensions of the posthumous dignity of the dead.

Body- and Property-related Duties

Article 1. The dead body is our necessary starting point. Article 1, however, has a paradoxical tinge, because what can "physical integrity" possibly mean when a body is slowly disintegrating? It means that, even then, the body should be handled with respect. Problems of compliance may arise in times of mass death (epidemics, natural disasters, wars, and political violence) when emergency burial is needed for public health reasons. Another problematic moment may be the regular clearance of old graves at cemeteries, as their maintenance in perpetuity is a sheer impossibility.[62] A typical area in which the balancing test has to be applied is in weighing the interest in the integrity of the dead body and the interest in organ and tissue donation to prolong the lives of patients. As a rule, the use of dead bodies for autopsies and for research for scientific or therapeutic purposes should be allowed, if carried out in accordance with the law.[63] However, sale of the body or its parts is never allowed because the dead body is not a property and cannot be inherited.

Although the dead body is a *res nullius,* Article 1 does contain some property aspects. Most legal systems provide relatives with *quasi-property rights* to custody of the body between death and burial. This means, according to Thomas Grey, "that they [the relatives, *adb*] have a legal duty to see that the body receives a prompt decent burial, and if anyone interferes with the body in a way that causes the family emotional distress, they can recover compensatory money damages."[64] Grey's explanation implies that a body should be returned to relatives when it is not in their custody and if they are not estranged from the deceased.

Articles 2 and 3. Like Article 1, Article 2 ("funeral") is a direct translation of the principles of dignity and respect. Indeed, organizing funerals or last rites is one of the distinguishing features of human beings. Universal though it may be, cultural and religious traditions should obligatorily be taken into account when this duty is performed. What is accepted as a respectful practice in one culture, is often perceived as strange (even indecent) in the next.[65] Normally, Article 2 ("funeral") and Article 3 ("burial") go together. However, a funeral can be held without a body (with the deceased represented symbolically), a burial without a rite. Both also have partly separate ramifications, a funeral with will and memory (Articles 4 and 9), and a burial with body and will (Articles 1 and 4). A burial is the act of depositing individual human remains below, on, or above the surface of the earth, usually as part of the funeral.[66] In fact, the destination of the remains can be earth (burial), fire (cremation), air (air burial) or water (sea burial). The remains are the body and what is eventually left of it (bones, ashes or cremains, mummies, embalmed bodies).

Article 3 raises problems in cases of group burials. A "group burial" means either that two or more unidentifiable sets of remains (for example, remains of victims of war or disaster) are buried or cremated together, or that two or more sets of identified remains are intentionally rendered unidentifiable, either partly (for instance, in family tombs) or wholly (when paupers are buried in common graves, or when cemeteries are cleared and exhumed remains stored together). These forms of collective disposal are different from a third form: mass graves as a result of violence. All forms have implications for Article 5 ("identity").

Also problematic is a concept seemingly at odds with privacy, that of a double burial. This concept, though, covers five situations and only some of them are an invasion of privacy. First, it is customary in many cultures to enclose the period of mourning between a provisional and a definitive burial.[67] Second, emergency burial may be necessary if a body cannot immediately be identified or transported to its permanent place of rest. Third, exhumation is sometimes required to regroup graves, to relocate cemeteries or to carry out autopsies, after which the bodies are reinterred. The fourth situation refers to the closure of a period of human rights abuses: at that moment, it frequently occurs that bodies from anonymous graves are reburied in a solemn manner. The last situation relates to periods of human rights abuses themselves. In the course of a genocide, perpetrators may exhume bodies and transport them to new mass gravesites in order to erase traces of the crime.

Burial sites contain graves and urns. They often also encompass such symbolic objects as effigies, ancestral masks, busts, tablets, funerary statues, altars for ancestor worship, or memorial monuments.[68] From this, it is clear that Article 3 has some important property aspects, which should be carefully regulated. They include architecture (crypts, mausoleums, charnel houses, columbaria, and shrines), and funeral offerings and grave goods. The ritual scattering of ashes in a place and on a time of personal significance, which can be considered as a dignified destination of remains, is perhaps the only legitimate exception to the rule that there has to be a place to rest.

Article 4. Perceptions of the wishes of the dead may vary considerably. Article 4 therefore applies to clearly formulated wishes in the first place and, in their absence, to cases where they can be established beyond a reasonable doubt. The article is body-related when it regulates the disposal of the remains and property-related when it regulates the estate (including both tangible and intangible property). As said before, the right of persons to choose the place and form of their burial is an aspect of their right to privacy. Indeed, these "wishes of the dead" can be seen as an extension of the freedom that they enjoyed while alive. Traditions and laws, of course, put limits to the execution of the will; for example, when the property bequeathed was acquired illegally or when burial wishes are unlawful, unreasonable, or not executable. Article 4 does not cover wishes of testators unrelated to body or property, such as those regarding the desired behavior of close relatives, although this does not mean that those wishes are unimportant. As the making of a will is an act implying rational decisions, the International Institute for the Unification of Private Law UNIDROIT recommends that testators draft wills in the presence of an authorized person and witnesses.[69]

Article 4 covers such diverse matters as intellectual property questions and endowments for memorials and commemorations (forms of posthumous maecenate). Indeed, the will is often used as a tool for saving certain personality characteristics (the subject of Articles 5 to 7) from oblivion.[70] A complication arises—not the least for archivists and historians—when the will reflects an urge to be forgotten instead of remembered, such as, for example, when it stipulates that personal papers should be destroyed after their author's death.

Personality-related Duties

Article 5. Whereas body- and property-related duties refer to what is left of the *human being* after death, personality-related duties refer to what is left of the *person* after death. Article 5 ("identity") is meant to protect against anonymous death. It signifies, first of all, searching for the dead when they have disappeared (during human rights abuses) or are missing (during wars and calamities). The "tomb of the unknown soldier" is a way to cope with the anonymity of death during war.[71] The article further includes official registration of certain individual particulars and the marking of graves and urns. This emphasis on personal identity is shared by most cultures. It also is a cornerstone of human rights philosophy. In a context of massive human rights abuses, identification of dead bodies is an act establishing an elementary form of historical truth. In recent decades, millions of surviving relatives demanded this form of truth (see Chapter 5).

Nevertheless, as we saw during the discussion of Article 4, the freely uttered wish to be forgotten should also be respected (to a certain extent). The complement of the wish to be forgotten, namely the wish to forget, is a characteristic of certain cultures. The custom of temporarily tabooing names of the dead and of mourners, we are told by the anthropologist James Frazer, existed in several cultures in order not to disturb the spirit of the deceased. Frazer wrote that in some cultures the tabooing of names hampered, and even made impossible, historical knowledge, for "how can history be written without names?"[72]

Articles 6 and 7. Article 6 ("image") does not refer to images of living people after their death, nor to images of people who are dying (e.g., during executions), but to the display of dead bodies, human remains, effigies, grave goods, and burial sites, and to pictorial representations (drawings, paintings, photographs, slides, and films) of them.[73] Public interest may override the private interest implied in Article 6, for example, in historical works, reports about war or human rights violations, or artistic endeavors. The question in particular of whether what is shown renders the dead identifiable has to be taken into account in any balancing test.

Article 7 ("speech") covers the whole range of relevant texts: tape recordings or descriptions of funerals, epitaphs, funerary orations, death notices, obituaries, commemorative addresses and texts, biographies, genealogies, and other historical works. As explained in Chapter 3, it is essential to emphasize that Articles 6 and 7 are applicable to facts only and not to opinions. Opinions are not susceptible to a truth proof and therefore enjoy greater protection than facts do (with the exception of those opinions amounting to wholly unfounded speculations). Without this essential provision, many conversations, writings, or images would be unduly hampered.

The crucial problem is how to maintain that the dead possess privacy and reputations without at the same time blocking access to sensitive archives or preventing critical research and writing about the dead. There is a solution in two steps. The first step involves *dejudicialization*. This means that not judges, but instead responsible historians and other researchers should be allowed to handle the problem. This step presupposes two conditions. The first is not to equate possible harm done to the privacy and reputation of the dead with invasion of privacy, respectively defamation. The second condition is not to perceive privacy and reputation as inheritable, that is, not to equate the interest of grieved relatives and friends in the untarnished privacy and reputation of the dead with the interest of the dead in their own privacy and reputation when they were still alive. The latter condition is the most important, because judges tend not to occupy themselves with the dead if no surviving relatives or other living complainants are involved (see Chapter 3).

The honest search for historical truth by responsible historians and others concerned with the past is the prime guarantee for complying with Articles 6 and 7. Nevertheless, the right of historians (and society as a whole) to know the truth can come into genuine conflict with their duty to respect the privacy and reputation of the dead. For such cases, a second step is needed: like judges, historians should apply a test in which they carefully weigh the issues at stake. This balancing test should determine whether in omitting sensitive facts (and even opinions) about the dead, the benefit gained in terms of privacy and reputation protection outweighs the harm inflicted on freedom of expression and historical truth. On the one hand, the expected benefit must be substantial. On the other hand, historians should be aware that the dead cannot defend themselves against the mention of certain facts or opinions about them anymore. If the test result favors privacy and reputation, the fact or opinion is not mentioned. Although such a test should form a *structural* part of the

critical method used by historians, it should not be mentioned obligatorily in their work. Otherwise, taking controversial or new positions
on historical facts would become exceedingly difficult, if not impossible. Moreover, it is not easy to justify the omission of facts without mentioning them. It is, however, recommended that historians
discuss in their work *substantive* objections of their subjects of study
or of the latter's surviving relatives, *if known*, to their statements or
theses. Historians should also resist the temptation to think that the
reasoned omission of a fact or opinion diminishes their prestige or
the importance of their work.

All of this leads to one conclusion. Historians should have a right to
silence: a right to omit sensitive privacy- and reputation-related facts
and opinions when the balancing test presses in that direction. This
should apply for the whole area of historical writing, even for biographies, where it is exactly the aim to describe, and possibly to evaluate,
public and private aspects of the person portrayed. The right to silence
expresses the idea that freedom of expression in public, however crucially important, is not absolute.

For balancing test purposes, however, there is an important distinction between privacy and reputation. While the test in reputation
cases should be executed with a presumption in favor of disclosure,
the test in privacy cases is a test between two interests of equal importance (omission and disclosure). Why is this so? Why should privacy
and reputation be treated differently? The fundamental reason lies in
the fact that the revelation of truth in reputation cases should not be
considered defamatory (reputations based on untruth are unearned),
while the revelation of truth in privacy cases, especially the privacy
of ordinary citizens, is often embarrassing for the victim but at the
same time rather futile information for the curious audience. In addition, defamation laws are frequently abused and have a *chilling* effect
on free speech, while the protection of privacy defends the autonomy
of the person and is generally seen as *encouraging* free speech. This
difference between reputation and privacy is expressed in the balancing procedure.[74]

Similar solutions apply, *mutatis mutandis*, to comments by other
groups, such as journalists and writers. The double approach of dejudicialization and balancing is possible only when historians are able
to convince all interested parties (enumerated in Table 6.2) of their
willingness to be accountable. A necessary condition for this is that
they operate on the basis of a transparent code of professional ethics,
in which the responsible handling of information and the balancing
test are described. That is part of the road walked in Chapter 6.

General Duties

Article 8. Article 8 ("heritage") does not require extensive comment here, as UNESCO has already done much pioneering work in this area during the last decades. Tangible cultural heritage covers monuments, buildings, and sites, which are of outstanding universal value from the historical, esthetic, or anthropological viewpoint. Intangible cultural heritage is manifested in oral traditions and expressions, including language, the performing arts, social practices, rituals and festive events, knowledge and practices concerning nature and the universe, and traditional craftsmanship. Natural heritage encompasses natural features, formations, sites, and areas of outstanding universal value from the viewpoint of science, conservation, or esthetics.[75]

The heritage that the dead leave engenders problems of intellectual property and copyright similar to those signaled in the discussions about posthumous privacy and reputation and about indigenous peoples and archaeologists. Another problem is that the UNESCO conception of heritage privileges its positive elements. It can be argued—and in the next chapters, it will—that certain negative aspects of the heritage of humanity should also be safeguarded. Public knowledge of the history of the repression of a people, for example, must be considered as part of that people's heritage.

On the Posthumous Reparation of Historical Injustice

In my *Universal Declaration of the Duties of the Living to the Dead,* no explicit duty regarding the reparation of injustices done to the dead when alive appears. According to the United Nations, reparation of injustice includes five forms: restitution, compensation, rehabilitation, guarantees of nonrepetition, and satisfaction.[76] The first two forms, restitution and compensation, are mainly financial. Financial claims to repair historical injustice, although sometimes urgently needed, clearly exceed the framework of the *Declaration.* Two reasons are that these claims are never applicable to all of the dead and that they necessarily fade over time—and these reasons go against the universality principle of the *Declaration.* Another reason is that the addressees of restitution or compensation cannot be the direct victims (they are dead), but their heirs. And even if the United Nations' definition limits "indirect victimhood" mainly to the immediate family or dependants, while excluding the extended family or other heirs, we are talking of a right of reparation for the living.[77] And a last reason is that as we are underinformed about the remote past and even about the recent past in which much injustice occurred, it is often exceedingly difficult to determine exactly who has to pay how much and to whom.[78] The third form, rehabilitation (understood as medical and psychological rehabilitation), is clearly not applicable to the dead, but only to the survivors of injustice. For a similar reason, the fourth form of reparation, guarantees of nonrepetition, is not applicable for a similar reason: the guarantees come too late for the dead.

In contrast, the last form of reparation, satisfaction, is present in almost all of the articles of the *Declaration*. Satisfaction often takes the name of symbolic reparation or posthumous rehabilitation. Forensic work with dead bodies in postconflict situations (Article 1) and solemn reburial (Article 3) are examples. Posthumous rehabilitation also contains a *social* aspect, that is, when collective symbolic measures of reparation (for example, official apologies from governments succeeding abusive regimes, commemorative ceremonies such as the collective minute of silence for the dead, or the erection of funerary monuments) are taken. Such measures are part of the mourning rituals covered by Article 2 (and Article 9). *Legally*, posthumous rehabilitation means that biased court judgments are reviewed or annulled, and that the reputation of former convicts is posthumously restored (Article 7); *politically*, it signifies that permission is given to publicly mention the formerly censored names of the dead again, to republish their works, and to publish biographies about them, in short, to restore their formerly censored legacy, identity, image- and speech- related characteristics, and heritage (Articles 4–8). In my *Declaration*, the form of reparation called "satisfaction," "posthumous rehabilitation," or "symbolic reparation" is covered well. Like posthumous privacy and reputation, it is an *empirical* dimension of posthumous dignity.

When Are the Duties of the Living to the Dead Unfulfilled?

The fact that the living *owe* respect to the dead does not mean that, in practice, they *have* respect for them. On the contrary, their actual attitude varies very much on a scale going from respect over fear to hostility. Therefore, it is time to ask how the living can fail to fulfill their duties to the dead. This question should be distinguished from another question, widely discussed among philosophers, namely whether the irreversible character of death itself can be seen as an irreparable harm.[79] Posthumous harm as understood in the latter discussion is different from the wrongs discussed in Table 4.2. The table specifies sixty wrongs, either legal or moral:

TABLE 4.2. *Moral and/or Legal Wrongs to the Dead* (tentative overview)

Related to duties 1 and 5, and to right 9:

* *Enforced disappearances of persons* (as crimes against humanity or otherwise) followed by execution and concealment or abandonment of dead bodies.[80]
* *Outrages upon the dignity of dead persons* (as war crimes or otherwise): violations of posthumous dignity, including intentional ill treatment (cannibalism/necrophagy; mutilation of dead bodies; necrophilia).[81]
* Unwarranted invasions of the privacy of the dead (understood as disturbing dead bodies).
* Suspension of, or obstruction to, *habeas corpus* to prevent identification of dead detainees.
* Intentional obstruction of the process of identification of human remains.[82]
* Unauthorized handling of human remains or tampering with the scene of death.
* Confiscation, illegal collection or theft of (parts of) dead bodies.
* Unlawful or unauthorized autopsy or *postmortem* research.
* Disrespectful treatment of dead bodies during or after autopsy or *postmortem* research.
* Routine salvaging of, or commerce in, dead body parts.

Related to duties 1–3 and 5, and to rights 9–10:

* *Outrages upon the dignity of dead persons* (as war crimes or otherwise): violations of posthumous dignity, including live burial, disrespectful funeral and burial (frequently, mass and anonymous burial), refusal of approval for burial.
* Unwarranted invasions of the privacy of the dead (understood as disturbing graves).
* Imposition of last rites or of a mode or moment of disposal culturally or religiously alien to the dead or their families.
* Illicit conditional return of bodies to relatives (as crimes against humanity or otherwise).
* Inappropriate delay of burial.
* Disrespectful, premature, or unauthorized exhumation of bodies.
* Obstruction of legitimate exhumation of bodies.
* Reburial or cremation to erase crime traces and forensic evidence.[83]

Related to duties 1–3, 5 and 7, and to rights 9–10:

* Anonymous grave or cemetery or unrecorded burial (unknown to all).
* Clandestine or unmarked grave or cemetery or secretly recorded burial (unknown to family and friends).
* Concealment of burial and location of graves and cemeteries.
* Distortion of religiously or culturally prescribed orientation of graves or position of bodies.

(continued)

TABLE 4.2. *Moral and/or Legal Wrongs to the Dead* (tentative overview) (continued)

Related to duties 1–3, 5 and 7, and to rights 9–10 (continued):

* Degrading location in cemeteries by refusing to bury in sacred ground.
* Degrading location in cemeteries by burying bodies together or not together.
* Obstruction of maintenance of grave or cemetery.
* Attack, desecration, destruction, and looting of grave and cemetery.
* Desecration or destruction of representations of the dead and their graves: effigies, portraits, relics, statues, ancestral masks, busts, and tablets, funerary statues, altars for ancestor worship, memorial monuments.
* Disrespectful or unauthorized use, or clearance, of cemetery.

Related to duties 4 and 8:

* Unwarranted invasions of the privacy of the dead (understood as illicit refusal to keep promises to the dead or honor their will.).
* Pillage of dead bodies; confiscation of property of the dead.
* Imposition of unreasonably high inheritance taxes.
* Infringement of posthumous copyright (including both moral and material interests).

Related to duty 5:

* Unwarranted invasions of the privacy of the dead (understood as malicious appropriation of the name or likeness of the dead).

Related to duties 6–7:

* Disrespectful display of human remains, including public autopsies when not in the public interest.
* Distorted reproduction or contextualization of images of the dead when not in the public interest.
* Unwarranted invasions of the privacy of the dead (understood as arbitrary or unlawful disclosure of privacy- or reputation-sensitive information about them or as putting them in a false light).
* Unwarranted insult to, and defamation of, the dead.
* Posthumous trial, sentence, and punishment.
* *Damnatio memoriae* and similar measures taken with intent to punish posthumously.
* Improper omission (including censorship and self-censorship) of facts about the dead.
* Denial of facts about the dead based on firm evidence (especially genocide, crimes against humanity, war crimes).

(continued)

TABLE 4.2. *Moral and/or Legal Wrongs to the Dead* (tentative overview) (continued)

Related to duties 6–7 (continued):

* Intentional distortion (lies, hate speech, falsification, manipulation) of facts and opinions about the dead.
* Malicious invention of facts about the dead.
* Posthumous annulment of awards and honors.

Related to duty 8:

* Intentional destruction or looting of, or damage to, heritage or cultural property.[84]
* Illicit traffic of cultural property.

Related to duty 8 and to right 10:

* Refusal to document the history of repression as a part of a people's heritage.

Related to right 9:

* Obstruction of legitimate search for the dead either by relatives, the Red Cross, or states.
* Desecration or destruction of memorials.
* Obstruction of mourners attending ceremonies or accessing cemeteries, graves, urns; insult of mourners.
* Suppression or obstruction of peaceful funerary cortèges and pilgrimages, wakes, and commemorations.
* Persecution (censorship, intimidation, arrest, detention), or killing, of mourners.
* (In many instances:) attendance of offensive persons at funerals and commemorations.
* Public ceremonies for deceased perpetrators of human rights abuses.[85]

Related to right 10:

* Noncompliance with the duty to investigate and with the right to the truth (*or* the right to know *or* the right to *habeas data*) in cases of gross human rights violations.
* *Archival cleansing:* removal, concealment, neglect, illegal destruction of archives.
* Illegal nondisclosure or excessive secrecy of archives; illegal prohibition of access to them.

(continued)

TABLE 4.2. *Moral and/or Legal Wrongs to the Dead* (tentative overview)
(continued)

Related to right 10 (continued):

* Intimidation and elimination of producers, owners, and custodians of sources.
* Obstruction of forensic anthropologists excavating graves and skeletons.
* Disinformation regarding bodies, graves, cemeteries

On Posthumous Punishment

It is not always simple to determine whether wrongs to the dead are committed with the intent to punish them. Ritual cannibalism, for example, reportedly often serves to absorb the power of the deceased. Although this is considered a crime, it is not a form of posthumous punishment, like other types of cannibalism.[86] Likewise, desecration of cemeteries by the military may be a strategic objective (and, as such, be a form of punishment), but also spring from negligence (the lowest grade of criminal intent) or may be the unplanned side effect of a campaign. Robbing the dead, stealing their organs, or confiscating their estate are crimes either motivated by profit for the perpetrator, desire to punish the deceased, or both. Likewise, mutilating corpses and abandoning them in mass graves can constitute an attempt to erase traces of their identities, to punish enemies, or both.

Strictly speaking, "posthumous punishment" is an illogical concept for two reasons. If it means that the dead punish the living, one needs to postulate a metaphysical world in which the living live on after their deaths—an assumption not made here. If it means that the living punish the dead (as in the reflections above), it is equally illogical, because the living cannot submit the dead to outrages, humiliation, or punishment, for it is not the dead who suffer, but their surviving near and dear and human beings in general. However, the fact that some *believe* that the dead can be punished is important in itself. I see five motives that explain the occurrence of posthumous punishment.

When driven by *revenge,* the living punish the dead because they consider either that the latter escaped just punishment while alive or that they did receive it, but, not having it fully served, have to endure it after death as well. In the first category of victims, we encounter the powerful of the earth who have posthumously fallen in disgrace; in the latter, enemies and insurgents. Outlaw and outcast groups to whom

TABLE 4.3. **Posthumous Punishment** (motives and strategies)

perpetrators	motive	targets	victims	strategy		efficiency
individuals, groups, government	revenge	dead	1: dead 2: living	repressive	direct	dis-advan-tages for the living
	hatred					
	fear			preventive		
	deterrence	living	1: living 2: dead	preventive	indi-rect	
	offense					

Sources are inspired by Barber, Canetti, Gittings, Human Rights Office of the Archdiocese of Guatemala, Iserson, Merridale, Middleton, Schreuer, Thomas, Verdery, and Vernant.[87]

an evil genius is ascribed may also belong to this broad category.[88] The second, closely related, motive is the *hatred* that blinds the perpetrator. Revenge- and hatred-driven punishment can be divided into two types. The aim of mutilation of the corpse (the first type) is to divest it of all its human traces—which was, as we saw, one of the sources of its posthumous dignity. Nonburial of the corpse (the second type) is believed to block the transition from living to dead. Abandoned and deprived of a recognizable individual identity, the dead are not properly dead. According to the perpetrators, they are not allowed admission to the circle of the purified dead and in this way, they are harmed in their afterlife.

The discussion about the third motive, *fear*, should be introduced by a general remark. I argued that the elementary duties of the living to the dead (like guaranteeing the integrity of the dead body and a decent burial) *have to be* performed *because* the dead possess posthumous dignity. I further argued that these duties *are* performed *because* most believe that the dead possess posthumous dignity. However, as stated above, this respect for the dead is often accompanied by another motive: fear. Such fear is widespread. If the duties to the dead cannot be performed for one reason or another or if their performance is deemed unsatisfactory, that fear is not assuaged. The living who share this fear may think that the dead do not find rest and that they will return to the earth in anger and take revenge. These returning "living dead" either appear as ghosts, as ghosts tied to a body, or as vampires feeding themselves with the blood or bodies of the living. The anger of the dead is explained by tying it to events before, during, or after their death: they had either a cursed life (as in the case of those human beings to whom an evil genius was ascribed), died a death caused by the violence or recklessness of others, or did not receive a (decent) funeral or burial. Alternatively, their body or grave was desecrated, or they were resentful because they no longer lived. They err restlessly or suffer in a hell, and are embittered by the lack of attention or care of the surviving relatives and acquaintances. Although these restless and angry dead are usually appeased with carefully executed rituals, this fear can also degenerate into a preventive attack to forestall the revenge of the dead. This motive is usually visible in the sort of punishment designed essentially to prevent the corpse from "moving." Preventive strategies are risky, however, because when they fail, the anger of the dead may increase. It is open to debate whether the outrages committed against the dead out of fear are indeed forms of punishment. They spring from a strategy of self-protection. The will to really injure the dignity of the dead often seems to be only secondary. This is supported by the fact that sometimes even deceased relatives and friends belong to the victims of this category.

The dead are targets of posthumous punishment, but the living also become its victims. The last two motives, deterrence and offense of the living, are almost always side effects of the first series of motives. But they are also at work autonomously. Where that is the case, the perpetrators intend to address the living over the heads of the dead. *Deterrence* means that the perpetrators issue a warning to the living that, like the mutilated dead, they risk a cruel fate. Funerals are prohibited or broken up to prevent the potential stimulation of social cohesion or political protest among the mourners.[89] Graves are destroyed to prevent them from becoming the focus of a pilgrimage. The last motive, *offense*, is, I think, particularly used in genocidal forms of repression: corpses are mutilated and cemeteries desecrated in order to humiliate and offend certain categories of adversaries singled out for destruction. It is also a motive guiding many deniers of genocide. By deriding and heaping scorn on the dead, they target the living. If this succeeds, in a sense the dead, who are the object of the posthumous punishment, are worse off than the anonymous dead: if the punishers go unpunished, their perverted version of facts survives with the eternal risk of becoming the version dominantly remembered.[90]

Universality: Do *All* of the Living Have Duties to the Dead?

Universality of duties to the dead does not mean that the execution of such duties cannot vary across cultures. On the contrary, cultural variation is broad and justly so. Universality means that all of the living are in charge of the duties to the dead, and that these duties apply to all of the dead. When we say that *all* of the living have duties to *all* of the dead, we formulate a general principle; a principle valid even if one were the last human being on earth. In practice, of course, duties for *specific* deceased human beings will be prescribed by law and taken care of by certain groups. We may then ask who exactly is in charge of which dead. In the following survey, it is important to distinguish the personal level from the social level, as these two may come into conflict with one another (as will be shown in Chapter 5).

Foremost among these caretakers, of course, are the dead themselves when they were still alive. By leading a life, developing a personality, having interests, uttering wishes, and writing wills, they leave indications of how and by whom they would like to be taken care of after their death. The next caretakers are the relatives, who bury and mourn the dead. The role of relatives is so special that it can be said that many of the duties to dead are also duties to their surviving relatives. Nevertheless, there may be no surviving relatives or, in the case of divided families, the relatives may be indifferent or even hostile toward the dead. A circle of family friends, acquaintances, religious counselors, and sometimes wider solidarity networks and the whole community support the relatives. The extent to which these groups—affiliated with the deceased through friendship, culture, and shared traditions—are allowed to intervene is preeminently culture-bound. The next caretakers are the physicians, who determine the moment of death and often play an important role in *postmortem* investigations. Notaries, lawyers, and judges also act on behalf of the dead, particularly to execute their wills and solve any ensuing problems with the heirs and others.

At the level of society as a whole, truth commissions investigating past human rights abuses, courts combating impunity, and civil groups organizing commemorations can be said to taking care of the dead. The same is true for governments and parliaments regulating cemeteries, making archives on past repression accessible, returning human remains of disappeared victims to families, or issuing public apologies for past abuses. Historians (and such related professionals as archivists, archaeologists, and curators) have a special place among the guardians of the dead because in principle, they occupy themselves *systematically* with *all* of the dead of history—the near and the distant, the known and the anonymous.

All of those caretakers have a specific duty to fulfill. Typically, groups representing the dead meet problems that can undermine their protective role. The first of these is the problem of which guardians have the authority to represent the dead. This is particularly important when conflicts arise between the rights of the living and their duties to the dead. Second, guardians risk misinterpreting the wishes of the dead. Even when the dead left clearly formulated wishes, vexing problems of interpretation may arise when circumstances for executing these wishes were unforeseen at the time when they were formulated. This may lead to a third risk, explored in Chapters 3 and 5: the abuse of the memory of the dead. Perhaps historians are more aware of these risks than are others; whether they are more immune to them remains to be seen. Much depends upon the ethical principles regulating their work.

Universality: Do the Living Have Duties to *All* of the Dead?

Let us now look at the other side of the universality principle: its applicability to all of the dead. This is a problem that can be approached either anthropologically or historically. *Anthropological* universality means that the duties of the living to the dead are applicable to all of the dead without discrimination. The wording of the nondiscrimination article of the *Universal Declaration of Human Rights* (Article 2) can serve as a source of inspiration for this discussion: "Everyone is entitled to all the rights and freedoms . . . without distinction of any kind, such as race, color, sex, language, religion, political or other opinion, national or social origin, property, birth, or other status." A considerable problem may arise, however, when the clause "other status" is taken to mean "moral quality." Is it acceptable to say that the duties of the living apply to all of the dead, regardless of whether they have led a morally gratifying or a shameful life? The answer is Yes. Applicability of duties does not refer only to the benefactors, heroes, and saints of humanity, but also to its tyrants, criminals, and mass murderers. Although this may sound too lenient for perpetrators of human rights abuses and too bitter for their victims, the duties cover all of the dead, regardless of their moral merit. Moreover, even deceased tyrants, criminals, and mass murderers have mourning relatives. If moral quality made a difference, we would be forced to exclude many from the protection engendered by these duties. In addition, we would have to decide whom to admit to the circle of those protected. This would render our whole operation senseless.

Historical universality—applicability to all of the dead in history—is more troubling because most duties seem to fade over time. Even if the passage of time gradually erases the possibility of discharging those duties, however, it does not seem to erode the feelings of awe and compassion to the dead entirely. To address this problem, it is advisable to distinguish two classes among the dead: on the one hand, the known, including the recent dead and the dead of longer ago who left traces (the rich, the powerful, the famous), and, on the other, the anonymous, including the dead of longer ago who left no traces or no recognizable traces. There are few problems with the recent dead, who usually have several caretakers. There are more, but still manageable, problems with the distant dead who were rich and could afford to build tombs, or with the powerful and famous, who survived in many historical sources.

What shall we do, however, with the countless anonymous dead of history who left no recognizable traces at all and about whose existence historical sources inform us only indirectly? Here, identification and remembrance of individual past human beings are impossible, and the sensibilities of the living are absent. Our power to imagine their abstract existence as at least a category—a category that encompasses the majority of the hundred billion dead—is a shallow basis for discharging duties to them. However, the fragile knowability of so many dead, while making irrelevant almost all the duties to them, is a *practical* obstacle. If we exclude the countless anonymous dead of past generations and therefore reject the universality of our duties to the dead on the basis of an epistemological criterion, there would exist a moving time barrier at one side of which are those dead who fall within the scope of the duties of the living because we know something about them, and at the other side of which is the rest who falls outside of that scope. Such a barrier would be arbitrary and, in cases where historical or archaeological research suddenly uncovered data about unknown people, absurd. By retaining the known dead and rejecting the anonymous, that is, by retaining knowledge about the dead as a criterion instead of the dead themselves, we would also violate the nondiscrimination principle on which anthropological universality is based. This principle, in fact, does not mention "knowledge" as a criterion. The fact that the group of the distant dead, and by implication the group about which we know nothing, steadily increases, complicates the practice, not the principle.

A similar reasoning seems to be valid for the distant unborn. With regard to future generations, Derek Parfit introduced the so-called "Social Discount Rate" (SDR)—the view that the moral importance of future events, especially benefits and losses, declines at a rate of n percent per year. The SDR means that we are less concerned about the effects of our conduct in the further future. Parfit, however, discussed and discarded six different defenses of the SDR. None of these defenses succeeded because, although it may often be morally permissible to be less concerned about the more remote effects of our conduct, this would never be because these effects were more remote but for other reasons. In general, remote effects of our acts matter. This is particularly so when they are *permanent*, for example, when irreplaceable parts of our cultural heritage are destroyed.[91]

Due to the asymmetry between past and future generations, the SDR discussion is not (or, at best, tangentially) applicable to past generations. Still, Parfit's approach is enlightening and his refutation of one of the arguments in favor of a SDR, the "argument from democracy," can be applied to our problem. On this argument from democracy, we are allowed to be morally less concerned with the further future because *many* people care less about it. But the fact that many care less about the distant unborn does not mean that the moral question of whether we have duties to the latter does not exist.

And so it is with the distant dead. The fact that many care less about the distant dead does not mean that a moral question of whether we have duties to the latter does not arise. One might add that, even if most are less concerned with, say, the dead from the epoch of the Crusades than with the dead of World War II, many others *do* care about that further past. Populations with a strong historical awareness continuously remember historical facts and figures from centuries ago (even if often mythified versions of them). Likewise, in scores of countries, the nation's origins and, concomitantly, archaeological findings are sensitive topics. Our memory has the unremarkable yet fantastic capacity to bridge centuries in a second. Remoteness in time, anonymity, and untraceability may suspend our duties toward the distant dead almost indefinitely, but they can never annul them entirely. As a matter of principle, then, the duties to the dead are not only anthropologically universal, but also retroactively universal.[92]

✿ 5

THE RIGHTS TO MEMORY AND HISTORY

Our days are ended. Think, then, of us,
Do not erase us from your memory, nor forget us.
　　　—*Popol Vuh*, sacred book of the Quiché Maya[1]

Yet meet we shall, and part, and meet again
Where dead men meet, on lips of living men.
　　　—*Mellonta tauta*, Samuel Butler[2]

My tears will not bring her back to life.
This is why I am crying.
　　　—Anonymous French epitaph[3]

The duties to the dead discussed in Chapter 4 can be discharged on two conditions only. The first is that the living have a right to "pay their last respects": a right to mourn, to bury and cremate, and to commemorate. The second is that they have a right to know the truth about the past, most notably the painful events of that past—the human rights abuses that occurred. I refer to these consequential rights as a right to memory and a right to history, respectively. They are consequential in the sense that without them the living would not be able to perform their duties to the dead. These rights to memory and history were already charted in Table 4.1 and wrongs related to them were identified in Table 4.2. I shall now demonstrate that both emanate from the *International Covenant on Civil and Political Rights* (hereinafter *Covenant*) and therefore belong to the family of human rights. When these two rights are guaranteed, the protection of the posthumous dignity of the dead—and indirectly the protection of human dignity—is guaranteed. Protecting the posthumous dignity of the dead enhances the humanity of the living. The *Covenant* contains three rights that cover the rights to memory and history: privacy (Article 17), freedom of thought and conscience (Article 18), and freedom of opinion and expression (Article 19).[4]

A Right to Memory

My thesis is that every human being has a right to memory. To explain this, I have first to probe briefly into the essential distinction between *habit memory* and *declarative memory*. Habit memory (or procedural memory) covers the skills of people. Galen Strawson used the example of the violinist to describe it: "[T]he past shapes and animates the present. The past is alive in the present without being alive as the past, alive in explicit memory—just as a violinist's phrasing flows from her practice sessions without her needing to have any explicit memory of them. I believe this shaping is what matters most; this is the deepest continuance of memory."[5] The ways in which the past is present in the present often resemble this violinist's phrasing. Declarative memory, in contrast, encompasses the recollection of facts and events. The content of that memory can be expressed in language. Containing both personal (or autobiographical) memory and factual (or semantic) memory, it refers to thought and opinion.[6] When I discuss the possibility of a right to memory, of course I am referring to this declarative memory, not to habit memory.

Consider first the connection between memory and thought. The view that memory is a form of thought is widely accepted among legal scholars and philosophers. Simon Blackburn, for example, defines memory as "[t]he power of the mind to think of a past that no longer exists . . ."[7] Thinking is a conscious or semi-conscious activity of the mind that can be directed toward the past, the present, or the future. When it is directed toward the past, it mobilizes declarative memory and produces memories. This implies that although not all thoughts are memories, all memories are thoughts. The link between memory and thought is so obvious that the opposite point of departure—that memories are not thoughts—would be much harder to argue. In languages such as German and Dutch, the linguistic proximity between both is telling.

Consider next the connection between "thought" and "opinion" as mentioned in Articles 18 and 19 respectively of the *Covenant*. The leading commentators on the *Covenant*, Karl Josef Partsch and Manfred Nowak, consider thought and opinion as intimately related phenomena: thinking is a process, and when that process leads to a result, that result is called an opinion.[8] The authoritative *Black's Law Dictionary* shares this view.[9] And this close connection allows me to consider memories, which I have already called thoughts, as opinions also.[10] This implies that statements about thoughts and opinions in the *Covenant* equally apply to memories.

Opinions, and by extension memories, can be formed, held, and expressed. Forming, holding, and expressing opinions are protected by the *Covenant*, although in a markedly different manner. According to the *Covenant*, the right to *form and hold* opinions, and by extension memories, is protected by the freedoms of thought and conscience (Articles 18 and 19[1]). It is absolute and hence it permits no exception or restriction. It cannot be derogated in times of public emergency.[11] From this, it follows that the right to memory includes the absolute right to form and hold memories. As it is difficult, even impossible, to imagine restrictions on, or punishment for, memories that are not uttered, this conclusion is obvious, but it will play a central role in the discussion about a duty to remember.

The right to freely *express* opinions, and by extension memories, can be exerted in private or in public. When opinions, including memories, are expressed in private, they are protected by the right to privacy (Article 17 of the *Covenant*). The reason is that the right to privacy protects the home of a person and the latter's identity, including "one's specific past as well as confession to a belief or some other conviction."[12] Like the right to hold memories, the right to express them in private is absolute. When, however, opinions, including memories, are expressed in public, they may be subject to restrictions. These restrictions are meant to protect respect for the rights or reputations of others, national security, public order, public health, or morals. This list of restrictions is devised for all opinions uttered in public and not just for memories. Of this list, only the rights or reputations of others and, especially, the protection of public order seem to be applicable grounds for banning public expressions of memory. Combined, however, with the hard requirements that these grounds have to be prescribed by law and have to be "necessary" (in the sense of responding to "a pressing social need" or "a clear and present danger"), few restrictions on the right to publicly express memories seem to be legitimate. What we see in practice is rather the opposite, as any annual *Amnesty International Report* abundantly shows.[13] Indeed, public commemorations are frequently perceived as a threat to public order and disturbed or annulled: mourners attending ceremonies or accessing cemeteries are obstructed; pilgrimages, funerary cortèges, and wakes suppressed; memorials desecrated; mourners are even persecuted. The right to memory and to mourn, alone or combined with the cognate right to peaceful assembly, is often violated.[14] But the thesis that every human being has a right to memory is based on solid philosophical and legal grounds.

I will now examine a stronger claim, the claim of a duty to remember. Memory is a dimension of the performance of all of the duties to the dead. When burying the dead and performing last rituals in their honor, when tending their graves and executing their will, when caring for their identity, privacy, reputation, and heritage, it is impossible not to think of them, of who they were, and what they did when they were alive. Not once or twice, but repeatedly. Is remembrance, then, not a duty to the dead in itself? My answer to this question is No.

A Duty to Remember: Arguments in Favor

Looking more closely at those pleading a duty to remember, we can distinguish three motives. The first and most important one does not need much elaboration: the living owe a moral debt (a debt of gratitude) toward all of those ancestors who achieved something positive—those who built society, its infrastructure and institutions, those who inspired us by their ideas, teachings, writings, or art, and those who initiated venerated traditions. It is the ancient idea expressed by Bernard of Chartres around 1126: "In comparison with the ancients, we stand like dwarfs on the shoulders of giants."[15] In short, we owe a debt of remembrance to those ancestors who set an example and created our heritage (see Article 8 of my *Declaration*). This attitude is common in all cultures, sometimes under the guise of an ancestor cult. Often, the first motive also reserves a place for a special subgroup of ancestors: the heroes who fell in successive battles while defending the freedom and achievements of the community.[16]

The second motive emphasizes commemoration of the dead who were victims of grave human rights abuses. Acknowledging and recounting the suffering of deceased victims of crime would, they say, posthumously restore dignity to them, a dignity that they were denied while alive. In his *Statement to the Inaugural Meeting of Judges of the International Criminal Court*, former United Nations Secretary-General Kofi Annan declared: "For those who have been slaughtered, all we can do is seek to accord them in death the dignity and respect they were so cruelly denied in life."[17] Remembering the victims is also a weapon against forgetting the deeds of their killers, especially when the latter spread falsified versions of their past crimes or when third parties deny that these crimes took place.[18]

Finally, there is a third motive based on the view that the living should accept the past in its entirety, whether good or bad, as the dead created it.

The first motive individualizes its claims. It likes to draw attention to the plethora of works that describe the numerous individual contributions to the history of civilizations. The second motive demands commemoration of individuals even more strenuously. This can be inferred from most truth commission reports: they contain long lists of victims of human rights abuses. The paradigmatic text in this respect is the dedication of *The Gulag Archipelago*, written by Aleksandr Solzhenitsyn, who formed a truth commission *avant la lettre* on his own long before any sign of *glasnost* or transition became visible:

> I dedicate this to all those who did not live to tell it. And may they please forgive me for not having seen it all nor remembered it all, for not having divined all of it . . . In this book there are no fictitious persons, nor fictitious events. People and places are named with their own names. If they are identified by initials instead of names, it is for personal considerations. If they are not named at all, it is only because human memory has failed to preserve their names. But it all took place just as it is here described.[19]

The first and second motives for a duty to remember coincide dramatically in those cases where bearers of tradition and heritage become targets of human rights abuses. We are all well aware that, in times of war and genocide, pregnant women and children are often killed for the mere fact that they represent future generations. It also happens, especially in the case of genocide of indigenous communities, that the elderly are targeted. Usually, the elderly are the leaders of such communities and killing the former is a strategy to destroy the latter. But the elderly are also sometimes killed because they represent past generations and are the guardians of cultural memory. According to their killers, they must die in order to break the chain of transmission from past to present and future generations.[20] One is reminded of the proverb variously attributed to the Malian oral traditionist Amadou Hampâté Bâ and the Argentinian literary historian Ricardo Rojas: "When an old man dies, it is a library that burns."[21]

A Duty to Remember: Arguments Against

Criticism of the first motive (gratitude to the dead) has its roots in the nineteenth century. In a famous reply to Edmund Burke, Thomas Paine declared in 1791: "I am contending for the rights of the *living* and against their being . . . controlled . . . by the manuscript assumed authority of the dead; and Mr. Burke is contending for the authority of the dead over the rights and freedom of the living."[22] In his *The Eighteenth Brumaire of Louis Bonaparte* (1852), Karl Marx wrote: "The tradition of all the dead generations weighs like an alp upon the brain of the living."[23] And in criticizing monumental and antiquarian approaches to history in 1874,

Friedrich Nietzsche in fact criticized this motive. He maintained that adherents of these approaches left no place for forgetting and allowed the dead to bury the living.[24] Criticism of the second motive (restoration of the dignity of victims) is relatively recent and warns of the danger of exalting the status of victimhood. Criticism of the third motive (acceptance of the entire past), like criticism of the first, has mainly come from outside the profession.[25] Henry Ford and Paul Valéry, among many others, belong to the famous family of debunkers of history, and, by implication, of any duty to remember.

This overview of former critics shows that the following refutation of the thesis of a duty to remember is not entirely new. How, then, should we weigh the three motives for a duty to remember? I recognize that gratitude for heritage, restored dignity for victims, and acceptance of the entire past are powerful motives to remember. Nevertheless, I believe that obligatory remembrance should be rejected for three reasons: it is impracticable, controversial, and contrary to the spirit of international law.

The duty to remember is impracticable if it would cover all of the dead of history, all of the hundred billion dead of Haub's estimate, including the forgotten. For how can we commemorate human beings we have never known? If obligatory remembrance is *not* meant to cover everyone who has ever died, it is likely to be controversial, because it creates the thorny problem of determining who will be those selecting and those selected. Who is vested with the authority to select the dead worthy of remembrance in the first place? Four facts should be recalled: that there are always many candidates to select; that they usually make very different selections; that any given selection is very restrictive and excludes much; and that such selection, though invariably presented as definitive, fluctuates over time. Any selection risks to be instrumentalized by present interests. A duty to remember may lead to distorted and false memories, to taboos, and to a dubious official history. It may either paralyze those who remember or mobilize them for an extreme cause. Under the pressure of special interest groups, parliaments may freeze selective collective memories into laws. Judges may see themselves constrained to rule against those breaching them. In the end, the path to revenge and violence may be initiated. A *strong* historical awareness is not necessarily a morally responsible awareness.[26]

And *who* should we remember? Most would say: our direct circle of deceased family members and friends because, having been so close, we have a *special* duty to them. But beyond that? Should we be obliged to remember individuals, be it martyrs or heroes, we have never personally known or never respected? To whom should we be grateful for their past works? And speaking of the victims of human rights violations, who exactly should we remember, especially when we notice that so many of these victims were brutally silenced without leaving any records from which we could learn what they thought? How, then, do we know what they stood for?[27] And should we commemorate the direct victims or also the indirect victims? If so, indirect to which degree?

And *how long* should our duty to remember last? Should our debt of gratitude for the work of the dead or the posthumous restoration of their dignity be eternal? If our duty should be eternal, do we not then grant immortality to human beings who, while alive, were mortal? Or should our duty fade? And if so, according to what timescale for which dead?

A Right to Silence

Finally, and most importantly, a duty to remember is contrary to the spirit of international law. The freedom to *hold* opinions, and by extension memories, without interference also covers the freedom *not to hold* them without interference. If there is a right to memory, there is a right to oblivion too. Likewise, the freedom to *express* opinions, and by extension memories, also necessarily covers the freedom *not to express* them and the freedom *not* to be informed of what happened; freedom of expression covers a right to silence and a right *not* to speak.

Consequently, a duty to remember forcefully imposed *on others* amounts to a violation of their human rights. In particular it violates Articles 17, 18, and 19 of the *International Covenant on Civil and Political Rights,* not coincidentally the very articles that guarantee the right to memory. Article 18 of the *Covenant* is very clear on this point: "Everyone shall have the right to freedom of thought, conscience and religion . . . No one shall be subject to coercion which would impair his freedom to have or to adopt a . . . belief of his choice." The leading authority on the interpretation of human rights, the United Nations Human Rights Committee (not to be confused with the former United Nations Human Rights Commission), adds: "No one can be compelled to reveal his thoughts or adherence to a . . . belief."[28] Commentaries on these fundamental texts concur. Partsch, for example, writes: "It would appear that compulsion to express one's views violates the right to hold opinions without interference under Article 18";[29] and Monica Macovei: "The freedom to hold opinions includes the negative freedom of not being compelled to communicate one's own opinions . . . Freedom of expression includes the negative freedom not to speak." [30]

The basic reason for rejecting a duty to remember lies in the origins of human rights: historically, human rights are meant as a shield for the dignity and autonomy of each individual person against the intrusion of others—and the state in particular—who are tempted all too often to indoctrination. The right to memory of a person would be seriously compromised by any duty to express memories that are not in truth held by this person.[31]

For all of these reasons, I reject the imposition on others of a duty to remember. Therefore, I list memory as a right, not a duty, in my *Declaration*. In order to fulfill our duties to the dead, gratitude, restoring posthumous dignity, and the courageous acceptance of the past in its entirety constitute strong motives, but their imposition on others is neither allowed nor necessary. The eight duties to the dead identified in Chapter 4 are *deep* duties: they are meant also for those to whom we are *not* grateful and for those who have *not* been victims. The duties to the dead are universal. But among them, there is no duty to remember.

The First Exception: The Self

Still, there are individual and collective exceptions to the rule that we have no duty to remember. The first exception is individual: it is the self-imposed duty to remember, which is perfectly legitimate. It is nothing else than a radical variant of the right to memory exercised by an autonomously deciding person. Indeed, scores of people impose on themselves such a duty to their near and dear. Many genocide survivors, for instance, have incessantly borne witness to the horrors they had seen and experienced. In the latter instance, however, the statement should be qualified, for their self-imposed duty to remember may not be the result of an autonomous decision but instead may hide a traumatic inability to forget. In a sense, many genocide survivors have a "bias toward the past," according to which the memory of a past agony persists and dominates any perception of the future. This is how one human rights activist put it:

> The question, should we remember, is usually asked by people who have a choice. For many of the people in Northern Ireland, however, as in South Africa and Guatemala and elsewhere, there is no choice about remembering. Many of those who have been traumatically affected by armed conflict wake up in the night with nightmares. Every time they pass a particular street or place, they remember the dreadful event that took place there. When the calendar moves towards certain dates, anni-

versaries of deaths or losses, the memories come flooding back unin-
vited. Remembering is not an option—it is a daily torture, a voice inside
the head that has no "on/off" switch and no volume control.[32]

Moreover, the temptation to instrumentalize memory for goals other
than mere remembering is ever present. "[M]emory is only ever as vir-
tuous as its users."[33]

The Second Exception: The Community of Historians

The third motive in favor of a duty to remember concerned the acceptance of the entire past. My objection against it was practical: it is
impossible to commemorate all of the dead. Because it is practical, my
objection leaves room for a second exception: the historical profession
(including archivists and archaeologists). In order to understand this
exception, it is necessary to clarify the tension between the freedoms
of individual historians on the one hand, and the duties of the scholarly community to which they belong, on the other. By the grace of
academic freedom, individual historians have the right to choose their
own subject of research. They are not obliged to study topics they do
not want to study nor should they be forced to a duty to remember. As
members of a worldwide community, however, they have the collective
responsibility, at least as a matter of principle, to investigate the past in
its entirety. They must look not only into its moments of glory, but also
into painful and half-forgotten episodes. They should shatter silences
and explode taboos. As they approach the past as experts, they should
accept a moderate form of the duty to remember. This collective duty
is "moderate" because it is tempered by the freedom of the individual
historian (see also Chapter 6). The difference with the group of those
with a self-imposed mission is that the latter limit themselves to a specific category of deceased human beings, while the global community
of historians directs their attention to all of the dead of history.

An Answer to Danto

The preceding analysis enables me to provide an answer to a question
of the philosopher Arthur Danto. While discussing Herodotus's well-
known exhortation to preserve the memory of the past by putting on
record the past achievements of people, Danto wondered: "Does history exist for the sake of the past which somehow has a right correlative

with our duty not to allow it to vanish from consciousness—a right not to be forgotten and a duty not to forget?"[34] Consider the following. A duty toward "the" past is possible only if it means a duty toward "persons of the past." Persons of the past, I argued, may have possessed rights while alive, but, once deceased, they do not have them anymore. The fact that past generations have no rights, does not imply, however, that the living do not have duties toward them. But a duty not to allow past generations and their achievements to vanish from consciousness is not part of these duties for most of us. Only those with a self-imposed mission and only historians, perceived not as individual teachers and researchers, but clustered as a worldwide scholarly community, have a duty to remember.

Like Peter Burke and many others before him,[35] Danto feared that what would survive as history would entirely consist of the heroic deeds Herodotus had in mind, because that would be the ultimate victory of the insidious censorship and propaganda of the rulers of the past. He hoped that a residue nearer to the truth would prevail, with as little falsity as possible and with a proper place for the painful facts of the past.

This was, of course, what dissenting historians living under dictatorships had in mind also. Under tyrannical circumstances, courageous historians sometimes fulfilled their duty to remember the whole past by criticizing the official rewriting of history with its blank spots and by explicitly claiming a right to historical truth. In the Soviet Union in a 1965 editorial, *Novy mir*'s chief editor Aleksandr Tvardovsky once wrote that the omission of facts was a lie. His article was promptly attacked by E. Vuchetich, who advanced the notion of "two truths:" the "truth of the event and the fact" and the "truth of the life and struggle of the people." Vuchetich attempted to introduce this novel notion with the aim of adapting epistemology to ideology. A group of prominent Soviet historians wrote an open letter to the newspaper *Izvestia*, in which the notion of "two truths" was attacked as an "attempt to distinguish between suitable and inconvenient facts," and in which the duty to search for the historical truth was emphasized. Submitted in May 1965, the letter was rejected for publication. It was instead published a month later in the *samizdat* journal *Political Diary*, edited by historian Roy Medvedev.[36]

In Czechoslovakia, a large debate about the nature of history took place among *samizdat* historians in 1984–85. It started in May 1984 with the publication of a *Charta 77* document, *The Right to History*. This document included a negative assessment of official historiography, a defense of the Catholic view of history, and a reappraisal of several episodes and persons in Czechoslovak history. It also criticized the severely restricted access to archives, especially for post–1918 sources. Some fifteen historians reacted to this *Charta 77* document. Many of the texts from this debate appeared in Milan Hübl's 1985 *samizdat* publication, *Voices on Czech History*.[37] In Poland, an article entitled, "The Right to Historical Truth," was accepted for publication in *Res Publica*—an independent but legally published monthly in the 1980s—but subsequently banned in 1987. The article, written by historian Adolf Juzweńko, described the problematic state of postwar Polish historiography. It eventually appeared in English in 1988.[38]

In a very different context, that of the transition in China in the late 1970s, a circle of writers around Hu Yaobang (the future Secretary-General of the Chinese Communist Party) initiated a major epistemological shift. These writers contended that practice rather than ideology was the criterion for truth. A major role in this shift was played by Sun Changjiang, a professor, journalist, and editor with a degree in Chinese history from the People's University of China. He was the main author of "Practice is the Sole Criterion of Truth," the article of May 1978 that sparked what became known as the "truth criterion controversy." Later, in the summer of 1987, Sun would nearly lose his Party membership for allegedly advocating "bourgeois liberalization" and criticizing leftist dogmatism. He was dismissed as an editor.[39]

Was the action of Tvardovsky, *Charta 77*, Juzweńko, and Sun futile? I strongly believe it was not. Although for a large part they wrote under pressure and with high risks, they kept burning the flame of truth. They did what may be expected of historians, but they did it under very unfavorable circumstances. Therefore, their action was important and courageous. A considerable chance existed that nobody would ever learn of their efforts. Indeed, like ancient trees that tumble down in a giant forest without any human ear to capture their sound, many similarly important efforts by similarly courageous historians have been forgotten. But these historians managed to leave traces of their actions. Therefore, their struggle for a right to history can be remembered here.[40]

The Third Exception: Postconflict Governments and the Right to the Truth

In each of the above examples, the government was actually asked to *abstain* from the field of historical research and guarantee freedom of expression and information to historians and others in their search for the truth. By contrast, the third and last exception to the rejection of the duty to remember implies that governments are urged on some occasions to *intervene* in the field of historical research. Many think, indeed, that governments are obliged to actively investigate past crimes and catastrophes. In a certain way, this duty is a duty to remember and in performing it by investigating the past, governments realize a principal condition for the execution of the population's right to the truth.

The desire for a right to the truth was prompted by (but not limited to) recent discussions about transitional justice, discussions that centered around the question of how societies emerging from dictatorships or internal conflicts marked by capital crimes could dispense justice. Both the scale and the gravity of these crimes (genocide, crimes against humanity, and war crimes) usually imply that the very institution charged with protecting human rights, the state, had been involved in their violation. This institutionalized violence led survivors to search for factual and existential truth, that is, for answers to questions such as: what exactly happened to the countless victims of human rights crises? Did they disappear and/or did they die? How, why, and where? Would the perpetrators and their accomplices be punished? Robert Darnton called this "Rankean rage"—the urge to know history "as it actually happened."[41] Some crimes remain unsolved and unpunished, sometimes for decades, sometimes forever. This is almost impossible for the humiliated survivors to bear.

To find answers for these serious questions, a new principle of international law was formulated in the mid-1970s and was called "the right to the truth" (or "the right to know" or "the right to be informed"). Such a right ought to entitle the relatives of victims to seek and obtain information on the fate and whereabouts of their dead. Two articles from the *International Covenant on Civil and Political Rights* formed the core of this new "right to the truth": Article 2, which stipulates the right of victims to an effective remedy, and Article 19, which covers freedom of expression and information. Both articles imply that a right to the truth is only effective when the state accepts the duty to investigate, reveal, and officially acknowledge past crimes (and, of course, prosecute and punish them).

Discussion of this principle is of cardinal importance for historians because, in a certain sense, what is called the "right to the truth" in international law today is nothing less than a crucial component of the "right to *historical* truth" or the "right to history." Indeed, the search for existential facts (facts about existence itself) is a first stage in the search for historical truth: these facts, if corroborated, fix the boundaries of any sound historical narrative and explanation of past human rights abuses. In this sense, forensic anthropologists, courts, and truth commissions act like protohistorians. In scores of countries, forensic anthropology teams excavate mass graves to find historical evidence for genocide and other crimes against humanity. In many countries, like Guatemala, these teams constantly receive death threats.[42] As it happens, all genocides (from the Armenian genocide and the Holocaust to Rwanda and Srebrenica) and many war crimes (like Nanking and Katyń) risk being subject to denial. Perpetrators continue the physical elimination of victims with the erasure of evidence. Denial starts while the very crimes are occurring—with the deletion of traces—and it continues afterward by the perpetrators and by others. Elsewhere, the facts about crimes are not denied, but their explanation is disputed. In Argentina and Uruguay, for example, discussions took place about the so-called theory of the two demons, a theory that depicts the violence of the state that occurred in the 1970s–1980s as a proportionate reaction to mounting subversive violence. Many called this theory a falsification of history. The idea that existential facts fix the boundaries of interpretation is keenly expressed by the Truth and Reconciliation Commission in South Africa:

> [O]ne can say that the information in the hands of the Commission made it impossible to claim, for example, that: the practice of torture by state security forces was not systematic and widespread; that only a few "rotten eggs" or "bad apples" committed gross violations of human rights; that the state was not directly and indirectly involved in "black-on-black violence"; that the chemical and biological warfare programme was only of a defensive nature; that slogans by sections of the liberation movement did not contribute to killings of "settlers" or farmers; and that the accounts of gross human rights violations in the African National Congress . . . camps were the consequence of state disinformation. Thus, disinformation about the past that had been accepted as truth by some members of society lost much of its credibility.[43]

The same thought was expressed previously. To those who at the Conference of Versailles asked what future historians would write about the First World War, the French Prime Minister Georges Clemenceau replied: "They will not say that Belgium invaded Germany."[44]

This emphasis on existential facts that exclude certain interpretations should not be confused with the naive nineteenth-century positivist conception that historians could write a definitive scientific historical account once they had at their disposal undisputed historical facts that did not need interpretation. Nor does it deny the importance of discussions about historical opinions and about sweeping explanations and representations of history. On the contrary, it allows for broad interpretations within the margins imposed by the available information, or within what Reinhart Koselleck called the "veto of the sources." But the attraction of historical opinions has obscured the role of existential facts in discussions about historical truth among historians. A good indicator of this is the secondary role that historians play in forensic anthropology, court cases about historical injustice, truth commission work, or the international discussions about the right to the truth within the United Nations. Some historians have been involved in several of these enterprises, but still far less than could have been expected.

The impact of human rights crises on historical consciousness is considerable. Herbert Butterfield suggested the existence of a causal relationship between war and historical consciousness. In his view, war is the pre-eminent experience that generates historical consciousness; it is a situation in which human beings of all classes are *compelled* to feel the impact of historical events. During the war, people ask how it came about; after it, who started it and what exactly happened. In short, they demand a satisfying narrative about the war, a story that also explains the behavior of their leaders, who acquire an interest in keeping "relevant records."[45] What Butterfield said about war can be applied to human rights catastrophes also. These crises also have a great impact on historical consciousness.

History of the Right to History

What I intend to do now is to sketch a history of this right to the truth or right to history.[46] The first formulation of the right in the mid-1970s was preceded by important changes in the thinking on time and suffering. Once tentatively formulated, the right was quickly followed by standard-setting and jurisdiction.

The new legal thinking about *time* began during the Nuremberg trials in 1945–46. During these trials, three exceptional crimes were identified: crimes against peace, war crimes, and crimes against humanity; later, the crime of genocide was added. At the time, it was agreed that these crimes had to be punished—a view reconfirmed in the 1966 covenants. The *International Covenant on Civil and Political Rights* (one of those covenants from 1966) stipulated that the rule that no one would be held guilty for acts that were not criminal at the time they were committed (the principle of nonretroactivity), could *not* apply to persons who had committed "any act or omission which, at the time when it was committed, was criminal according to the general principles of law recognized by the community of nations."[47]

In 1968, the United Nations determined that time limits did not apply for prosecuting these crimes (genocide, crimes against humanity, war crimes), *irrespective of the date of their commission.*[48] This principle of imprescriptibility has slowly become a norm of international law.

Another important step in the thinking about time and law was taken with the 1992 approval of the *Declaration on the Protection of All Persons from Enforced Disappearance.* This declaration (converted into a convention in 2006) was the first to call enforced disappearances crimes against humanity. It perceived them not as crimes of the past, but as *ongoing* crimes—as kidnappings without an end—as long as perpetrators did not convincingly acknowledge the fate of their victims.[49] In addition to disappearances, another phenomenon that stimulated the discussion about time perception was the kidnapping of babies during the military regime in Argentina (1976–83). Born to dissident women during the latter's detention, these babies were taken away for adoption by families of military or security officials who were unable to have children of their own. Some of these children attempted to establish their real identity afterward.

Previously used to applying the norms prevalent at the time of the occurrence of the crimes in formulating legal or historical judgments, judges and historians are now forced by these developments also to take into account the norms flowing from the imprescriptibility of major crimes. The impact of these developments is considerable: on the one hand, they optimize the execution of the rights to memory and history, and on the other, they risk to entail the introduction of a certain anachronism in judgments made long after the facts.

Not only did the legal conception of time change, so did the legal conception of *suffering.* This notion was gradually expanded to include not only the suffering of direct victims of abuses, but also the pain of their families. The crucial turn here was the adoption in 1985 of the United Nations *Declaration of Basic Principles of Justice for Victims of Crime and Abuse of Power.* It was slowly made clear that the lack of will to inform relatives about the fate of the disappeared or the dead was itself a breach of human rights, in particular the right of relatives to be protected from psychological torture and the right to respect for private and family life.[50] The 1989 *Convention on the Rights of the Child* also recognized the right of families to information about absent family members.[51] The right of victims or their next of kin to obtain clarification of the facts of repression was also increasingly seen as a basis for reparation claims. Indeed, knowledge of these facts constitutes a form of reparation itself. Learning about the circumstances in which a loved one died enables the family and friends to start an appropriate process of mourning. Not only for direct victims and their families, but also for circles of friends and larger communities is it traumatic that they do not know what happened to the victims. Moreover, the duty of governments to investigate, reveal, and acknowledge the truth was perceived as a means to gain insight into the repressive methods of dictatorships and to prevent the atrocities of the past from recurring in the future.

Although the new views on time and suffering lay a fertile infrastructure for the right to the truth, the genealogy of this right itself should be traced back to the seventeenth century. In 1679, *habeas corpus* was introduced, the remedy that enables someone to ask that a judge command authorities to produce detainees in person before the court. This is necessary to determine whether they are still alive, safe, and lawfully detained. But the story of the right to the truth in the strictest sense starts in 1974 when, inspired by a resolution of a Red Cross conference the previous year, the United Nations General Assembly itself adopted a resolution that called the desire to know the fate of the missing and the dead a basic human need.[52] In 1977, the *First Protocol added to the Geneva Conventions* switched the emphasis from "need" to "right" and stressed the right of families to know the fate of their missing and dead relatives as a general principle.[53]

The "right to know" and the "right to the truth" were explicitly mentioned for the first time in the 1980s. In 1982, the United Nations Human Rights Committee emphasized the duty of states to investigate cases of disappearances.[54] In a crucial decision in the 1983 *Quinteros versus Uruguay* case, submitted by the mother of a woman who had been missing for several years, the committee spoke of:

> the anguish and stress caused to the mother by the disappearance of her daughter and by the continuing uncertainty concerning her fate and whereabouts. The [mother] has the *right to know* [my emphasis, *adb*] what has happened to her daughter. In these respects, she too is a victim of the violations of the *Covenant* suffered by her daughter, in particular of article 7 [that is, the right not to be treated inhumanly, *adb*].[55]

In 1988, the Inter-American Court of Human Rights delivered a pioneering judgment in a disappearance case, *Velásquez Rodríguez versus Honduras*, concerning the duty to investigate past crimes and, implicitly, on its inextricable complement, the right to the truth. The court emphasized that changes of government did not affect the duties of states to prevent, investigate, punish, and compensate human rights violations. It declared: "According to the principle of the continuity of the State in international law, responsibility exists both independently of changes of government over a period of time and continuously from the time of the act that creates responsibility to the time when the act is declared illegal."[56] The principle of obligatory investigation of past abuses *even after a change of regime* gradually became entrenched. A growing body of case law, especially from the Inter-American Court of Human Rights, emphasized the individual (reparatory) and collective (preventive) role of the right to the truth: reparation and prevention are not complete without truth.[57] In 1995, Leandro Despouy, the United Nations Special Rapporteur on States of Emergency, called the right to the truth "a rule of customary international law," and made a plea to recognize it as nonderogable.[58] In the meantime, many official and unofficial truth commissions and fact-finding missions had put this new right into practice. Many others would soon follow.

Finally, in 1997, United Nations Special Rapporteur on Impunity Louis Joinet brought the various strands together into a coherent set of *Principles to Combat Impunity* (hereinafter the *Impunity Principles*). The *Impunity Principles* maintain that victims of gross human rights violations have three legal rights: a right to the truth (still called a "right to know" by Joinet), a right to justice, and a right to reparation. I summarize those *Impunity Principles* dealing with the right to the truth only and will not discuss the other two rights. The right to the truth includes seventeen principles: four general ones, eight on truth commissions, and five on archives containing evidence of the violations. The *Impunity Principles* call the right to the truth imprescriptible and inalienable for individuals as well as for society. Legal measures favoring perpetrators (pardon, amnesty, and prescription) or victims (reparation) do not extinguish it. In doing so, the *Impunity Principles* implicitly acknowledge that there does not exist a moment in the near or distant future from which the right to the truth becomes completely meaningless. Public knowledge of the history of repression is considered as a part of a people's heritage and is explicitly linked to a duty to save archives in order to preserve collective memory from extinction. It is not entirely clear whether by "the duty to preserve memory" the *Impunity Principles* mean more than preserving archives. It is certain, however, that this duty does *not* mean that governments monitor or manipulate commemorations and other expressions of collective memory, but quite the contrary, that they play a facilitating role and create adequate conditions for such expressions to flourish.

The Sub-Commission on Prevention of Discrimination and Protection of Minorities (later called the Sub-Commission on the Promotion and Protection of Human Rights) adopted the *Impunity Principles* without a vote in 1997. They were distributed widely both within and outside the United Nations and frequently quoted as an essential instrument by many international human rights bodies and national states. Year after year, they were noted and recommended in resolutions by the Commission on Human Rights. During this process, several reports and studies on impunity in member states of the United Nations were drafted by the Secretary-General, Kofi Annan. In 2005, after many discussions, the *Impunity Principles* were updated by an independent expert, Diane Orentlicher. Hence, the story is not yet complete. The updated *Impunity Principles* must be formally approved by the United Nations General Assembly. Up to 2005, the right to the truth was discussed mainly within the impunity framework, but since, it has increasingly been seen as an autonomous right: following two separate resolutions on the "right to the truth" in 2005 (by the Commission on Human Rights) and 2006 (by the Human Rights Council), the Office of the High Commissioner for Human Rights produced two studies on this right in 2006 and 2007, in which it was called inalienable, autonomous, nonderogable, and imprescriptible, and fundamental to the inherent dignity of the human person.

The Right to the Truth: An Evaluation

And so the contours of this important right have gradually become visible. Three conditions make the concept of the right to the truth broader than the right to freedom of expression and information enshrined in Article 19 of the *International Covenant on Civil and Political Rights*.[59] First, while it emanates from the individual right to freedom of expression and information, the right to the truth is not only held by individuals but also by society as a whole. It transcends individual needs and can be claimed even after the parties involved in the human rights crises are all deceased.

Second, while the right to freedom of expression and information can be restricted (in the case of public commemorations, inter alia), the right to the truth is nonderogable. In this connection, the right to the truth is sometimes called a *procedural right,* a remedy that is necessary to protect other fundamental human rights: like *habeas corpus,* it arises after the latter are violated; it is itself violated when the information relating to the first violations is not provided.[60] Surprisingly, claims for access to official information appear to be most successful when they are based on the right to privacy.[61] When citizens seek information about themselves or on behalf of the disappeared and the dead in official files, the right to the truth is sometimes called the right to *habeas data.* It usually gives the individual the right to access and update sensitive personal or family information in public (and sometimes private) databases.[62]

The third condition that makes the right to the truth broader than the right to freedom of expression and information is the concomitant duty to investigate. International courts have repeatedly confirmed that the right to the truth, like the right to free expression and information, is a *positive* right: governments must not only abstain from unjustified control of these rights, but also implement measures to allow citizens to exercise them.[63] On top of this, the right to the truth imposes on governments an *affirmative* duty to conduct investigations of human rights violations themselves. This duty appears to include the active compilation of data (regardless of whether they are in the possession of the government) and their analysis, preservation, and access, as well as the publication of reports about these data. On the one hand, everything must be done not only to respect the right to the truth but also to *ensure* respect for it. On the other hand, what counts are means and conduct, not results: if it is really impossible to provide the information, there is no violation of the right to the truth.[64] In addition, the right to the truth and the right to access official information are seen as applications of the principles of democratic transparency and accountability.[65] The right to the truth should not, however, cause harm to, or threaten the safety and interests of the victim, the victim's relatives, or of witnesses. Hence, the right to the truth is nonderogable, but not absolute.

At the collective level, some cultures apparently do not prefer to deal with the past in a way that involves the search, and especially the expression, of truth. The reason for this is that these cultures believe that the assassinated victims belong to the realm of those dead who have to be placated—and that speaking about them brings bad fortune and opens the door for bad spirits. Think of the custom, mentioned in Chapter 4, of tabooing names of the dead and of mourners during a certain period.[66] Where these taboos do not exist, the part of successor governments in the search for truth has to be large, given that surviving victims, relatives, or civil society associations are often intimidated, and that they frequently lack the resources, authority, expertise, and time to investigate large-scale, structural violations.

One question about the right to the truth remains unresolved. Although the notion was developed in a context of transitional justice and discussion about impunity, and initially referred to recent past injustice, it was clear from the start, and especially since 2005, that this notion could not be restricted to experiences called "transitions to democracy."[67] It remains a question, however, how far back it stretches in time. Several arguments are pleading against an application of the right to the truth to the further past: the past cannot be altered, the parties involved in injustice die and generations succeed each other, and, in addition, it is impossible to reevaluate all of the past all of the time (see Chapter 3). Pleading in favor is the circumstance that historical awareness of a people often goes back to centuries-old events of pride and shame. As a right of societies, truth is imprescriptible. Even when the parties involved are dead, even when time goes by, it is never too late to reopen cases and challenge amnesia. It is never too late to claim the historical truth. This was the opening thought of Chapter 4. In principle, therefore, the right to the truth stretches back endlessly in time.

Conclusion

The web of relationships between rights and duties regarding history can now be disentangled. The global form of this web is presented in Table 5.1.

Governments have a duty to remember in at least two senses. They have the permanent duty to facilitate historical research and teaching at all levels (with decent budgets and responsible archival and information policies). In addition, in the context of restoration of, or transition to democracy, they have a duty to actively investigate, reveal, officially acknowledge, and punish crimes perpetrated during preceding dictatorships or conflicts. The source for this duty is located in the fact that

TABLE 5.1. *Relationships Between Rights and Duties Regarding History*

A duty to remember understood as a duty
to facilitate and to investigate
for governments and for the global community of historians

↑   ↓

A universal right to freedom of expression and information,

understood as a right to the truth or as a right to history (and to silence)

↑↓

and as a right to memory (and to oblivion)

↑   ↓

Universal duties to the dead
(see Table 4.1)

democratic governments are accountable to their citizens because they are in charge of the state in the name of these citizens.

Like governments, historians also have a collective duty to remember. This means that, as members of a global community, historians should responsibly investigate the entire past, including its painful parts, and teach about it. The source for this duty lies in the fact that the historical profession is accountable to society—not only the local and national society, but also the global society—because it charges them with the production of expert knowledge about the past (see Chapters 1 and 6). There is a special relationship between the duty to remember of the government and the duty to remember of the community of historians in that the governmental duty is a necessary condition for historians to be able to comply well with their duty. Strictly speaking, the condition is "quasi-necessary," because historians can exercise their duty even when the government itself fails to perform its duty, albeit under far less favorable circumstances.

On their turn, compliance with both duties is a necessary condition for the sound exercise of universal human rights, and, as far as we are concerned here, in particular the right to freedom of expression and information (Article 19 of the *International Covenant on Civil and Political Rights*.) Strictly speaking, here also the condition is "quasi-necessary," because the right to freedom of expression and information can be exercised even in the absence of the performance of these duties, albeit under far less favorable circumstances. The universal right to freedom of expression and information can adopt several shapes, two of which are important here. First, it can present itself as a right to the truth or as a right to history, in particular as a right to know the truth about past human rights abuses. This right includes a right to silence (narrowly restricted for facts; absolute for opinions). The right to history is *not* (only) a right of historians, but a right of all citizens in a society. In addition to the right to history, there is, secondly, the right to memory, that is, the right to mourn, to bury and cremate, and to commemorate. The right to memory lies on a continuum between a duty to remember imposed on oneself on one side, and a right to oblivion, on the other. Sometimes, tensions arise between the individual urge to forget—or to remember in private—and the right of the public to the truth, between the right not to remember and the right not to forget. These tensions are inevitable and painful.

At the same time, there is a relationship between the rights to history and memory. The right to know the truth about history is a necessary condition for proper commemoration and mourning, and in its turn, the right to memory is a necessary condition for giving past events their proper meaning and place, and, even if forgetting is often simply impossible, to reach some peace and go on with one's life. In combination, the rights to history and memory are necessary conditions for citizens to decently discharge their universal duties to the dead (see Table 4.1 for the list of these duties). Conversely, a sound exercise of these duties constitutes a basis to claim the (consequential) rights to history and memory. And the rights to history and memory are themselves conditions for governments and historians to perform their duties to remember.

APPENDIX 5.1

Selected International Instruments As Sources of Inspiration for a
Universal Declaration of Duties of the Living to the Dead

Items marked (*) also refer to the rights to memory and history.

UNITED NATIONS (<http://www.ohchr.org>)

Universal Declaration of Human Rights (1948)
[Inspired my Articles 1–10.]

Article 2: "Everyone is entitled to all the rights and freedoms . . . without distinction of any kind, such as race, color, sex, language, religion, political or other opinion, national or social origin, property, birth, or other status . . ."
Article 8: "Everyone has the right to an effective remedy by the competent national tribunals for acts violating the fundamental rights granted him by the constitution or by law." (*)
Article 12: "No one shall be subjected to arbitrary interference with his privacy, family, home or correspondence, nor to attacks upon his honour and reputation . . ." (*)
Article 15: "Everyone has the right to a nationality . . ."[68]
Article 17: " . . . No one shall be arbitrarily deprived of his property."
Article 18: "Everyone has the right to freedom of thought, conscience and religion . . ." (*)
Article 19: "Everyone has the right to freedom of opinion and expression; this right includes freedom to hold opinions without interference and to seek, receive and impart information and ideas through any media and regardless of frontiers." (*)
Article 29(2): "In the exercise of his rights and freedoms, everyone shall be subject only to such limitations as are determined by law solely for the purpose of securing due recognition and respect for the rights and freedoms of others and of meeting the just requirements of morality, public order and the general welfare in a democratic society." (*)

International Covenant on Civil and Political Rights (1966)
[Inspired my Articles 1, 9–10.]

Article 2(3): "Each State Party to the present Covenant undertakes: (a) To ensure that any person whose rights or freedoms . . . are violated shall have an effective remedy . . ." (*)

Article 17(1): "No one shall be subjected to arbitrary or unlawful interference with his privacy, family, home or correspondence, nor to unlawful attacks on his honour and reputation." (*)

Article 18: "(1) Everyone shall have the right to freedom of thought, conscience and religion. This right shall include freedom to have or to adopt a . . . belief of his choice, and freedom, either individually or in community with others and in public or private, to manifest his . . . belief. . . . (2) No one shall be subject to coercion which would impair his freedom to have or to adopt a . . . belief of his choice. (3) Freedom to manifest one's . . . beliefs may be subject only to such limitations as are prescribed by law and are necessary to protect public safety, order, health, or morals or the fundamental rights and freedoms of others." (*)

Article 19: "(1) Everyone shall have the right to hold opinions without interference. (2) Everyone shall have the right to freedom of expression; this right shall include freedom to seek, receive and impart information and ideas of all kinds, regardless of frontiers, either orally, in writing or in print, in the form of art, or through any other media of his choice. (3) The exercise of the rights provided for in paragraph 2 . . . carries with it special duties and responsibilities. It may therefore be subject to certain restrictions, but these shall only be such as are provided by law and are necessary: (a) For respect of the rights or reputations of others; (b) For the protection of national security or of public order (ordre public), or of public health or morals." (*)

International Convention for the Protection of All Persons from Enforced Disappearance (2006) [Inspired my Article 10.][69]

Article 24(2): "Each victim has the right to know the truth regarding the circumstances of the enforced disappearance, the progress and results of the investigation and the fate of the disappeared person." (*)

UNITED NATIONS COMMISSION ON HUMAN RIGHTS
(<http://www.ohchr.org>)

Updated Set of Principles for the Protection and Promotion of Human Rights through Action to Combat Impunity (E/CN.4/2005/102/Add.1; 2005) [Inspired my Articles 1–3, 5, 9–10.][70]

Preamble: "*[A]ware* that forgiveness . . . implies, insofar as it is a private act, that the victim or the victim's beneficiaries know the perpetrator of the violations and that the latter has acknowledged his or her deeds. . . . *Convinced,* therefore, that . . . measures must be taken . . . to securing . . . observance of the right to know and, by implication, the right to the truth, the right to justice and the right to reparation, without which there can be no effective remedy against the pernicious effects of impunity . . ." (*)

I   Combating impunity: general obligations

Principle 1: "*General obligations of states to take effective action to combat impunity.* Impunity arises from a failure by States to meet their obligations to investigate violations; . . . [and] to ensure the inalienable right to know the truth about violations." (*)

II   The right to know

A. General principles

Principle 2: "*The inalienable right to the truth.* Every people has the inalienable right to know the truth about past events concerning the perpetration of heinous crimes and about the circumstances and reasons that led . . . to the perpetration of those crimes. Full and effective exercise of the right to the truth provides a vital safeguard against the recurrence of violations." (*)

Principle 3: "*The duty to preserve memory.* A people's knowledge of the history of its oppression is part of its heritage and, as such, must be ensured by appropriate measures in fulfilment of the State's duty to preserve archives and other evidence concerning violations of human rights . . . and to facilitate knowledge of those violations. Such measures shall be aimed at preserving the collective memory from extinction and, in particular, at guarding against the development of revisionist and negationist arguments." (*)

Principle 4: "*The victims' right to know.* Irrespective of any legal proceedings, victims and their families have the imprescriptible right to know the truth about the circumstances in which violations took place and, in the event of death or disappearance, the victims' fate." (*)

Principle 5: "*Guarantees to give effect to the right to know.* States must take appropriate action . . . to give effect to the right to know. . . . Societies that have experienced heinous crimes perpetrated on a massive or systematic basis may benefit in particular from the creation of a truth commission or other commission of inquiry to establish the facts surrounding those violations so that the truth may be ascertained and to prevent the disappearance of evidence. Regardless of whether a State establishes such a body, it must ensure the preservation of, and access to, archives concerning violations of human rights and humanitarian law." (*)

B. Commissions of inquiry

Principle 6: "*The establishment and role of truth commissions* . . . In recognition of the dignity of victims and their families, investigations undertaken by truth commissions should be conducted with the object in particular of securing recognition of such parts of the truth as were formerly denied."[71] (*)

Principle 8: *"Definition of a commission's terms of reference . . .* (e) Commissions of inquiry shall endeavour to safeguard evidence for later use in the administration of justice; (f) The terms of reference of commissions of inquiry should highlight the importance of preserving the commission's archives. At the outset of their work, commissions should clarify the conditions that will govern access to their documents, including conditions aimed at preventing disclosure of confidential information while facilitating public access to their archives." (*)

C. Preservation of and access to archives bearing witness to violations

Principle 14: *"Measures for the preservation of archives.* The right to know implies that archives must be preserved. Technical measures and penalties should be applied to prevent any removal, destruction, concealment or falsification of archives, especially for the purpose of ensuring the impunity of perpetrators . . ."[72] (*)

Principle 15: *"Measures for facilitating access to archives* . . . Access to archives should also be facilitated in the interest of historical research, subject to reasonable restrictions aimed at safeguarding the privacy and security of victims and other individuals. Formal requirements governing access may not be used for purposes of censorship." (*)

Principle 16: *"Cooperation between archive departments and the courts and non-judicial commissions of inquiry.* (. . .)" (*)

Principle 17: *"Specific measures relating to archives containing names.* (. . .)" (*)

Principle 18: *"Specific measures related to the restoration of or transition to democracy and/or peace* . . . (c) Third countries shall be expected to cooperate with a view to communicating or restituting archives for the purpose of establishing the truth." (*)

III   The right to justice

Principle 24: *"Restrictions . . . relating to amnesty* . . . (b) Amnesties and other measures of clemency . . . shall not prejudice the right to know." (*)

IV   The right to reparation / guarantees of non-recurrence

Principle 34: *"Scope of the right to reparation.* The right to reparation . . . shall include measures of restitution, compensation, rehabilitation, and satisfaction. . . . In the case of forced disappearance, the family of the direct victim has an imprescriptible right to be informed of the fate and/or whereabouts of the disappeared person and, in the event of decease, that person's body must be returned to the family as soon as it has been identified, regardless of whether the perpetrators have been identified or prosecuted." (*)

Principle 36: "*Reform of state institutions* . . . (b) Habeas corpus . . . must be considered a non-derogable right." (*)

GENERAL ASSEMBLY OF THE UNITED NATIONS
(<http://www.un.org/ga>)

Basic Principles and Guidelines on the Right to a Remedy and Reparation for Victims of Gross Violations of International Human Rights Law and Serious Violations of International Humanitarian Law (United Nations General Assembly Resolution 61/177) (<http://www.un.org/ga>; 2006) [Inspired my Articles 1–3, 5, 9–10.]

Principle 11: "Remedies for gross violations of . . . human rights . . . include the victim's right to . . . : (a) Equal and effective access to justice; (b) Adequate, effective and prompt reparation for harm suffered; and (c) Access to relevant information concerning violations and reparation mechanisms." (*)

Principle 18: "[V]ictims of gross violations of . . . human rights . . . should, as appropriate and proportional to the gravity of the violation and the circumstances of each case, be provided with full and effective reparation, . . . which include the following forms: restitution, compensation, rehabilitation, satisfaction and guarantees of non-repetition." (*)

Principle 22: "*Satisfaction* should include . . . : (b) Verification of the facts and full and public disclosure of the truth to the extent that such disclosure does not cause further harm or threaten the safety and interests of the victim . . . ; (c) The search for the whereabouts of the disappeared, for the identities of the children abducted, and for the bodies of those killed, and assistance in the recovery, identification and reburial of the bodies in accordance with the expressed or presumed wish of the victims, or the cultural practices of the families and communities; (d) An official declaration or a judicial decision restoring the dignity, the reputation and the rights of the victim and of persons closely connected with the victim; (e) Public apology, including acknowledgement of the facts and acceptance of responsibility; . . . (g) Commemorations and tributes to the victims; (h) Inclusion of an accurate account of the violations that occurred in . . . human rights . . . training and in educational material at all levels." (*)

Principle 24: "[V]ictims and their representatives should be entitled to seek and obtain information on the causes leading to their victimization . . . and to learn the truth in regard to these violations." (*)[73]

Pre-Draft Declaration on Human Social Responsibilities (E/CN.4/2003/105, Annex I; 2003) [Inspired my Article 8.]

Article 23: "Every person has the responsibility to preserve the positive elements of the cultural heritage of the community/society in which he or she lives and that has been handed down by previous generations, as well as to enrich them for the benefit of future generations."

UNESCO
(<http://www.unesco.org>)

Declaration on the Responsibilities of the Present Generations towards Future Generations (1997) [Inspired my Article 8.]
Article 7: "*Cultural diversity and cultural heritage* . . . The present generations have the responsibility to identify, protect and safeguard the tangible and intangible cultural heritage and to transmit this common heritage to future generations."[74]

Universal Declaration on the Human Genome and Human Rights (1997) [Inspired my Article 8.]
Article 1: "The human genome underlies the fundamental unity of all members of the human family, as well as the recognition of their inherent dignity and diversity. In a symbolic sense, it is the heritage of humanity."

WORLD HEALTH ORGANIZATION
(<http://www.who.int>)

Guiding Principles on Human Organ Transplantation (1991) [Inspired my Article 1.]
Principle 5: "The human body and its parts cannot be the subject of commercial transactions. Accordingly, giving or receiving payment (including any other compensation or reward) for organs should be prohibited."

WORLD INTELLECTUAL PROPERTY ORGANIZATION
(<http://www.wipo.int>)

Berne Convention for the Protection of Literary and Artistic Works (1886, 1979) [Inspired my Articles 4, 7–8.]
Article 6bis: "(1) Independently of the author's economic rights, and even after the transfer of the said rights, the author shall have the right to claim authorship of the work and to object to any distortion, mutilation or other modification of, or other derogatory action in relation to, the said work, which would be prejudicial to his honor or reputation. (2) The rights granted to the author . . . shall, after his death, be maintained, at least until the expiry of the economic rights, and shall be exercisable by the persons or institutions authorized by the legislation of the country where protection is claimed." (*)
Article 7: "(1) The term of protection granted by this Convention shall be the life of the author and fifty years after his death."
Article 7bis: "The provisions of the preceding Article shall also apply in the case of a work of joint authorship, provided that the terms measured from the death of the author shall be calculated from the death of the last surviving author."

INTERNATIONAL COMMITTEE OF THE RED CROSS
(<http://www.icrc.org>)

Geneva Conventions of August 12, 1949: Third Geneva Convention (1949) [Inspired my Articles 2–5, 9–10.]
Article 120: "Wills of prisoners of war shall be drawn up so as to satisfy the conditions of validity required by the legislation of their country of origin . . . The death certificates . . . shall show particulars of identity as set out in . . . Article

17 [surname, first names, . . . date of birth, . . . the signature or the fingerprints, *adb*], and also the date and place of death, the cause of death, the date and place of burial and all particulars necessary to identify the graves. . . . The detaining authorities shall ensure that prisoners of war who have died in captivity are honourably buried, if possible according to the rites of the religion to which they belonged, and that their graves are respected, suitably maintained and marked so as to be found at any time. Wherever possible, deceased prisoners of war who depended on the same Power shall be interred in the same place. Deceased prisoners of war shall be buried in individual graves, unless unavoidable circumstances require the use of collective graves . . ." (*)

Protocol I Additional to the Geneva Conventions and Relating to the Protection of Victims of International Armed Conflicts (1977)
[Inspired my Articles 1, 2, 5, 9–10.]

Part II, section III: Missing and dead persons[75]
Article 32: "*General principle:* . . . [T]he right of families to know the fate of their relatives." (*)
Article 34: "*Remains of deceased:*"
Article 34(1): "The remains of persons . . . shall be respected, and the gravesites of all such persons shall be respected, maintained and marked."
Article 34(2)(a): "To facilitate access to the gravesites by relatives of the deceased . . ." (*)
Article 34(2)(b): "To protect and maintain such gravesites permanently."
Article 34(2)(c): "To facilitate the return of the remains of the deceased and of personal effects to the home country upon its request or, unless that country objects, upon the request of the next of kin."
Article 34(4)(b): "A High Contracting Party in whose territory the gravesites . . . are situated shall be permitted to exhume the remains only: . . . Where exhumation is a matter of overriding public necessity, including cases of medical and investigative necessity, in which case the High Contracting Party shall at all times respect the remains, and shall give notice to the home country of its intention to exhume the remains together with details of the intended place of reinterment." (*)

Protocol II Additional to the Geneva Conventions and Relating to the Protection of Victims of Non-International Armed Conflicts (1977)
[Inspired my Articles 1–3, 10.]
Article 8: "*Search:* Whenever circumstances permit . . . all possible measures shall be taken, without delay, . . . to search for the dead, prevent their being despoiled, and decently dispose of them." (*)[76]

INTERNATIONAL CRIMINAL COURT

(<http://www.icc-cpi.int>)

Rome Statute (1998) [Inspired my Articles 1 and 3.]
Articles 8(2)(b)(xxi) and 8(2)(c)(ii) of the Rome Statute concern the war crime of "committing outrages upon personal dignity, in particular humiliating

and degrading treatment" [during international and internal armed conflicts respectively.] (See below.)[77]

Assembly of States Parties to the Rome Statute of the International Criminal Court (2002) [Inspired my Articles 1 and 3.]

"Elements of Crimes," in *First Session: Official Records* (ICC-ASP/1/3; 2002), 108–55, here 140, 146:

The first element of the war crime of "committing outrages upon personal dignity" (see above, *adb*) as defined by the Assembly of States Parties reads: "1. The perpetrator humiliated, degraded or otherwise violated the dignity of one or more persons." A note attached to this element adds: "For this crime, 'persons' can include dead persons."

A legal advisor of the Red Cross commenting on this element explains that "outrages upon the dignity of dead persons" include (1) mutilation of bodies and (2) refusal of decent burial.[78]

INTER-PARLIAMENTARY UNION
(<http://www.ipu.org>)

Universal Declaration on Democracy (1997) [Inspired my Articles 9 and 10.]

Article 14: "Public accountability, which is essential to democracy, applies to all those who hold public authority . . . and to all bodies of public authority . . . Accountability entails a public right of access to information about the activities of government, the right to petition government and to seek redress through impartial administrative and judicial mechanisms." (*)

Article 19: "A sustained state of democracy . . . requires a democratic climate and culture constantly nurtured and reinforced by education and other vehicles of culture and information." (*)

Article 21: "The state of democracy presupposes freedom of opinion and expression." (*)

INTERNATIONAL COUNCIL OF MUSEUMS
(<http://www.icom.museum>)

Code of Ethics for Museums (1986; revised 2001, 2004) [Inspired my Article 6.]

Article 4.3: "*Exhibition of sensitive materials.* Human remains and materials of sacred significance must be . . . presented with great tact and respect for the feelings of human dignity held by all peoples."[79]

WORLD ARCHAEOLOGICAL CONGRESS
(<http://www.worldarchaeologicalcongress.org>)

Vermillion Accord on Human Remains (1989) [Inspired my Articles 1, 3–4, 6.]

Article 1: "Respect for the mortal remains of the dead shall be accorded to all, irrespective of origin, race, religion, nationality, custom and tradition."

Article 2: "Respect for the wishes of the dead concerning disposition shall be accorded whenever possible, reasonable and lawful, when they are known or can be reasonably inferred."[80]

6

A Code of Ethics for Historians

Science without conscience is but ruin of the soul.

—François Rabelais[1]

Before the 1990s, historians often kept questions of professional ethics at the back of their minds, but seldom on the tips of their tongues. Traditionally, moral awareness within the profession has been rather high but also rather invisible. Questions of historical truth and method have been central to the professional training of history students for two centuries. At the same time, many historians were reluctant to talk about "big principles" and some even believed that values and ethics were not a legitimate part of historical writing. As an additional factor, many of the most problematic moral questions did not arise during, but before or after research and teaching, and consequently they were—and are—seldom discussed in historical works themselves. These moral questions typically emerged when historians trained their students, marked essays, appointed new staff, sought access to closed archives, quoted from confidential documents, or undertook commissioned research. And, sometimes, these questions were woven into historical works, preferably in the introduction (especially in the paragraphs explaining the background to the work), the conclusion, or the footnotes. They also occasionally popped up after publication, for example, when book reviews provoked heated debate, when subjects of research felt defamed and sought redress in court (see Chapter 3), or when authors played to the gallery and made too many concessions to the marketplace.

The 1990s

Perhaps this cluster of factors explains why professional ethics did not receive the attention it deserved among academic historians for much of the twentieth century.[2] This changed around 1990 under the impulse of three long-term trends. The first was the downfall of a series of dictatorships notorious for their rewriting of history: this resulted in the gradual spread of democracy and in better conditions for writing history responsibly (see Chapter 1). The second trend was the increase in human rights awareness after World War II. Human rights related topics such as the growing sensitivity to freedom of information issues, the protection of human research subjects, the notion of informed consent, the attention to privacy and reputation, the frequent dependence of science upon political, military, or economic powers, and the potentially negative effects of applied knowledge led many scientific disciplines to develop codes of ethics after 1960.[3] The third trend was the overwhelming acceptance of contemporary history as a fully-fledged part of historical writing. From the days of Leopold von Ranke (1795–1886) until long after World War II, contemporary history had been a suspected branch of history, because it did not seem to satisfy the scientific requirement of distance, but contemporary issues with a high ethical profile—such as genocide, slavery, racism, and colonialism—eventually placed themselves almost effortlessly at the heart of numerous polemical exchanges throughout the century's last decade. These issues forced many to examine increasingly the extent to which historical injustices could and had yet to be rectified with reparatory measures. In addition, most of the survivors of the Armenian genocide, the Holocaust, and scores of crimes against humanity in colonial countries had died in the meantime; this disappearance of witnesses made the denial of these crimes easier. Reacting against this denial of history, many began to speak about an ethical "duty to remember" (Chapter 5).

On top of these three general trends, a number of specific developments in the 1990s made ethics the subject of intense debate in the domain of history. The opening up of secret archives at the end of the Cold War was a first factor. More emphatically than ever before, it revealed the enormous extent to which history could be and had been falsified. A second factor was the information overload instantly accessible via the Internet after 1995. The growing number of producers of nonscholarly versions of history increased the risk of abusing it (Chapter 1), because not all of them were inclined to maintain the essential standards of integrity. They reminded historians that an assiduous application of the historical-critical method remains an indisputable necessity. A third factor (in some countries, at least) was the proliferating cult of memory, which made some wonder whether, under the guise of commemorations and heritage, the past had become a new kind of secular religion.[4] In the West, they argued, the gradual loss of authority suffered by traditional institutions such as the state, the school, and the church since at least the 1960s had left a vacuum which for many people had apparently been filled with a history of a moralistic brand. A final factor had bearings on history and all other academic subjects. The growing dominance of economy-led managerial perspectives at universities and the concomitant trend to cut budgets and augment funding from private partners threatened the academic profession at its core. It gradually dawned on academics that they should organize a defense against what constituted nothing less than a frontal assault on academic freedom and the tenure system, and that they should shield themselves from attempts at *de*professionalization (attempts of managers to take away power from professional experts).[5] A reflection on basic principles was an essential part of this defense.

Standing in the eye of all of these storms, historians were in trouble themselves. A severe epistemological crisis engendered by postmodernism had cast doubts on the possibility to attain any historical truth. This situation inside and outside the profession compelled historians to think more deeply about the essentials of their scholarship and profession and its ethical foundations. Curiously, all of these developments did not yet crystallize into an internationally adopted code of ethics for historians.

Codes of Ethics in the Field of the Humanities

The historical sciences lag behind other branches of scholarship in codifying their professional ethics, in spite of the fact that UNESCO published important guidelines for academic ethics in 1997. It stipulated: "[H]igher education institutions should be accountable for . . . the creation, through the collegial process and/or through negotiation with organizations representing higher-education teaching personnel, . . . of statements or codes of ethics to guide higher education personnel in their teaching, scholarship, research and extension work."[6]

In the last three decades, ethical codes have been drafted in such allied disciplines as museum governance, archaeology, and archival science. For museums, reflection about ethical issues began in the early 1970s when they saw that their acquisitions and the international circulation of cultural property were taking place under poorly defined conditions.[7] In archaeology, scholars had to deal with the concerns of the living people whose ancestors they studied. The tense relationships between the profession and indigenous peoples in the run-up to the 1990 Native American Graves Protection and

Repatriation Act in the United States and analogous developments elsewhere led archaeologists to codify professional conduct in this area (Chapter 4).[8] For archivists, debates about freedom of, and access to, information, copyright, and privacy protection were crucial.[9]

In these disciplines, affairs and scandals accelerated the process. For example, the debate on professional ethics among American archivists was intensified by the case of historian Francis Loewenheim, professor at Rice University, in Houston, Texas. In 1968, Loewenheim accused the Roosevelt Library of concealing six letters from the American ambassador (and historian) to Germany, William Dodd, to President Franklin Roosevelt, which he needed for his edition of the Dodd-Roosevelt letters. Loewenheim declared that he had been the victim of discrimination because the letters were subsequently used by library archivist Edgar Nixon in his 1969 book, *Franklin D. Roosevelt and Foreign Affairs, 1933–37*. The charges were investigated by a joint committee of the American Historical Association and the Organization of American Historians. In its report of August 1970, the committee found no deliberate and systematic withholding of documents and rejected the charges. This affair triggered a debate in the archival profession.[10]

One of the first to think systematically about the duties of historians was the Belgian legal historian John Gilissen in 1960. Curiously, his position was paradoxical: he spoke out against a code of ethics because he found it a rigid instrument, but at the same time maintained that if historians did not develop customary rules for their profession, judges would do this in their place. After careful analysis of jurisprudence in which historians were defendants, he formulated ten such customary rules.[11] Today, few national historical associations possess codes of ethics. The American Historical Association, which adopted a *Statement on Standards of Professional Conduct* in 1987 (after discussions stretching back to the early 1970s), is a pioneer.[12] In 2001, the Australian Council of Professional Historians Associations also endorsed a *Code of Ethics and Professional Standards;* in 2003, the Australian Historical Association did the same.[13] In 2004, the Swiss historians developed their own code.[14] And in the Netherlands, the Royal Netherlands Academy of Arts and Sciences launched its *Principles for Commissioned Historical Research* in 2007. In particular, subdisciplines working with oral or confidential written materials show sensivity to ethics and receive more incentives to develop codes. The subdiscipline of history most sensitive to the codification of ethics is oral history.[15]

The International Committee of Historical Sciences has no code of ethics itself. As explained in Chapter 1, Article 1 of its *Constitution* was amended in 2005 and reads: "It [= the International Committee of Historical Sciences] shall defend freedom of thought and expression in the field of historical research and teaching, and is opposed to the misuse of history and shall use every means at its disposal to ensure the ethical professional conduct of its members."[16] That is a recent and clear, but rather laconic statement on professional ethics by the International Committee of Historical Sciences. In short, progress in the codification of ethics has been slow. A possible explanation is Rolf Torstendahl's assertion that, at the end of the twentieth century, there was no unanimity in the historical profession about common norms or a common identity.[17] Why this is so remains unclear, although the epistemological crisis alluded to earlier presumably played a considerable role.

Reasons to Reject a Code of Ethics

Why indeed, one might ask, should historians adopt a code of ethics? There are many arguments against such a code. We should weigh them one by one and draw lessons from them.

1. We Do Not Need Codes

The argument. The traditional view is that no code is needed because all historians know and apply the essential maxim: that historical truth is searched for and discussed, not imposed. Or, as a variant, all that historians need is a democratic and public debate in which the evidence of all of the parties is weighed.

The reply. The argument is correct, but too laconic. I also firmly believe that historical truth must be searched for, not imposed, and that historians should use the power of argument, not coercion, to further their common aim. And a democratic and public debate is the oxygen of historical scholarship. The trouble is that abusers of history either avoid a public debate because their activities flourish in secrecy (for example, in cases of plagiarism and censorship) or attempt to manipulate that public debate and, if need be, sue others to propagate their convictions (for example, in cases of genocide denial). Naturally, abusers who do not respect the rules of the public debate will not respect codes of ethics either. However, the argument that codes of ethics are superfluous because abusers do not consult them and responsible historians do not need them, is too simple: codes of ethics may assist those responsible historians and abusers who are in doubt, and give advice to the former and deter the latter.

2. A Code is a Political Instrument

The argument. Values and ethics are not a part of historical writing, but of politics.

The reply. Those defending this thesis do not seem to believe that it makes sense, or that it is even possible, to discuss ethics rationally and that some moral decisions are objectively better than others.[18] Because this is possible—as I hope to have shown throughout this book—the discussion about ethics does not belong more or less to the realm of politics than any other aspects of historical writing. It is true that moral wisdom depends, to a certain degree, on historical circumstances and may gradually change. Therefore, a code of ethics should be perceived as a set of principles that have to be perfected continuously. Such a set of principles is perhaps the best we have at a certain moment, but they should nonetheless be tested continuously as every code is always subject to improvement.

3. We Already Have Codes

The argument. The rights and duties of historians are already formulated in *general* guidelines, such as the 1948 *Universal Declaration of Human Rights* and UNESCO's 1997 *Recommendation Concerning the Status of Higher-Education Teaching Personnel,* and consequently no *special* charter is necessary.

The reply. It is true that codes often overlap. However, general guidelines alone are insufficient. Texts such as those mentioned appeal to historians as human beings or experts, but do not touch upon ethical questions specific to the historical profession. A specific code should be complementary to the general ones.

4. Codes Can Be Abused

The argument. Once adopted, a code can be manipulated and abused.

The reply. Indeed, the risks are not imaginary: in the wrong hands, a code may stifle, discourage, or unjustifiably narrow legitimate historical debate and unleash witch hunts against "heretical" historians. Therefore, first, a code should emanate from a recognized, democratically organized association of historians. Second, a code should stipulate that all of its principles are connected and that none may be interpreted with arguments that are contrary to the spirit of the code.

5. Codes Are a Form of Abuse Themselves

The argument. A code of ethics restricts the freedom of historians and their discussions; therefore, it is unethical itself.

The reply. First, the freedom of historians is not limitless (see Chapters 3 and 5). A code of ethics does not restrict or compromise that freedom, but it does clarify its limits. The principles of the code are concerned with the *intention and conditions* accompanying the conduct of historians, rather than with its *content*. The code is a procedural rather than a substantial tool. Second, whereas it became clear in Chapter 1 that the demarcation between the responsible and irresponsible use of history is sometimes difficult to determine, a code assists historians in drawing that demarcation and in opposing history that is unambiguously irresponsible. Finally, codes support historians in assessing the risks involved in their roles as guardians of the dead (Chapter 4) and in weighing questions of posthumous privacy and reputation (Chapter 3). Codes do not offer, as some contend, an idealized profile of the profession. They help to solve problems, but they are not master keys. Codes are compasses that orient us while answering pressing questions about responsible conduct.

6. Codes Are Rigid Instruments

The argument. A code of ethics is rigid and bureaucratic; its application slows down the daily work. It is a corporatist rather than a professional tool. Historian August Ludwig von Schlözer (1735–1809) already regarded skeptically the standardization of rules and saw it as an imprisonment.[19]

The reply. This practical objection can be answered easily. A code is not a corporatist tool because history is not a guild. In contrast to university degrees in history, the title "historian" itself is not protected by exams or certificates, anyone writing a historical work can claim it. With a title so open to abuse, history is a profession in the sense and to the extent only that its practitioners voluntarily accept and apply certain standards to their work. In addition, to a large degree, handling a code is a question of habit. Sometimes, it will indeed slow down work. If the delay is caused by code-specific deficiencies, a better version should substitute the old one. If it is caused by a process of reflection, it rightly slowed down the work. Sometimes too, the code will accelerate the work, because it solves doubts and provides answers to important questions. Hence, in general, historiographical progress is not in jeopardy.

7. Codes Are Ineffective

The argument. A code is doomed to remain theoretical; it cannot be enforced efficiently and will not prevent harm.

The reply. The debate over the efficient implementation of codes centers around two poles: repression and prevention. The repressive strategy addresses the question of whether it is desirable to impose *imperative* measures, such as the establishment of an "International Order of Historians" to adjudicate disputes, or *prohibitive* measures, such as organizing boycotts, suing *mala fide* historians, or advocating legislation to criminalize genocide denial. Although few historians would advocate prohibitive measures or the establishment of an "Order of Historians," the question of adjudication as such has received much attention.

I shall briefly relate the American experience. In 1987, the American Historical Association adopted an *Addendum on Policies and Procedures* (last revised in 1997), which described how its Professional Division had to handle alleged breaches of its *Statement on Standards of Professional Conduct*. The introduction to the 1999 edition of this *Statement* included the following: "Although enforcement of these standards is part of its work, the division hopes that policing activities will diminish as historians become more cognizant of their professional responsibilities." In May 2003, the Professional Division's President William Cronon estimated that there were 50 to 100 inquiries for adjudication annually, but that fewer than ten of these required formal investigation. Most regarded plagiarism. In the introduction to the 2003 edition of the *Statement*, the Council of the American Historical Association announced that it would no longer investigate acts of misconduct by historians. The reasons given were limited resources and lack of power to impose sanctions. In January 2005, a thoroughly revised *Statement* appeared, this time without the *Addendum*.[20] In 1995, the American Anthropological Association had also taken the decision not to adjudicate any longer, but the American Psychological Association, the American Sociological Association, and the American Political Science Association continue their adjudication programs.

The American experience seems to confirm the argument that a code is not efficient because its implementation is (too) difficult. It is certainly the case that adjudication as a form of code enforcement is difficult. On the other hand, one should see the three stages in developing standards (codifying them, making them binding, and implementing them) as a long-term process. The American experience does not teach us, however, that adjudication is impossible or undesirable. Nor did the abolition of adjudication lead to the abolition of the *Statement on Standards of Professional Conduct* itself. In addition, judges appear to be sensitive to the use of professional standards; at least they increasingly take into account standards of professional journalism in press cases. The leading specialist in media law, Eric Barendt, commented on this development: "The imposition of a standard of 'responsible journalism' . . . may deter or chill the exercise of free speech and press rights. But that might be a desirable chill."[21]

In principle, a society of historians should never refuse to give formal or informal advice, if so requested by members or others involved in ethical disputes or dilemmas. Any society of historians from which a code emanates, even when it does not have an adjudication program, should systematically gather documentation about the current state of ethical issues in history and about affairs of irresponsible use and abuse of history that come to its attention. This task of collecting materials on ethical issues provides a bridge to the other implementation strategy: prevention. The preventive approach, already discussed in Chapter 1, holds that a code is the focus of moral awareness and debate among historians. Therefore, the code should form an obligatory part of the curriculum, embedded in a program of discussing ethical questions for historians, and taught to history students. Table 6.1 gives an outline of such a program:

TABLE 6.1. **Suggestions for a Subject *Ethical Problems For Historians***

Parts	Items
	Ethics and ~
codes	Comparative study of codes of ethics for historians on the one hand, and those for archivists, museum professionals, archaeologists, anthropologists, journalists, and judges on the other hand Study of codes of ethics as sources

the abuse and irresponsible use of history	Abuse of history (= its use with intent to deceive) and irresponsible use of history (= either its deceptive or negligent use):
	  * *heuristic level* (data as sources): irresponsible destruction, collection, use of sources of others; fabrication of own sources
	  * *epistemological level* (data as words): irresponsible description and analysis of data
	  * *pragmatic level* (data as works): lies about oneself or about the works; reception of works by censors; providers of information, assignments, contracts, funding; editors and publishers; peer reviewers; audiences
	History of the abuse of history
	The detection of the abuse of history

	Sociology of ~
the historians	Study of types of historians such as Nobel prize winners, destroyers of myths, mentors, institution builders, rectors and deans, founders of journals, history textbook authors, source editors, autodidactic historians, politically active historians, television personalities, court historians, pseudohistorians . . . Values, motives, commitment, retroactive moral evaluations of historians
the profession	Historians as scholars and as professionals The historical profession: demographic evolution of the profession; the curriculum; awarding of degrees, admission of students, and recruitment (selection and promotion) and dismissal of staff Persecuted historians: dissidents, exiles/refugees Historians and resistance against persecution Historians and solidarity: human rights activism of historians
the historical work	Abuse-sensitivity of historiographical genres, in particular source editions, genealogies, biographies, obituaries, chronicles, chronologies, annals, maps, photographs, bibliographies, historical dictionaries, encyclopedias, statistics, indexes, archive catalogs, and history textbooks Censorship; self-censorship; propaganda; taboos; omissions

(continued)

TABLE 6.1. **Suggestions for a Subject** *Ethical Problems For Historians* (continued)

Parts	Items
	Sociology of ~ (continued)
archaeology	Fraud in archaeology: motives and cases Archaeology and indigenous peoples
archives	Archival cleansing: removal, concealment, neglect, illegal destruction of archives Archival access and secrecy Intimidation and elimination of producers, owners, and custodians of sources Archives of dictators, of truth commissions, of courts and tribunals
heritage	Intentional damage, destruction, looting of heritage Illegal collection of, and trade in, objects of heritage
teaching	Curricula determinants History textbooks: selection, use, manipulation, controversies
research subjects	Privacy: invasion of privacy cases against historians Reputation: defamation cases against historians
legislation	Laws concerning copyright; concerning freedom of expression, freedom of information, official secrets, habeas data, and archives; concerning privacy and defamation
judges	Differences between judges and historians; between legal and historical truth Lawsuits about historical issues before national and international courts
groups	Groups as commissioning entities Public commemorations
sponsors	Pressure and control of sponsors
government	Government as commissioning entity Official histories; official commemorations; official historical projects (museums, etc.) History as official propaganda Heads of state and government with an active interest in history
political context	The relationship between historiography on the one hand and democracy or dictatorship on the other
UNESCO	Discussions on academic freedom Discussions on tangible and intangible heritage, on positive and negative elements of heritage
United Nations Human Rights Council	Discussions on impunity for, and reparation of, historical injustice; on the right to the truth Historians, truth commissions, forensic anthropology, mass graves Postconflict traumas, apologies

8. Codes Should Be National, Not Universal

The argument. Every country has its own historiographical traditions and particularities and these should be reflected in a code. Therefore, if a code is needed at all, it should be national.

The reply. History teaching and historical research, despite their strong national bias in terms of organization, funding, and archives, constitute a universal enterprise.[22] Therefore, a universal, not a national, outlook should dominate the spirit of a code. It cannot be otherwise. Although the American, Australian, Swiss, and Dutch codes of ethics are conceived in diverging ways, they are not in the least incompatible. They overlap, but emphasize different principles. Work has to be done to unify these approaches to a certain extent, but there should always remain considerable room for the special region- or country-dependent preoccupations of any code-drafting society of historians.

An Evaluation of the Reasons to Reject a Code of Ethics

The arguments against a code cannot be neglected. They yield useful warnings and lessons. Among these are the following: first, a code is not eternal but provisional; it should be regularly revised. A code is a compass that offers guidance for making wise ethical decisions, but it is not an infallible device. A compass does not guarantee that one arrives safely in the harbor, but, at critical moments, it may indicate a good direction. Combined with training, experience, good equipment, perseverance, cooperation, and wisdom, it is indispensable. Second, a code should be firmly universal in approach, but should leave room for national particularities. Third, to prove its transparency, a code should explicitly mention relevant texts of larger scope and influence; to prove its surplus value, it should address questions specific to the historical profession. Fourth, the guardian of the code should be a recognized association of professional historians, democratically organized, trusted for its professionalism, and with an open mind for the ethical discussion. Such an association should gather documentation on that discussion in the broadest sense. Fifth, although some mixture of repression and prevention will probably be necessary, a code that recommends and prevents is certainly preferable to one that condemns. Sixth, without exception, the existing body of literature narrows the problem of historians' ethics down to historians' duties. This (justified) traditional emphasis on duties must, however, be put within a larger theoretical framework in which the rights of historians have their place also. Like all citizens, historians possess universal rights. In addition, as academics they enjoy academic freedom. Academic freedom is the right to combine, without outside interference, the rights to free expression and to culture and science (mentioned in Articles 19 and 27 of the *Universal Declaration of Human Rights* respectively). Although firmly based on universal human rights, academic freedom itself is also duty-dependent, in that it protects academic historians only if and while they are performing their core professional duty, that is, the honest search (in its broadest sense) for historical truth in research and teaching. Finally, the question whether historians need a code does not solely depend on themselves; it also depends on outsiders and how the latter perceive the former. Table 6.2 surveys all of the players in the field:

TABLE 6.2.   **Parties Interested in a *Code of Ethics for Historians***

Inside the profession

Professional historians (academic professional historians, history teachers, others)
History students
Boards of history departments and of historical institutes of academies
Associations of historians

Outside the profession

Amateur historians
Other scholars (archivists, archaeologists, social scientists, others)
Boards of faculties and universities
Ministries of education
(Potential) providers of:
    * information (producers, owners, and custodians of sources; informants, witnesses, respondents)
    * assignments and contracts (government, others)
    * funding (sponsors)
Subjects of research:
    * living subjects
    * relatives and caretakers of deceased subjects
The media
Parties involved in conflicts with historians:
    * dissatisfied source holders, commissioning entities, sponsors
    * complainants, judges

Tensions Between Accountability and Autonomy, and Between Scholarship and Profession

Codes of ethics provide general principles governing the methodical and organizational aspects of history, and therefore contain both scholarly and professional elements. These principles refer to freedom and integrity (of historians), respect (for those surrounding them), and the careful and methodically executed search for truth (as the result of this interaction). However, together they do not constitute a code of practice with exhaustive rules for every problem that can arise. As mentioned in Chapter 1, two types of tension exist here: tensions between scholarship and profession, and within the profession, tensions between autonomy and accountability. Codes of ethics are a solution for the second type of tension, the tension between autonomy and accountability. This is so because the adoption of a code of ethics by the historical profession is a form of accountability to society with the aim of maximizing its autonomy.[23]

But tensions of the first type—between scholarship and profession—may survive despite the use of a code of ethics, as the following example demonstrates. It concerns the professional secrecy regarding a source that gives information in confidence. "Source" should not be understood here as information, but as the author of that information. The right not to disclose sources of confidential information means that it is permitted to make the sources anonymous while mentioning the facts and opinions from these sources. (This right should not be confused with the right to silence, discussed in Chapter 3, which allows for the omission of some facts and opinions themselves). The right to nondisclosure is a widely recognized right of journalists.[24] But is it a right of historians too? The answer has two sides, a professional and a scholarly one.

For the professional side, we can take the Council of Europe *Principles Concerning the Right of Journalists Not To Disclose Their Sources of Information* (2000) as our guide.[25] These principles recommend an "explicit . . . protection of the right of journalists not to disclose information identifying a source" and prescribe that any breaches of this right be painstakingly justified.[26] Interestingly, the *Principles* define the term "journalist" very broadly, that is as "any natural or legal person who is regularly or professionally engaged in the collection and dissemination of information to the public via any means of mass communication." This clearly covers historians also, particularly contemporary historians. Similar provisions exist for Africa and the Americas.[27] Therefore, professionally, historians have a right to nondisclosure of sources similar to the one accorded to journalists.

At the scholarly level, matters are more complicated. In order to be able to test statements of fact and opinion, scholars have developed principles of transparency and accountability. These principles include *maximal* acknowledgement of sources of information. Clearly, this duty of verifiability, including the acknowledgement of sources, clashes with the right not to reveal sources of confidential information. As progress in scholarship is crucially dependent on verifiability, and hence on transparency and accountability—more dependent, I believe, than the public debate is—it is natural that scholars weigh these two interests (verifiability and secrecy) with a presumption in favor of verifiability. This means that historians are only allowed *not* to disclose their sources of information if they are able to give a solid justification for their decision.[28] This also means that there is a clear difference between the professional and scholarly role of historians: as experts, historians have an undiluted right to nondisclosure; as scholars, they have to satisfy higher standards of accountability than journalists.[29]

In short, this situation is different from the first. Whereas journalists have a right to nondisclosure that can be restricted by others only exceptionally, historians also have such a right, but, given that they, unlike journalists, possess countervailing scholarly duties as well, they should themselves restrict and sufficiently justify uses of this right. In this, the right to nondisclosure of sources is similar to the right to silence for historical facts about reputations: both should be balanced against disclosure with a presumption in favor of disclosure.

Reasons to Adopt a Code of Ethics

Against this background, I see ten reasons to adopt a code of ethics. A code:

* is the focus of moral awareness and debate among historians;
* formulates the rights and duties of historians;
* is an instrument to teach the core of the profession to students;
* is a compass to detect irresponsible uses and abuses of history;
* is an instrument to evaluate and to adjudicate conflicts;
* helps reduce and prevent irresponsible uses and abuses of history;
* clarifies the foundations and limits of the historical profession for those in and outside of it;
* helps to protect historians against pressure;
* enhances the autonomy, transparency, and accountability of the historical profession;

* and increases public trust in, and understanding of, the historical profession.[30]

The following proposal for a code of ethics for historians contains a mixture of three types of principles. Many principles contain classic ideas that were formulated and tested during the past centuries. Their classic character indicates that the code belongs to a long tradition of reflection about the ethics of historians. Other old principles are reworded to fit into a consistent language of rights and duties, the pressing relevance of which is shown throughout the book. And, finally, as the structure and logic of the proposed code intend to systematically cover the entire area of ethics for historians, some principles are new, or appear as such for historians, although they are already applied in other domains of science and society.

Historians should do everything that lies in their power to guarantee that they take good care of history. It is our professional expertise—our access to, and production of, expert knowledge about the past—that distinguishes us from others interested in the past.[31] This does not mean in the least that historians own the past—history is too important to be left to historians alone; rather it means that they have specific duties. The philosopher André Mercier aptly summarized the core message:[32]

Sagesse oblige.

A CODE OF ETHICS FOR HISTORIANS (proposal)

Introduction

Article 1: Scope

This code is intended for academic historians (further abbreviated as "historians.") Its use is recommended for other professional and non-professional historians. It is also a tool for the general public wanting to be informed about the standards of the historical profession. It constitutes a set of principles about the historians' rights and duties and expresses a vision on its four irreducible values: freedom and integrity (of historians), respect (for those they study), and the careful and methodically determined and executed search for historical truth (as the result of the interactions between historians and others).

The code flows from the UNESCO *Recommendation Concerning the Status of Higher-Education Teaching Personnel* (1997), Article 22(k):

"[H]igher education institutions should be accountable for . . . the creation, through the collegial process and/or through negotiation with organizations representing higher-education teaching personnel, consistent with the principles of academic freedom and freedom of speech, of statements or codes of ethics to guide higher education personnel in their teaching, scholarship, research and extension work," and from the *Constitution* of the International Committee of Historical Sciences (2005), Article 1: "It shall defend freedom of thought and expression in the field of historical research and teaching, and is opposed to the misuse of history and shall use every means at its disposal to ensure the ethical professional conduct of its members."

Article 2: Implementation

Historians shall use, discuss, and promote this code at congresses and during their research and teaching. It must be interpreted as a whole; nothing in it may be explained on the basis of arguments that are contrary to its spirit. Complaints about breaches of the code, when supported with evidence, merit investigation by a representative, authoritative, and independent body of historians, which, if necessary, takes the advice of experts.

Core Tasks

Article 3: Research; Teaching

Historians have two equal and connected core tasks: the search for historical truth (historical research) and its transmission (publishing and history teaching).

Universal Rights

Article 4: Freedom of Expression and Information; Peaceful Assembly; Intellectual Property

Historians' rights are based on the *Universal Declaration of Human Rights* (1948) and the international covenants derived from it. Particularly important are Article 19(1) and 19(2) of the *International Covenant on*

Civil and Political Rights that protect the freedom of information necessary for historical research and the freedom of expression necessary for
publishing and the teaching of history. Article 19 stipulates that: "(1)
Everyone shall have the right to hold opinions without interference; (2)
Everyone shall have the right to freedom of expression; this right shall
include freedom to seek, receive and impart information and ideas of
all kinds, regardless of frontiers, either orally, in writing or in print, in
the form of art, or through any other media of his choice." In addition,
Article 21 of the *Covenant* states that historians have the right to organize meetings and form professional associations. Equally important
is Article 15(1)(c) of the *International Covenant on Economic, Social and
Cultural Rights* that protects the intellectual property of historians. It
stipulates that, "States Parties to the present Covenant recognize the
right of everyone . . . to benefit from the protection of the moral and
material interests resulting from any scientific . . . production of which
he is the author."

Duty-Dependent Rights

Article 5: Academic Freedom; Autonomy; International Contacts

Duty-dependent rights can be claimed and exercised only while
historians discharge their duties. While historians discharge their
duties inside or outside of academe, Articles 15(2), 15(3), and 15(4)
of the *International Covenant on Economic, Social and Cultural Rights*
(1966) are applicable, in particular that "the States Parties to the present Covenant" will take steps "necessary for the conservation, the
development and the diffusion of science and culture," that these
states "undertake to respect the freedom indispensable for scientific
research," and "recognize the benefits to be derived from the encouragement and development of international contacts and cooperation
in the scientific and cultural fields." These articles imply that historians are entitled to academic freedom, including the right to organize
themselves autonomously. Paragraph 27 of the UNESCO *Recommendation* defines academic freedom as follows: "[T]he right [of higher-
education teaching personnel], without constriction by prescribed
doctrine, to freedom of teaching and discussion, freedom in carrying
out research and disseminating and publishing the results thereof,
freedom to express freely their opinion about the institution or system in which they work, freedom from institutional censorship and

freedom to participate in professional or representative academic bodies." This academic freedom also extends to expressions and activities in the public sphere if those are unambiguously performed as part of the academic work. Historians are allowed to exchange information at an international level, which includes the right to travel for scientific purposes. The tasks of historians demand long-term commitments and, therefore, the academic freedom of historians is best protected by a system of tenure.

Article 6: Choice of Topics

Historians have the right to choose and design their research topics and their curricula of teaching topics without political or other nonscientific interference.

Article 7: Selection of Information

Historians have the right to work on the basis of equitable laws on copyright, freedom of information, archives, and privacy and defamation. They are entitled to demand that archival selection criteria (that is, criteria to preserve or destroy records) are not politically inspired and take due account of the historical interest; that maximal, free, and equal access to information is the rule and that restrictions are exceptional and only for purposes prescribed by law and necessary in a democratic society. It should be possible to contest any restriction through a procedure independent of the executive branch.

Duties in General

Article 8: Complementarity

In their capacity as human beings, citizens, professionals, and academics, historians have general duties stipulated in international instruments. To these general duties, their specific duties are complementary. Historians have specific duties because they obtain expert knowledge about the past. In order to discharge these specific duties, they should have the rights described above. If these rights are lacking in whole or in part, historians shall still attempt to discharge their specific duties to the best of their ability. Furthermore, they shall discuss conflicts between general and specific duties (in particular, between their duties as loyal citizens and those as critical scholars) at congresses and during their research and teaching, and balance them in the spirit of this code.

Duties Regarding Subjects of Study

Article 9: Respect

Aware of the universal rights of the living and the universal duties to the dead, historians shall respect the dignity of the living and the dead they study. The *International Covenant on Civil and Political Rights* (1966) is applicable, in particular Article 17(1): "No one shall be subjected to arbitrary or unlawful interference with his privacy, family, home or correspondence, nor to unlawful attacks on his honour and reputation," and Article 19(3): "[The right to freedom of expression] may . . . be subject to certain restrictions, but these shall only be such as are provided by law and are necessary: (a) for respect of the rights or reputations of others; (b) for the protection of national security or of public order . . . , or of public health or morals."

Duties Regarding Work

Article 10: Integrity; Historical Truth

Integrity is the moral foundation of the historians' work. It shall be the intent of historians to honestly search for the historical truth, even if they are aware that their knowledge is provisional and fallible, and even if there are limits to that search as stipulated in Article 9 ("Respect"). Historians shall always oppose the abuse of history (its use with intent to deceive) and the irresponsible use of history (either its deceptive or negligent use).

Article 11: Access to Information

When accessing information, historical and otherwise, historians shall respect: (1) embargoes provided by the laws on freedom of information and on archives, (2) the informed consent principle governing interviews, and (3) pledges of confidentiality. Historians accessing confidential information on individuals, private institutions, or the government under certain conditions—conditions such as: monopolistic access; privileged access; selective access; approval of research design; oath of secrecy about the information during and/or after research; anonymization of information or its sources (informants, witnesses, and respondents); manuscript approval; pre-publication review and clearance by third parties; partial or total or temporary publication ban—shall fairly balance, in the spirit of this code, the benefit in terms of the estimated information surplus against the harm for all parties involved in terms of unequal access, biased information, or nonidentifiability of persons. Historians have a right to nondisclosure of sources of confidential information, but given their scholarly duties of transparency and accountability, they should balance any nondisclosure against disclosure with a presumption in favor of disclosure.

Article 12: Disclosure of Information

The disclosure of information is governed by Articles 10 and 11, and restricted by Article 9. Publication of information, and speaking freely about it, is the rule; confidentiality is the exception. As part of their right to silence—itself an integral part of the universal right to free expression—historians have the right, after balancing the individual against the public interest, not to disclose historical facts harming the privacy and reputation of persons, either living or dead. The balancing test takes place as follows: in privacy cases, the interests in disclosure and secrecy are of equal importance; in reputation cases there is, in principle, a presumption in favor of disclosure.

Article 13: Critical and Objective Method; Independence

Historians shall adopt a critical attitude and use a method based on: (1) accuracy (transparency; respect for evidence and argumentation; control of bias and anachronism; impartiality and objectivity) at the levels of statements of fact and description, and (2) plausibility at the levels of statements of opinion and analysis. Historians shall be candid about their perspective on the past and disclose the names of institutions or persons from whom they are dependent. They shall aspire to political, ideological, and intellectual independence and to as much financial independence as possible from government, commissioning entities, and sponsors.

Article 14: Free Debate; Accountability; Universalism

Free and public exchange of ideas is the oxygen of historical scholarship. Historians shall publish and disseminate their corroborated research findings as much as possible. Reports with a secret or confidential character shall be kept to a minimum. Peer review shall be carried out objectively and impartially; it shall be anonymous only when absolutely necessary. Peers with a conflict or harmony of interests, real or perceived, with the historians under review, shall abstain from reviewing them. Historians shall check their findings in a free and public debate among informed and verifying colleagues, students, and third parties. They shall be tolerant of divergent informed and *bona fide* opinions of mainstream historians and their opponents. Their orientation shall be universalistic in that their research shall not be audience-relative but shall allow, in principle, worldwide verification.

Article 15: Moral Evaluations

Historians shall be sensitive to their implicit moral evaluations. As part of their right to silence, historians have an absolute right not to mention their own explicit moral evaluations about the past. However, they shall be allowed to make such explicit moral evaluations on their subjects of study, on the condition that these have sufficient factual basis, are prudent and fair, and are a contribution to the public debate about history. In such evaluations, historians shall at all times clearly distinguish the values of contemporaries of the epoch studied, those of themselves, and those embodied in universal human rights standards. Although historians are not obliged to make statements about responsibility and guilt of historical actors or to draw moral lessons from the past, in cases of imprescriptible crimes, such as genocide, crimes against humanity, and war crimes, they shall try, to the best of their ability, to indicate the range of well-founded evaluations.

Duties Regarding Society at Large

Article 16: The Right to History

The first duty of historians regarding society—understood as their local, national, and global community—is the discharge of the other duties mentioned in this code. Article 13(1) of the *International Covenant on Economic, Social and Cultural Rights* stipulates that "The States Parties . . . agree that education shall be directed to the full development of the human personality" and its Articles 15(1)(a) and 15(1)(b) recognize the right of every one "to take part in cultural life," and "to enjoy the benefits of scientific progress and its applications." Therefore, historians shall attempt to answer important historical questions asked by their society to the best of their ability. They shall further the historical awareness of their society and facilitate its right to history, provided that such promotion corresponds to the spirit of this code. When performing activities in the public forum, historians shall avoid every ambiguity as to whether they operate with professional or scholarly authority. Historians shall help enhance the quality of history teaching in primary and secondary education, including the contents of history curricula and history textbooks.

Article 17: The Right to Memory

Memories are opinions and, as such, they are protected by Article 19(1) of the *International Covenant on Civil and Political Rights.* Holding opinions, and by extension memories, permits no exception or restriction. Every individual has a right to memory. The right to have memories implies the right not to be forced by others to have specific memories. No duty to remember can be imposed on others. Expressing opinions, and by extension memories, is subject to the restrictions of Article 19(3) of the *International Covenant on Civil and Political Rights* (quoted above). Although historians should reject the duty to remember and although individually they have the freedom to choose their research and teaching topics, they form a global professional community that, when perceived as such, has the collective duty, in principle, to study and teach the past in its entirety, including suppressed, generally forgotten, or controversial historical issues.

Article 18: Democracy

Historians shall support democracy because a democratic society—a society that recognizes and respects the human rights set forth in the *Universal Declaration of Human Rights*—is a necessary condition for a sound historiography. Conversely, a sound historiography reflects and strengthens the democratic society.

Duties Regarding the Historical Profession

Article 19: Protection

Historians shall protect and promote the historical profession and its infrastructure of sources. They shall oppose external threats to the autonomy of the profession. They shall also oppose internal threats to the integrity of the profession, that is, the abuse and irresponsible use of history mentioned in Articles 1, 2 and 10, the unfair treatment of colleagues and students, and inequality under equal conditions.

Article 20: Solidarity

Historians shall treat colleagues and history students with respect and sympathy. They shall work for the rights of all members of the profession worldwide. They shall show solidarity with colleagues and history students whose rights are violated.[33]

✥ Epilogue

Most persons are more inclined to the future than to the past. In some situations, however, a bias toward the past may be inevitable. In particular, I am thinking of all of those who experienced past sufferings compared to which any future happiness and suffering are perceived as bleak, if not trivial, as is the case with survivors of gross violations of human rights. For that reason, they speak of a past that does not go away. Here is one such view, expressed by Imre Kertész: "Memories are like stray dogs. They surround you, stare at you while they gasp, and howl, baying at the moon. You would like to chase them but they do not disappear. Instead, they eagerly lick your hand. But once they are behind you, they bite you."[1] At the other side of the spectrum of memories about experiences, pride in past performance is also a reason for a bias toward the past.

And the same motives work in peoples. Some peoples are more concerned with their past than others. Here too, pain and pride are at work. Those peoples whose identity is threatened by defeat in war or loss of roots, and those whose identity is boosted by freshly gained autonomy, tend to display a more acute sense of historical awareness than other peoples.

Even without such a special bias, the past is real and important. Its secret is that it is the great absentee from history, and yet it will not go away.[2] And if the absent past is also still there, the question is, how we can conceive of it meaningfully? This book suggested two perspectives: as an area of conflict and abuse (Chapters 1–3) and as an area of reconciliation and responsible use (Chapters 4–6). Both perspectives can adopt low and high degrees of intensity; thus, four possibilities arise.

Historians and others dedicated to the search of historical truth have a straightforward high-intensity conflict with the enemies of the past—the dictators, the abusers of history, and the assassins of memory. These are heavy clashes. In addition, they also have permanent low-intensity conflicts in which it is less clear who the enemy is and even whether there is an enemy in the traditional sense at all. The adversaries in these low-intensity conflicts are not the assassins of memory. On the contrary, they are the contemporaries of historians who feel wronged because historians supposedly misrepresented them in their works. If these contemporaries or their relatives are right, their complaints point to the boundaries of the historian's freedom. The adversaries in these conflicts may also be the historians themselves when they neglect their elementary duties and use the tools of their trade irresponsibly to manufacture a comfortable history.

The past can also be conceived as an area of reconciliation. Low-intensity reconciliation with the past means that historians and others dedicated to the search for historical truth approach their subjects of study with both irreverence and respect. If they want to create a novel picture of the past, they should be untamably curious and be prepared to leave the well-trodden tracks, open new doors, and travel to the unknown. And still, once this quest is over, a few topics may remain cloaked in silence for reasons of reputation and secret, or, above all, for reasons of privacy—the signpost not of censorship, but of prudence and respect—and always the result of careful balancing tests. I strongly prefer this low-intensity reconciliation: it is a moderate approach where professional ethics serve as a guide. In this view, a code of ethics, far from being a sterile tool that hampers our practice, is an instrument to guarantee our scholarly and professional quality and autonomy. There is another approach also, that of high-intensity reconciliation. Those advocating it attach more importance to respect for the past than to an irreverent approach to the past. They include a duty to remember the dead among their tasks. The high-intensity approach is ambitious (I admire it), but it is not mine, because I think—and I hope to have argued this convincingly—that it does not reflect sufficiently the complex character of the past. As Nietzsche said, the dead should not bury the living.

If the past as an area of conflict and reconciliation is present despite its absence, *how*, then, is it present? The past is always there in our conduct. We called this habit memory. In addition, it is very much alive in our thoughts, in our declarative memory. Our mind is more versatile than our conduct and it cannot be pinned down to the dimensions of space and time. Not long ago, the writer György Konrad said that the ability to remember is, "both a benefit and a curse. It is a curse because it will not leave us in peace and a benefit because it overcomes death. Thus, in recollection, we may speak with both the living and the dead. As long as we are remembered, we live on. Forgetting puts the seal on death."[3] In its operations of declarative memory, the mind is able to connect us instantly with the dead. But historical writing is not an ordinary operation of memory. It is a rather peculiar operation of factual memory, based on freedom and integrity, respect, and the careful and methodically determined search for truth.

Thinking of the past, either via memory or via history, enables us to meet the inhabitants of its lands. With muffled drums, the echoes of previous generations come to our ears. If we choose the path of responsible history, the road to these strange lands is long. To read the landscape at critical junctures, this book argued, it is best to use a code of ethics. That is, a compass for sovereign walkers into the past.

NOTES

Introduction

1. In *Censorship of Historical Thought: A World Guide, 1945–2000* (Westport, CT, and London: Greenwood Press, 2002), xi–xiv, I explained how that passion emerged during the years that I worked for Amnesty International in 1980–82.
2. See <http://www.concernedhistorians.org>.
3. The preamble of the United Nations *Convention on the Prevention and Punishment of the Crime of Genocide* (<http://www.ohchr.org>; 1948) contains a historical clause: "The Contracting Parties, . . . recognizing that at all periods of history genocide has inflicted great losses on humanity, and being convinced that, in order to liberate mankind from such an odious scourge, international cooperation is required . . ."
4. See Bernard Williams, *Truth & Truthfulness: An Essay in Genealogy* (Princeton and Oxford: Princeton University Press, 2002), 84–148.
5. See Antoon De Baets, "The Impact of the *Universal Declaration of Human Rights* on the Study of History," *History and Theory*, 48, no.1 (February 2009).

Chapter 1

1. Marcus Tullius Cicero, *De oratore I, II* (originally Latin, 55 BCE; translation E.W. Sutton; Cambridge, MA: Harvard University Press, and London: Heinemann, 1976), II, 62 (242–45).
2. International Committee of Historical Sciences, *Constitution* (<http://www.cish.org>; 1926, as amended in 1992 and 2005), Article 1.
3. For example, Marc Ferro, *The Use and Abuse of History, or How the Past Is Taught to Children* (London and Boston: Routledge, 2003); Moses Finley, *The Use and Abuse of History* (London: Chatto & Windus, and New York: Viking, 1986); Pieter Geyl, *The Use and Abuse of History* (New Haven, CT: Yale University Press, 1955); Bernard Lewis, *History Remembered, Recovered, Invented* (Princeton, NJ: Princeton University Press, 1987); Tzvetan Todorov, "The Abuses of Memory," *Common Knowledge*, 5, no. 1 (Spring 1996), 6–26. My own analysis of the censorship of history was also centered on the basic notion of legitimation. See Antoon De Baets, *Censorship of Historical Thought: A World Guide 1945–2000* (Westport, CT, and London: Greenwood, 2002), 1–36. Essays by Friedrich

Nietzsche and W.B. Gallie carrying the phrase "use and abuse of history" in their titles do not deal with abuse as understood here. Throughout this chapter, I have generally deliberately abstained from giving concrete examples of abuses. For many examples, see De Baets, Censorship, passim, and Chapters 2 and 3 of the present book.

4. More background in Philip Altbach, "The Academic Profession," in Altbach, ed., International Higher Education: An Encyclopedia, vol. 1 (New York and London: Garland, 1991), 23–45.

5. Miroslav Kusý, "On the Purity of the Historian's Craft," Kosmas, 1984–85, III, no. 2 & IV, no. 1, 29–31, 38. He referred to Marc Bloch's Apologie pour l'histoire ou métier d'historien (originally 1949; Paris: Colin, 1967) and Edward Carr's What Is History? (originally 1961; Harmondsworth: Penguin, 1973).

6. Natalie Zemon Davis, "Censorship, Silence and Resistance: The Annales during the German Occupation of France," Historical Reflections, 24, no. 2 (Summer 1998), 351–74.

7. This is partly the case in the (interesting) piece of Laurent Wirth, "Facing Misuses of History," in The Misuses of History (Strasbourg: Council of Europe [Council for Cultural Co-operation], 2000), 23–56. Wirth approaches, however, the core of the problem when discussing intentional omission (pages 46–47.)

8. Edward Shils, The Calling of Education: The Academic Ethic and Other Essays on Higher Education, ed. Steven Grosby (Chicago: Chicago University Press, 1997), 160–61. John Dewey expressed the same idea in 1902. See his "Academic Freedom" (1902) in Jo Ann Boydston, ed., John Dewey: The Middle Works, 1899–1924, vol. 2, 1902–1903 (Carbondale and Edwardsville: Southern Illinois University Press; and London and Amsterdam: Feffer & Simons, 1976), 55. On the value of truth, see Bernard Williams, Truth & Truthfulness: An Essay in Genealogy (Princeton and Oxford: Princeton University Press, 2002), 6–7.

9. Karl Popper, Logic of Scientific Discovery (London: Hutchinson, 1980), 34–42 and 278–82; and Popper, Conjectures and Refutations: The Growth of Scientific Knowledge (London: Routledge & Kegan Paul, 1963, 1974), 33–41, 253–58. For an overview of demarcation theories, see Marcello Truzzi, "Pseudoscience," in Gordon Stein, ed., The Encyclopedia of the Paranormal (Amherst, NY: Prometheus, 1996), 560–74, and Riki Dolby, Uncertain Knowledge: An Image of Science for a Changing World (Cambridge, etc.: Cambridge University Press, 1996), 159–65, 184–225. See also David Stump, "Pseudoscience," in Maryanne Horowitz, ed., New Dictionary of the History of Ideas, vol. 5 (Detroit: Scribner's, 2005), 1950–51. Dolby enumerated the following demarcation principles: authoritative classification (Auguste Comte), induction (John Stuart Mill), convention (Henri Poincaré), operationalism (Percy Bridgman), true protocol statements (logical positivists), falsifiable hypotheses (Karl Popper), progressive research programs (Imre Lakatos), heuristic value (pragmatists), correct ideology (Marxists), and no demarcation (Paul Feyerabend). See Dolby, Uncertain Knowledge, 163–64.

10. The power of myths to give meaning is clear from George Schöpflin's taxonomy, which distinguishes eight motifs in myths: territory; redemption and suffering; unjust treatment; election and civilizing mission; military valor; rebirth

and renewal; ethnogenesis and antiquity; and kinship and shared descent. See his "The Functions of Myth and a Taxonomy of Myths," in Geoffrey Hosking and George Schöpflin, eds., *Myths and Nationhood* (London: Hurst, 1997), 28–35. See also David Lowenthal, "Fabricating Heritage," *History & Memory*, 10, no. 1 (Spring 1998), 5–25. For further reflections on myths, see William McNeill, "Mythistory, or Truth, Myth, History, and Historians," *American Historical Review*, 91, no. 1 (February 1986), 6–9; for reflections on the excusability of historical myths, see David Gordon, *Self-determination and History in the Third World* (Princeton, NJ: Princeton University Press, 1971), 177–82; for reflections on the coexistence of contradictory beliefs in the human mind, see Paul Veyne, *Les Grecs ont-ils cru à leurs mythes? Essai sur l'imagination constituante* (Paris: Seuil, 1983).

11. For the concept of deception (and the distinction with self-deception), see Mark Bevir, *The Logic of the History of Ideas* (Cambridge, Cambridge University Press, 1999), 265–78. Bevir defines deception as the attempt to make others believe something the deceiver believes to be false (page 267).

12. Joel Feinberg, *Harm to Others* (New York and Oxford: Oxford University Press, 1984), 187–91.

13. Applying Immanuel Kant's argument in "On a Supposed Right to Lie from Altruistic Motives" (originally German 1785), in Peter Singer, ed., *Ethics* (Oxford: Oxford University Press, 1994), 281: "For a lie always harms another; if not some other particular man, still it harms mankind generally, for it vitiates the source of law itself." For criticism of Kant's thesis, see Williams, *Truth & Truthfulness*, 84–85, 117.

14. See also Eric Barendt, *Freedom of Speech* (fully revised and updated second edition; Oxford: Oxford University Press, 2005), 226.

15. De Baets, *Censorship*, 22.

16. Hyman Gross, *A Theory of Criminal Justice* (New York: Oxford University Press, 1979), 13–18.

17. Shils, *Calling of Education*, 160–61; Frederick Schauer, *Free Speech: A Philosophical Inquiry* (Cambridge: Cambridge University Press, 1982), 92, 102.

18. Illegal abuses are usually covered by one of the following types of rights or laws. Regarding the author who is abused: freedom of expression or copyright; regarding the message content: freedom of information or archives; regarding the historians' subjects: privacy or reputation.

19. For a survey of pseudohistorical theories, see Robert Carroll, *The Skeptic's Dictionary* (Hoboken, NJ: Wiley, 2003); Karl Corino, ed., *Gefälscht! Betrug in Politik, Literatur, Wissenschaft, Kunst und Musik* (Reinbek: Rowohlt, 1992); Kenneth Feder, *Frauds, Myths, and Mysteries: Science and Pseudoscience in Archaeology* (Mountain View, CA, London, and Toronto: Mayfield, 1999); Werner Fuld, *Das Lexikon der Fälschungen* (Frankfurt am Main: Eichborn, 1999); William Williams, ed., *Encyclopedia of Pseudoscience* (Chicago and London: Fitzroy Dearborn, 2000).

20. See, among others, Daniel Woolf, "Historiography," in Horowitz, ed., *New Dictionary*, vol. 1, passim, for examples.

21. Donald Cameron Watt, "The Political Misuse of History," *Trends in Historical Revisionism: History As a Political Device* (London: Centre for Contemporary Studies, 1985), 11. See also Martin Sabrow, Ralph Jessen, and Klaus

Große Kracht, eds., *Zeitgeschichte als Streitgeschichte: Grosse Kontroversen seit 1945* (Munich: Beck, 2003), 9–18.

22. Antoon De Baets, "Archives," in Derek Jones, ed., *Censorship: A World Encyclopedia* (London and Chicago, Fitzroy Dearborn: 2001), 76–82.

23. This is the domain of *historical propaganda:* the systematic *manipulation* of historical facts or opinions, usually by, or with the connivance of, the government or another power; see De Baets, *Censorship,* 18.

24. Related to irresponsible omission is the notion of *historical taboos:* historical facts or opinions that cannot be mentioned for reasons of privacy, reputation, or the legitimation of power and status.

25. For background to the discussion about narrative in historiography, see Chris Lorenz, "History: Forms of Representation, Discourse, and Functions," in Neil Smelser and Paul Baltes, eds., *International Encyclopedia of the Social and Behavioral Sciences,* vol. 10 (Oxford, etc.: Elsevier-Pergamon, 2001), 6836–42.

26. American Historical Association, *Statement on Standards of Professional Conduct* (<http://www.historians.org>; Washington, May 1987; entirely revised January 2005); *Berne Convention for the Protection of Literary and Artistic Works* (<http://www.wipo.int>; Berne and Paris: World Intellectual Property Organization, 1886, 1979), Articles 3, 6bis–7bis, 10, 15–16; Ernst Bernheim, *Lehrbuch der Historischen Methode und der Geschichtsphilosophie* (Leipzig: von Duncker & Humblot, 1903), 300–358; Bloch, *Apologie,* 41–52; William Broad and Nicholas Wade, *Betrayers of the Truth* (New York: Simon and Schuster, 1982), 29; Dino Brugioni, *Photo Fakery: The History and Techniques of Photographic Deception and Manipulation* (Dulles, VA: Brassey's, 1999), 196–202; Daryl Chubin and Edward Hackett, *Peerless Science: Peer Review and US Science Policy* (Albany: State University of New York Press, 1990), 136; Umberto Eco, "Fakes and Forgeries," in Eco, *The Limits of Interpretation* (Bloomington and Indianapolis, IN: Indiana University Press, 1990), 174–202; David Fischer, *Historians' Fallacies: Toward a Logic of Historical Thought* (New York etc.: Harper Torchbooks, 1970), 82–87; Anthony Grafton, *Forgers and Critics: Creativity and Duplicity in Western Scholarship* (Princeton, NJ: Princeton University Press, 1990), 36–68; Ian Haywood, *Faking It: Arts and the Politics of Forgery* (Brighton: Harvester Press, 1987), 1–18, 131–43; Alain Jaubert, *Le Commissariat aux archives: les photos qui falsifient l'histoire* (Paris: Barrault, 1986); Otto Kurz, *Fakes: A Handbook for Collectors and Students* (London: Faber and Faber, [1948]), 316–21; Marcel LaFollette, *Stealing into Print: Fraud, Plagiarism, and Misconduct in Scientific Publishing* (Berkeley and Los Angeles: University of California Press, 1992), 32–67; Charles-Victor Langlois and Charles Seignobos, *Introduction aux études historiques* (originally 1898; Paris: Éditions Kimé, 1992), 133–58; Gilbert Ouy, "Les Faux dans les archives et les bibliothèques," in Charles Samaran, ed., *L'Histoire et ses méthodes* (Paris: Gallimard, 1961), 1367–83; Pierre Pradel, "Les Musées: l'authenticité des témoignages—faux et demi-faux," in Samaran, ed., *L'Histoire et ses méthodes,* 1784–89; Jan Vansina, *Oral Tradition As History* (London: James Currey, 1985), 95–114.

27. See, among others, Glanville Williams, *The Mental Element in Crime* (Jerusalem: Magnes Press, 1965), 20.

28. Also failures to act can occur either purposely, knowingly, recklessly, or negligently. See the diagram in Joel Feinberg, *Harm to Others* (New York and Oxford: Oxford University Press, 1984), 257–58n34.

29. Gross, *Theory of Criminal Justice*, 93–98 (quotation on 94).

30. See also Joe Nickell, *Pen, Ink, & Evidence: A Study of Writing and Writing Materials for the Penman, Collector, and Document Detective* (originally 1990; New Castle, DE: Oak Knoll Press, 2000), 192–94 ("genuine fakes").

31. Toby Mendel, *Study on International Standards Relating to Incitement to Genocide or Racial Hatred—For the UN Special Advisor on the Prevention of Genocide* (N.p., April 2006), 49.

32. See also LaFollette, *Stealing into Print*, 47, 60. For a reflection on the boundaries of sound historical scholarship, see Jürgen Kocka, "Objektivitätskriterien in der Geschichtswissenschaft," in Kocka, *Sozialgeschichte* (Göttingen: Vandenhoeck & Ruprecht, 1977), 40–47. Likewise, I identified six types of restrictions put upon historians living in democracies that form borderline cases of censorship: see De Baets, *Censorship*, 6–10.

33. Gross, *Theory of Criminal Justice*, 103–13.

34. *Black's Law Dictionary*, B.A. Garner ed. (originally 1891; St. Paul, MN: West Group, 2004), 825.

35. Table 1.3 offers a comprehensive overview of authors' motives for *writing* history. As motives of authors are indicators for the motives of readers, the table also reflects types of motives for *reading* history. Therefore, it also globally indicates the social functions, meaning, and utility (or "uses") of historical writing. The table also happens to contain implicitly many motives for deception. I hope, therefore, that it refutes, partially at least, Marc Bloch's belief (Bloch, *Apologie*, 43) that it would be in vain to enumerate the range of motives that persons may have to lie.

36. Bernheim, *Lehrbuch*, 301–2; Bloch, *Apologie*, 43; Feder, *Frauds*, 9–10; W.B. Gallie, "The Uses and Abuses of History," in Gallie, *Philosophy & the Historical Understanding* (originally 1964; New York: Schocken Books, 1968), 126–39; Grafton, *Forgers and Critics*, 37–49; Haywood, *Faking It*, 8–9; Kurz, *Fakes*, 318–19; Langlois and Seignobos, *Introduction*, 141–45; Vansina, *Oral Tradition*, 91–93.

37. See for the political use and abuse of history, for example, "Historical Consciousness and Political Action," *History and Theory*, 17, no. 4 (December 1978) (theme issue).

38. The only authors who make the essential distinction between intent and motive are Bevir, *The Logic*, 286–304, and Elizabeth Brown, "Falsitas pia sive reprehensibilis: Medieval Forgers and Their Intentions," in *Fälschungen im Mittelalter*, vol. 1 (Hannover: Hahnsche Buchhandlung, 1988), 103.

39. See also Andrus Pork, "History, Lying and Moral Responsibility," *History and Theory*, 29, no. 3 (October 1990), 329.

40. For the distinction between facts and opinions, see Chapter 3.

41. Pork, "History," 327.

42. De Baets, *Censorship*, 17.

43. See, for example, Nickell, *Pen, Ink, & Evidence*, 186–94 ("Questioned documents").

44. For examples of blameworthy negligence, see Jon Wiener, *Historians in Trouble: Plagiarism, Fraud, and Politics in the Ivory Tower* (New York and London: The New Press, 2005), 71–116.

45. Alfred Housman as quoted in Carr, *What Is History?*, 10.

46. This is the case of historian Ferdinand Nahimana. See International Criminal Tribunal for Rwanda, *Prosecutor v. Ferdinand Nahimana, Jean-Bosco Barayagwiza, Hassan Ngeze; Case no. ICTR-99-52-T: Judgement and Sentence* (<http://www.grandslacs.net/doc/2905.pdf>; 2003), especially paragraphs 5, 8, 13, 620–96, 978–1033, 1091–1105.

47. Yosef Yerushalmi, *Zakhor: Jewish History and Jewish Memory* (New York: Schocken, 1989), 116.

48. See Karl Erdmann, Jürgen Kocka, and Wolfgang Mommsen, *Toward a Global Community of Historians: The International Historical Congresses and the International Committee of Historical Sciences, 1898–2000* (New York and Oxford: Berghahn, 2005), 142–43 (on the Charter of 6 July 1932), 330, 397, 400 (amendments of the *Constitution* of 1992 and 2005).

49. I am grateful to Jean-Claude Robert, secretary-general of the International Committee of Historical Sciences, for clarifying the history of the different versions of the clause (e-mail correspondence of 22, 24, and 25 September, 1 and 3 October, 26 and 28 November 2006). See for that history the following minutes at <http://www.cish.org>: (1) the Bureau meeting (Oslo, 13 August 2000), item 5 ("Other matters," regarding the Indian situation); (2) the Bureau meeting (Paris, 30–31 August 2003), which concluded item 9.3 ("History research in India") in the following terms: "The Sydney Congress [of 2005] should prominently deal with the present problem of the relationship between politics and history, including censorship and political intervention into the discipline"; (3) the "Bureau restreint" meeting (Lausanne/Crans, 21–22 February 2004), which under item 2 ("ICHS operations/amendments to the statutes") spoke of "abuse of history" and also stated: "The advantage of the new wording [i.e., 'abuse'] is that it spells out the ICHS's attitude towards the use of history for political ends"; (4) the Bureau meeting (Berlin, 27–28 August 2004), which under item 3.1 ("Motion to amend the statutes of the ICHS: Article 1") changed "abuse" into "misuse"; (5) the General Assembly (Sydney, 3 July 2005), which under item 6 ("Amendments to the statutes of the ICHS") spoke of "abusive use." In the final text, the term "misuse" was chosen. For the situation of history under the Bharatiya Janata Party in India, see, for example, Romila Thapar, "Politics and the Rewriting of History in India," *Critical Quarterly*, 47, nos. 1–2 (July 2005), 195–203.

50. See also Council of Europe (Parliamentary Assembly), *History and the Learning of History in Europe: Report (Doc. 7446)* (<http://www.assembly.coe.int>; 1995), paragraph 40: "Any abuse of history should be combated and avoided."

51. Michael Grossberg, "Plagiarism and Professional Ethics: A Journal Editor's View," *Journal of American History*, 90, no. 4 (March 2004), 1337–38.

52. The discussion was mainly triggered by Hans-Werner Goetz's paper that later appeared as "Historical Consciousness and Institutional Concern in European Medieval Historiography (11th and 12th centuries)," in Sølvi Sogner,

ed., *Making Sense of Global History: The 19th International Congress of Historical Sciences, Oslo 2000, Commemorative Volume* (Oslo: Universitetsforlaget, 2001), 350–65. In the discussion, Goetz maintained that the distinction between the use and abuse of history is a modern one because medieval historians were convinced that, when they distorted history, they acted in good faith or for the sake of a larger interest. But perhaps Goetz confused intention and motive.

53. Not all literature, though: see Vansina, *Oral Tradition*, 54–56, 129–30; Wilfred C. Smith, "A Human View of Truth," *Studies in Religion: A Canadian Journal*, 1, no. 1 (1971), 6–24; Felipe Fernández-Armesto, *Truth: A History and a Guide for the Perplexed* (London: Bantam Press, 1997).

54. See LaFollette, *Stealing into Print*, 43; Grafton, *Forgers and Critics*, 61–62; De Baets, *Censorship*, 17.

55. Bloch, *Apologie*, 43; Gilles Constable, "Forgery and Plagiarism in the Middle Ages," *Archiv für Diplomatik*, 29 (1983), 1–2; Jacques Le Goff, *Histoire et mémoire* (Paris: Gallimard, 1988), 303; Grafton, *Forgers and Critics*, 67, 125; Gary Minkley and Martin Legassick, "'Not Telling': Secrecy, Lies, and History," *History and Theory, Theme Issue 39* (December 2000), 1–10; Luise White, "Telling More: Lies, Secrets, and History," *History and Theory, Theme Issue 39* (December 2000), 11–22.

56. See for many examples Umberto Eco, "The Force of Falsity," in Eco, *Serendipities: Language & Lunacy* (New York: Columbia University Press, 1998), 1–21.

57. See note 10.

58. Schauer, *Free Speech*, 26, 74–75; Schauer, "Reflections on the Value of Truth," *Case Western Reserve Law Review*, 41, no. 3 (1991) 699–724; Williams, *Truth & Truthfulness*, 14–15.

59. Bloch, *Apologie*, 41; Schauer, *Free Speech*, 74–75; Le Goff, *Histoire et mémoire*, 22; Grafton, *Forgers and Critics*, 5–6, 28, 123–27.

60. Barendt, *Freedom of Speech*, 8, 21, 176, 231; Joel Feinberg, "Limits to the Free Expression of Opinion," in Feinberg and Hyman Gross, eds., *Philosophy of Law* (Encino, CA, and Belmont, CA: Dickenson, 1975), 136–37; Schauer, *Free Speech*, 15, 25, 32–33, 74–75.

61. See note 9.

62. Herbert Butterfield, "Delays and Paradoxes in the Development of Historiography," in Kenneth Bourne and Donald C. Watt, eds., *Studies in International History* (London: Longmans, 1967), 6–8; Butterfield, "Historiography," in Philip Wiener, ed., *Dictionary of the History of Ideas: Studies of Selected Pivotal Ideas*, vol. 2 (New York: Charles Scribner's Sons, 1973–74), 484, 485, 487; Grafton, *Forgers and Critics*, 83–85, 92–93, 95–98, 117, 126.

63. For China, see Ku Chieh-kang (Gu Jiegang), *The Autobiography of a Chinese Historian, Being the Preface to A Symposium on Ancient Chinese History (Ku Shih Pien)* (translation and annotation: Arthur Hummel; Leyden: Brill, 1931), xxii–xxviii, 151 (and passim).

64. Ouy, "Les Faux," 1371, 1373; Constable, "Forgery and Plagiarism," 16; M.T. Clanchy, *From Memory to Written Record, England 1066–1307* (Oxford: Blackwell, 1993), 321, 325; Brown, "Falsitas pia," 101, 106, 118; Grafton, *Forgers and Critics*, 36–37.

65. Grafton, *Forgers and Critics*, 45, 48–49; Clanchy, *Memory to Written Record*, 319; Goetz, "Historical Consciousness," 351, 358.

66. Williams, *Truth & Truthfulness*, 63, 163, 271, 276, 285n17, 290n12.

67. Fernández-Armesto, *Truth*, 3–4. See also Arthur Danto, "Prudence, History, Time, and Truth," in David Carr, Thomas Flynn, and Rudolf Makkreel, eds., *The Ethics of History* (Evanston: Northwestern University Press, 2004), 80–81; Derek Parfit, *Reasons and Persons* (Oxford: Clarendon Press, 1984), 457–61.

68. Williams, *Truth & Truthfulness*, 257–58.

69. The answer to the question *why* truth is intrinsically better than error and lie is complex. It would require the study of the history of modernity and democracy. See Williams, *Truth & Truthfulness*, 263–69, and the afterword of Chapter 2 of the present book.

70. John Finnis, "Scepticism, Self-refutation, and the Good of Truth," in P.M.S. Hacker and J. Raz, eds., *Law, Morality, and Society: Essays in Honour of H.L.A. Hart* (Oxford: Clarendon Press, 1977), 247–67; Williams, *Truth & Truthfulness*, 2–3; Simon Blackburn, *Truth: A Guide for the Perplexed* (Harmondsworth: Penguin, 2006), 23–44.

71. For the link between truth, democracy, and dignity, see Office of the United Nations High Commissioner for Human Rights, *Study on the Right to the Truth* (<http://www.ohchr.org>; E/CN.4/2006/91; 2006), paragraphs 46, 56–57 and *Right to the Truth* (<http://www.ohchr.org>; A/HRC/5/7; 2007), paragraphs 16, 83; see also Schauer, *Free Speech*, 15–34, especially 17.

72. Williams, *Truth & Truthfulness*, 149–71, 276. This new conception may even have led to a change in the vocabulary expressing the concept of truth.

73. Clanchy, *Memory to Written Record*, 148–49; Smith, "A Human View of Truth," passim; Constable, "Forgery and Plagiarism," 13, 16, 23–26, 30, 33, 36, 38. See, however, Brown, "Falsitas," 105–6.

74. Constable, "Forgery and Plagiarism," 27; Eco, "Fakes and Forgeries," 187; Vansina, *Oral Tradition*, 129–30; Fernández-Armesto, *Truth*, 46–81; Thomas Mallon, *Stolen Words: Forays into the Origins and Ravages of Plagiarism* (New York: Ticknor & Fields, 1989), 3.

75. Constable, "Forgery and Plagiarism," 30.

76. Bloch, *Apologie*, 43–44.

77. Butterfield, "Historiography," 464, 475–77, 484–85, 487.

78. Haywood, *Faking It*, 10.

79. Clanchy, *Memory to Written Record*, 318–19; Constable, "Forgery and Plagiarism," 11–13; Grafton, *Forgers and Critics*, 24, 36–37.

80. Clanchy, *Memory to Written Record*, 322–23.

81. Clanchy, *Memory to Written Record*, 193, 298; Mallon, *Stolen Words*, 4.

82. Williams, *Truth & Truthfulness*, 170, 276, 290n12.

83. Williams, *Truth & Truthfulness*, 151.

84. Williams, *Truth & Truthfulness*, 172–205.

85. Anthony Grafton, *The Footnote: A Curious History* (Cambridge, MA: Harvard University Press, and London: Faber and Faber, 1997), 191. See also Constable, "Forgery and Plagiarism," 29, 39.

86. Mallon, *Stolen Words*, xii, 2, 24, 39.

87. Arnaldo Momigliano, "Ancient History and the Antiquarian," in Momigliano, *Studies in Historiography* (London: Weidenfeld and Nicolson, 1966), 2, 6–7, 9–10, 24–25, 27. See also Carlo Ginzburg, "Checking the Evidence: The Judge and the Historian," *Critical Inquiry*, 18, no. 1 (Autumn 1991), 80, 91.

88. Paradoxically, these processes also made historians financially more dependent on governments, and this dependence often transformed them into purveyors of official historical myths that they presented with pretensions of objectivity, but, in fact, saw as indispensable for nation-building. See Georg Iggers, "The Uses and Misuses of History, the Responsibility of the Historian, Past and Present," in Sogner, ed., *Making Sense of Global History*, 314–16; Williams, *Truth & Truthfulness*, 252. Many others have emphasized this point.

89. *Berne Convention*, Article 6bis (1).

90. World Intellectual Property Organization, *Copyright Treaty* (<http://www.wipo.int>; 1996), preamble; Barendt, *Freedom of Speech*, 247–67.

91. Peter Walcot as quoted in Williams, *Truth & Truthfulness*, 277; also 93.

92. Williams, *Truth & Truthfulness*, 213–16.

93. The United Nations Development Programme calculated that the share of the world's countries with multiparty electoral systems that met the wider criteria for democracy rose from 39% in 1990 to 55% in 2003. See its *Human Development Report 2005* (New York and Oxford: Oxford University Press, 2005), 20 (adapting earlier estimates on pages 14–15 of its *Human Development Report 2002*).

94. Blackburn, *Truth*, 167.

95. See also Michael Schudson, "Dynamics of Distortion in Collective Memory," in Daniel Schacter, ed., *Memory Distortion: How Minds, Brains, and Societies Reconstruct the Past* (Cambridge, MA, and London: Harvard University Press, 1995), 355.

96. Voltaire, *Questions sur les miracles* (1765), here "Onzième lettre écrite par le proposant à M. Covelle." According to <http://en.wikiquote.org/wiki/Voltaire>, this famous quotation is an adaptation from "Certainement qui est en droit de vous rendre absurde est en droit de vous rendre injuste" (to be translated as "Truly, whoever is able to seduce you to absurdity, is able to seduce you to injustice.")

Chapter 2

1. See R. Andrew Nickson, "Paraguay's Archivo del Terror," *Latin American Research Review*, 30, no. 1 (1995), 125–29; *Amnesty International Report 1994* (London: Amnesty International, 1994), 237–38; Stella Calloni, "Los archivos del horror del Operativo Cóndor" (originally in *Covert Action Magazine*, August 1994; consulted at <http://www.derechos.org>).

2. Antonio González Quintana, "Archives of the Security Services of Former Repressive Regimes," *Janus: Archival Review*, 2 (1998) (citations from the

1996 version found at <http://www.unesco.org>), 11–12. This article should be read together with its sequel: González Quintana, "Los archivos de la represión: balance y perspectivas," *Comma: International Journal on Archives,* 4, no. 2 (2004), 59–74.

3. González Quintana, "Archives," 4. See also Henry Kamen's analysis, *The Spanish Inquisition: A Historical Revision* (New Haven and London: Yale University Press, 1997), 174–213.

4. Eric Johnson, *Nazi Terror: The Gestapo, Jews, and Ordinary Germans* (New York: Basic Books, 1999), 495n32.

5. *Czechoslovakia:* Stéphane Alonso, "Slowaakse politiek siddert voor archieven," *NRC Handelsblad* (7 March 2005), 4; *Guatemala:* Kate Doyle, "The Guatemalan Police Archives" (<http://www.gwu.edu/~nsarchiv>; Washington: National Security Archive, November 2005) and Idem, "The Atrocity Files: Deciphering the Archives of Guatemala's Dirty War," *Harper's Magazine* (December 2007), 52–64; *Brazil:* Lawrence Weschler, *A Miracle, a Universe: Settling Accounts with Torturers* (New York: Pantheon Books, 1990), 15–16; *Ethiopia:* Tore Engelschiøn, "Prosecution of War Crimes and Violations of Human Rights in Ethiopia," *Jahrbuch für afrikanisches Recht,* 8 (1994), 41–55; *Cambodia:* David Chandler, *Voices from S-21: Terror and History in Pol Pot's Secret Prison* (Berkeley and Los Angeles: University of California Press, 1999), 49; *Iraq:* International Center for Transitional Justice, *Briefing Paper: Creation and First Trials of the Supreme Iraqi Criminal Tribunal* (New York: International Center for Transitional Justice, 2005), 15; *Paraguay:* see note 1. For other examples, see Kamen, *Inquisition,* 183 (Inquisition); Robert Conquest, *The Great Terror: A Reassessment* (New York: Oxford University Press, 1990), 107 (tsarist Russia); J. Sweeney, "Seized Serb Documents Link Milosevic to Mass Killings," *Observer* (27 June 1999) (Serbia's 1999 conflict with Kosovo).

6. Étienne François, "Les 'trésors' de la Stasi ou le mirage des archives," in Jean Boutier and Dominique Julia, eds., *Passés recomposés: champs et chantiers de l'histoire* (Paris: Autrement, 1995), 145–46; Bruce Ackerman, *The Future of Liberal Revolution* (New Haven and London: Yale University Press, 1992), 80–89, 136–39; Timothy Garton Ash, *The File: A Personal History* (New York: Vintage Books, 1997); Joachim Gauck, "Zum Umgang mit den Stasi-Akten—eine Zwischenbilanz," in Bernd Faulenbach, Markus Meckel, and Hermann Weber, eds., *Die Partei hatte immer recht: Aufarbeitung von Geschichte und Folgen der SED-Diktatur* (Essen: Klartext Verlag, 1994), 38–40; Jürgen Kocka, "Chance und Herausforderung: Aufgaben der Zeitgeschichte beim Umgang mit der DDR-Vergangenheit," in Faulenbach, Meckel, and Weber, eds., *Die Partei,* 244–46.

7. *Keesings historisch archief,* 75 (2005), 274, and 76 (2006), 84.

8. Marc Bloch, *Apologie pour l'histoire ou métier d'historien* (Paris: Colin, 1967), 31.

9. In the case of conflicting information, it is usually not simple to know whose version—from the security service or from the opposition—is the more reliable. Janet Cherry has convincingly demonstrated the complexity of establishing historical truth with contradictory and sanitized evidence. See her "Historical Truth: Something to Fight for," in Charles Villa-Vicencio and Wilhelm

Verwoerd, eds., *Looking back, Reaching forward: Reflections on the Truth and Reconciliation Commission of South Africa* (Cape Town: University of Cape Town Press, 2000), 137–42.

10. Robert Gellately, *The Gestapo and German Society: Enforcing Racial Policy, 1933–1945* (Oxford: Clarendon Press, 1990), 130.

11. For a definition of denunciation, see Sheila Fitzpatrick and Robert Gellately, eds., *Accusatory Practices: Denunciation in Modern European History, 1789–1989* (Chicago and London: University of Chicago Press, 1997), 91. See also Johnson, *Nazi Terror*, 15; Serge Rumin, "Gathering and Managing Information in Vetting Processes," in Alexander Mayer-Rieckh and Pablo de Greiff, eds., *Justice as Prevention: Vetting Public Employees in Transitional Societies* (New York: Social Science Research Council, and Washington: International Center for Transitional Justice, 2007), 425–26.

12. Kamen, *Inquisition*, 191; Gellately, *Gestapo*, 130.

13. See Trudy Huskamp Peterson, *Final Acts: A Guide to Preserving the Records of Truth Commissions* (Washington: Woodrow Wilson International Center Press, and Baltimore: Johns Hopkins University Press, 2005), 4–6.

14. Antoon De Baets, *Censorship of Historical Thought: A World Guide, 1945–2000* (Westport, CT, and London: Greenwood, 2002); De Baets, "Archives," in Derek Jones, ed., *Censorship: A World Encyclopedia* (London and Chicago: Fitzroy Dearborn, 2001), vol. 1, 76–82.

15. François, "Trésors," 145–46; Kamen, *Inquisition*, 183.

16. Weschler, *Miracle*, 15–16; Conquest, *Great Terror*, 130.

17. "Revisiting the Horrors of the Holocaust," *CBS News* (17 December 2006); David Banisar, *Freedom of Information Around the World 2006: A Global Survey of Access to Government Records Laws* (<http://www.freedominfo.org>; Washington: Freedominfo.org, 2006), 50.

18. Conquest, *Great Terror*, 130–31.

19. Chandler, *Voices from S-21*, 49–51, 104–9. See also Tom Fawthrop, "The Secrets of S21," *Index on Censorship*, 34, no. 1 (2005), 78–81.

20. *Truth and Reconciliation Commission of South Africa Report* (London: Macmillan, 1998), vol. 1, 201–43 (quotation on 201), and vol. 5, 345–47.

21. Human Rights Watch, *Iraq: State of the Evidence* (Washington: Human Rights Watch, 2004), 4–14.

22. *Soviet Union:* Stephen Kotkin, "Terror, Rehabilitation, and Historical Memory: An Interview with Dmitrii Iurasov," *Russian Review*, 51 (April 1992), 238–62; *Brazil:* Weschler, *A Miracle*, 7–79; *China: Keesings historisch archief*, 71 (2001), 116–17, and *Index on Censorship*, 30, no. 2 (March–April 2001), 100. See also the case of Gao Wenqian, in John Pomfret, "A Chinese Hero Is Taken Off His Pedestal: Biography Depicts Zhou Enlai as a Tragic Backroom Schemer," *Washington Post* (9 December 2003), A18.

23. Human Rights Watch, *Bureaucracy of Repression: The Iraqi Government in Its Own Words* (Washington: Human Rights Watch, 1994), ix–x.

24. David Banisar, *The www.freedominfo.org Global Survey: Freedom of Information and Access to Government Record Laws around the World* (Washington: Freedominfo.org, 2003), 76; Diane Orentlicher, *Independent Study on Best*

Practices, Including Recommendations, to Assist States in Strengthening Their Domestic Capacity to Combat All Aspects of Impunity (http://www.ohchr.org; E/CN.4/2004/88; 2004), paragraph 20.

25. Doyle, "Guatemalan Police Archives." For finds of repression archives in other countries, see González Quintana, "Los archivos," 68–70.

26. William Shawcross, *The Quality of Mercy: Cambodia, Holocaust and Modern Conscience* (originally 1984; London: Deutsch, 1985), 360.

27. Nissim Rejwan, *Nasserist Ideology, Its Exponents and Critics* (New York: Wiley, 1974), 15.

28. *Spain:* González Quintana, "Archives," 6; *East Germany:* Ackerman, *Future,* passim. For Chile, see M.J. Errázuriz, "Piden regular acceso: preocupa uso de archivos de C. Rettig," *El Mercurio* (Santiago de Chile; 22 September 1996), A1, A13. Regional variation may be important: in the Western Balkans, for example, public access to files of the secret services of former regimes is generally excluded in countries where screening laws (so-called "lustration laws") were passed (Albania, Serbia), while in countries without such laws (Bosnia-Herzegovina, Croatia, Macedonia), various regulations allow for some form of public access to these files. See Magarditsch Hatschikjan, ed., *Manual on Lustration, Public Access to Files of the Secret Services and Public Debates on the Past in the Western Balkans* (Thessaloniki: Center for Democracy and Reconciliation in Southeast Europe, 2005), 9.

29. *Index on Censorship,* 27, no. 2 (March-April 1998), 90.

30. Irena Maryniak, "The Epic That Will Not Die," *Index on Censorship,* 31, no. 4 (October 2002), 56. When Havel signed legislation expanding access to the Communist police files in March 2002, he said, however, that the need for truth prevailed over the risks of releasing information. See David Banisar, *Freedom of Information and Access to Government Records around the World* (<http://www.privacyinternational.org>; London: Privacy International, 2002), 11–12.

31. Ackerman, *Future,* 81–83; Hiroko Yamane, "Preservation or Destruction of Personal Files," in *International meeting on Impunity of Perpetrators of Gross Human Rights Violations* (Geneva: International Commission of Jurists, 1993), 264.

32. Ackerman, *Future,* 88.

33. Rumin, "Gathering and Managing," 412.

34. Neil Kritz, ed., *Transitional Justice: How Emerging Democracies Reckon with Former Regimes* (Washington: United States Institute of Peace Press, 1995), vol. 1, 52.

35. Peter Green, "Czechs Seek to Indict Officials Who Assembled Lists of Jews: Communists' Registries Used Some Nazi-Period Data," *International Herald Tribune* (9 October 1998), 13.

36. "Paraguay: Hitler im Brunnen," *Der Spiegel* (1993, no. 18), 170.

37. *Keesings historisch archief,* 71 (2001), 458, and 72 (2002), 204; Banisar, *Freedom of Information Around the World 2006,* 51.

38. "Revisiting the Horrors."

39. Importance level 1 is awarded each time the European Court considers a case as making a significant contribution to the development, clarification, or modification of its case law.

40. European Court of Human Rights, *Case of Rotaru versus Romania: Judgement* (<http://www.echr.coe.int>; 2000), paragraphs 7–24, 44, 55, 57; see also the concurring opinion. See also Ursula Kilkelly, *The Right to Respect for Private and Family Life: A Guide to the Implementation of Article 8 of the European Convention on Human Rights* (Strasbourg: Council of Europe, 2001, 2004), 28.

41. European Court of Human Rights, *Case of Turek versus Slovakia: Judgement* (<http://www.echr.coe.int>; 2006). Parts of the judgment (notably paragraphs 48, 52, 54, 102–3, 106–8, 115–16) give a good impression of the inner workings of a security service.

42. Ackerman, *Future*, 89.

43. *Truth and Reconciliation Commission of South Africa Report*, vol. 1, 201–43 (quotation on 235) and vol. 5, 226–27; Verne Harris, "The Archival Sliver: A Perspective on the Construction of Social Memory in Archives and the Transition from Apartheid to Democracy," in Carolyn Hamilton, et al., eds., *Refiguring the Archive* (Cape Town: David Philip, 2002), 135, 137–42, 146.

44. Even here, more conventional motives were also at play—the archives were allegedly purged of controversial or embarrassing records. Rejwan, *Nasserist Ideology*, 15; Fekri Hassan, "Memorabilia: Archaeological Materiality and National Identity in Egypt," in Lynn Meskell, ed., *Archaeology under Fire: Nationalism, Politics and Heritage in the Eastern Mediterranean and Middle East* (London and New York: Routledge, 1998), 207–9.

45. Derek Jones, ed., *Censorship: A World Encyclopedia*, vol. 2 (London and Chicago: Fitzroy Dearborn, 2001), 744.

46. González Quintana, "Archives," 6.

47. Geoffrey Pridham and Susannah Verney, "The Coalitions of 1989–90 in Greece: Inter-Party Relations and Democratic Consolidation," *West European Politics*, 14, no. 4 (1991), 59, 69.

48. On the symbolic force of secret archives, see Rumin, "Gathering and Managing," 410–11.

49. R. Michael Malek, "Rafael Leonidas Trujillo: A Revisionist Critique of His Rise to Power," *Revista/Review Interamericana*, 7, no. 3 (1977), 440.

50. Human Rights Watch, *Iraq*, 4–14.

51. *Keesings historisch archief*, 62 (1992), 612–13 and 63 (1993), 544, 843; Tina Rosenberg, *The Haunted Land: Facing Europe's Ghosts after Communism* (New York: Random House, 1995), 250–51; Timothy Garton Ash, "The Truth about Dictatorship," *New York Review of Books*, 45, no. 3 (19 February 1998), 38; Jon Elster, *Closing the Books: Transitional Justice in Historical Perspective* (Cambridge: Cambridge University Press, 2004), 193.

52. "Poland in Uproar over Leak of Spy Files," *Guardian* (5 February 2005).

53. Elster, *Closing the Books*, 117.

54. P. Finn, "Smear Campaigns Target Post-Communist Leaders in Eastern Europe," *International Herald Tribune* (14 August 2000), 7.

55. *Keesings historisch archief*, 66 (1996), 251–52, 613–14, and 75 (2005), 85; Tina Rosenberg, "Political Intrigue and Poland's Past," *International Herald Tribune* (14 August 2000), 8.

56. Ruti Teitel, *Transitional Justice* (Oxford: Oxford University Press, 2000), 95–103 (quotation 96).

57. Banisar, *Freedom of Information Around the World 2006,* 51; see also Elster, *Closing the Books,* 117.

58. Human Rights Watch, *Iraq,* 8.

59. González Quintana, "Archives," 4, 7.

60. Ackerman, *Future,* 86; Banisar, *Freedom of Information Around the World 2006,* 51; see also Elster, *Closing the Books,* 117.

61. "Openbaarheid van archief uit Portuese dictatuur inzet twist," *NRC Handelsblad* (25 April 1996), 6.

62. See also Huskamp Peterson, *Final Acts,* 9–10. See for an overview of types of users of court records, Peterson, "Temporary Courts, Permanent Records," *United States Institute of Peace Special Report,* no. 170 (August 2006), 7–8.

63. United Nations Commission on Human Rights, *Updated Set of Principles for the Protection and Promotion of Human Rights Through Action to Combat Impunity* (<http://www.ohchr.org>; E/CN.4/2005/102/Add.1; 2005), principles 3, 5, 8, 14–18 (see Appendix 5.1 of this book for an overview). See also Office of the United Nations High Commissioner for Human Rights, *Right to the Truth* (<http://www.ohchr.org>; A/HRC/5/7; 2007), paragraphs 21, 58–70, 88, also 37; International Council on Archives, *Code of Ethics* (<http://www.ica.org>; 1996); González Quintana, "Archives," 10–11; Perrine Canavaggio and Louis Joinet, "Les archives contre l'oubli," *Le Monde* (23 June 2004); Article 19, *The Public's Right to Know: Principles of Freedom of Information Legislation* (<http://www.article19.org>; London: Article 19, 1999), 3–4. Principle 1 of *The Public's Right to Know* ("Maximum Disclosure") emphasizes that to prevent any attempt to doctor or otherwise alter records, the obligation to disclose should apply to the records themselves and not just to the information they contain.

64. Third countries can possess revealing archives. The example of Gestapo files in Moscow was already given. The United States declassified thousands of files—sometimes as part of large-scale declassification projects, often after freedom of information requests by truth commissions or by nongovernmental organizations such as the National Security Archive (http://www.gwu.edu/~nsarchiv)—on dozens of repressive regimes (and withheld many others).

65. Bertram Wolfe, "Totalitarianism and History," in Carl Friedrich, ed., *Totalitarianism* (New York: The Universal Library, 1964), 265.

66. *Universal Declaration of Human Rights,* Articles 19, 21. Article 21 is considered the key to democracy: "The will of the people shall be the basis of the authority of government." Regional declarations on free expression also mention that free expression is a determinant of democracy; see the preambles of: Council of Europe, *Declaration on the Freedom of Expression and Information* (<http://www.assembly.coe.int>; 1982); Inter-American Commission on Human Rights, *Inter-American Declaration of Principles on Freedom of Expression* (<http://www.cidh.oas.org>; 2000); African Commission on Human and People's Rights, *Declaration of Principles on Freedom of Expression in Africa* (<http://www.achpr.org>; 2002).

67. See Inter-Parliamentary Union, *Universal Declaration on Democracy* (<http://www.ipu.org>; 1997; adopted without a vote), preamble, Articles 3, 6–9, 12–14, 19, 21, 27, and others.

68. For the mutual relationship between a liberal society and truthful history, see Bernard Williams, *Truth & Truthfulness: An Essay in Genealogy* (Princeton and Oxford: Princeton University Press, 2002), 265.

69. Williams, *Truth & Truthfulness*, 217.

70. For the link between truth and democracy, see Chapter 1.

71. Williams, *Truth & Truthfulness*, 209.

72. See for this discussion, among others, Barbara Misztal, "Memory and Democracy," *American Behavioral Scientist*, 48, no. 10 (June 2005), 1320–38.

Chapter 3

1. Globally, historians have indeed been accused of every crime conceivable, from the smallest to genocide, although not always in their capacity as historians. Numerous examples appear in Antoon De Baets, *Censorship of Historical Thought: A World Guide 1945–2000* (Westport, CT, and London: Greenwood, 2002).

2. See, for example, the cases of Appendices 3.3 and 3.4.

3. Quoted in Appendix 5.1.

4. Fernando Volio, "Legal Personality, Privacy, and the Family," in Louis Henkin, ed., *The International Bill of Rights: The Covenant on Civil and Political Rights*(New York: Columbia University Press, 1981), 198; Manfred Nowak, *U.N. Covenant on Civil and Political Rights: CCPR Commentary* (Kehl am Rhein, Strasbourg, Arlington, VA: Engel, 1993), 306. For the distinction between honor and reputation, see Article 19, *Defamation ABC: A Simple Introduction to Key Concepts of Defamation Law* (<http://www.article19.org>; 2006), 5, 9.

5. *Examination of the Alignment of the Laws on Defamation with the Relevant Case-Law of the European Court of Human Rights, Including the Issue of Decriminalisation of Defamation*(Strasbourg: Council of Europe [Steering Committee on the Media and New Communication Services], 2006), 5. For the distinction between defamation and concepts such as insult, hate speech, blasphemy, and privacy invasion, see Article 19, *Defamation ABC*, 1–3, 5, 10; and Eric Barendt, *Freedom of Speech* (fully revised and updated second edition; Oxford: Oxford University Press, 2005), 170–92, 227–46, 295–302.

6. For the distinction, see Article 19, *Defamation ABC*, 6, 12–16.

7. See also Article 19, *Defamation ABC*, 16–19, and Article 19, *Rights vs Reputations: Campaign against the Abuse of Defamation and Insult Laws* (<http://www.article19.org>; 2003), 3–4.

8. For the distinction between facts and opinions, see Joel Feinberg, "Limits to the Free Expression of Opinion," in Feinberg & Hyman Gross, eds., *Philosophy of Law* (Encino, CA, and Belmont, CA: Dickenson, 1975), 138–39; Frederick Schauer, *Free Speech: A Philosophical Inquiry* (Cambridge: Cambridge University Press, 1982), 18, 31–32, 169; Volio, "Legal Personality,"199; Nowak, *Covenant*, 305–6; Barendt, *Freedom of Speech*, 216–17, 222–23; *Examination*, 15, 19, 23–27;

Monica Macovei, *Freedom of Expression: A Guide to the Implementation of Article 10 of the European Convention on Human Rights* (Strasbourg: Council of Europe, 2004), 9–10, 13, 51–52; and many other legal sources. See also Chapters 1 and 5 of this book. The nongovernmental organization Article 19 defines opinions as statements "which either do not contain a factual connotation which could be proved to be false, or cannot reasonably be interpreted as stating actual facts given all the circumstances, including the language used (such as rhetoric, hyperbole, satire or jest)." See Article 19, *Defining Defamation: Principles on Freedom of Expression and Protection of Reputation* (London: Article 19, 2000), Principle 10 ("expressions of opinion"); see also Principle 7 ("proof of truth").

9. Toby Mendel, *Study on International Standards Relating to Incitement to Genocide or Racial Hatred—For the UN Special Advisor on the Prevention of Genocide* (N.p., April 2006), 60. Feinberg, "Limits," 138–39, discusses an exception to the truth defense: the case of the true but useless exposure of past misdeeds of a "reformed sinner." Indeed, such true but useless exposure of a reformed sinner's acts could give a judge reason to reject the truth defense. But it is not always as simple as shown by the discussion about amnestied crimes.

10. Schauer, *Free Speech,* quotations at 174, 176–77.

11. See Bernard Edelman, "L'Office du juge et l'histoire," *Droit et société: revue internationale de théorie du droit et de sociologie juridique,* 14, no. 38 (1998), 48–51. See for the difference between journalists and historians also Chapter 6.

12. See European Court of Human Rights, *Case of Lingens versus Austria: Judgement* (<http://www.echr.coe.int>; 1986).

13. There are other defenses, such as "innocent publication" and "consent"; see Article 19, *Defamation ABC,* 19, and Article 19, *Rights vs Reputations,* 4.

14. European Court of Human Rights, *Case of Lehideux and Isorni versus France: Judgement* (1998), paragraph 55 (but see also "dissenting opinion of judge Casadevall," paragraph 3); *Case Law Concerning Article 10 of the European Convention on Human Rights* (Strasbourg: Council of Europe [Directorate General of Human Rights], 2001), 17.

15. *Joint Declaration by the UN Special Rapporteur on Freedom of Opinion and Expression, the OSCE Representative on Freedom of the Media and the OAS Special Rapporteur on Freedom of Expression* (London: Article 19, 2000). There have been several other joint declarations.

16. See, for example, Czechoslovakia (Ivan Jirous), Poland (Robert Moczulski), Soviet Union (Viktor Artsimovich, Vasyl Barladianu, Ivan Dzyuba, Abulfaz Elchibey, Valery Marchenko, Valentin Moroz, Anatoly Nazarov), in De Baets, *Censorship,* 161, 384–85, 519, 526, 532–37.

17. See, for example, Appendix 3.3 under Iran (Kasravi cases); and also Peter Gran and Nasr Abu-Zayd in the Egypt entry and Hichem Djaït in the Tunisia entry in De Baets, *Censorship,* 195–97, 463–64.

18. See Thai cases of Appendices 3.3 en 3.5.

19. See cases of Appendices 3.3 and 3.4.

20. Herbert Butterfield, "Historiography," in Philip Wiener, ed., *Dictionary of the History of Ideas: Studies of Selected Pivotal Ideas,* vol. 2 (New York: Charles Scribner's Sons, 1973–74), 465, 480.

21. See Turk cases of Appendix 3.5.

22. See Iranian cases of Appendix 3.5.

23. All leader-related cases: all cases of Appendices 3.3, 3.4, and 3.5, plus case 13 of Appendix 3.1 (66 cases); cases regarding leaders deceased more than half a century previously: cases marked (**) in Appendices 3.3, 3.4, and 3.5 (32 cases).

24. In Chapter 4, we will describe the case of cultures according to whose customs it is even temporarily forbidden to pronounce the names of the dead. The reports of the World Press Freedom Committee, *Insult Laws: An Insult to Press Freedom*(<http://www.wpfc.org>; Reston, VA: World Press Freedom Committee, 2000) and *It's a Crime: How Insult Laws Stifle Press Freedom: A 2006 Status Report*(<http://www.wpfc.org>; Reston, VA: World Press Freedom Committee, 2006) list eighteen countries with provisions, mostly in criminal codes, for protecting the memory of the dead and against defaming them or their living close relatives: Cameroon, Germany, Greece, India, Japan, Mexico, Netherlands, Nigeria, Philippines, Russia, Senegal, Serbia (Kosovo), South Korea, Sweden, Taiwan, Thailand, Tunisia, and Turkey. See also John Gilissen, "La Responsabilité civile et pénale de l'historien," *Revue belge de philologie et d'histoire*, 38 (1960), 304, 321–29 ("Respect dû à la mémoire des morts.")

25. See, for example, *Lehideux and Isorni*. Marie-François Lehideux, born in 1904, and Jacques Isorni, born in 1911, lodged an application with the European Commission of Human Rights in 1994. Isorni died in May 1995 and in June 1996 his widow was given standing to continue the proceedings on her late husband's behalf. In 1997, the case was referred to the European Court of Human Rights. In June 1998, Lehideux died. In September 1998, the court delivered a judgment.

26. Questions of posthumous reputation or privacy played a substantial or primary role in 56 lawsuits mentioned in the Appendices; they are marked with (*). For a (Swiss) case about posthumous reputation where a historian was the complainant, see *Willi Wottreng versus Präsident des Obergerichts des Kantons Zürich* (2000–2001).For appeals by historians to file lawsuits against a deceased leader: see Soviet Union (Pyotr Yakir *versus* Joseph Stalin; Igor Bestuzhev-Lada *versus* Joseph Stalin) in De Baets, *Censorship*, 508, 522.

27. Article 19, *Defining Defamation, 7*. See also Gilissen, "La Responsabilité civile et pénale," 325–29.

28. Jean-Denis Bredin, "Le Droit, le juge et l'historien," *Le Débat*, no. 32 (November 1984), 98, 107. See also Gilissen, "La Responsabilité civile et pénale," 295, 304.

29. See De Baets, *Censorship*.

30. Appendices 3.1 to 3.5 constitute an attempt to approximate the universe of defamation cases.

31. *Examination*, 6–11.

32. Case 18.

33. Case 3.

34. Cases 1, 2.

35. Case 10.

36. Cases 6, 17, 18.

37. Cases 15, 16.

38. Defendants total 21 because two were sued twice (cases 1–2 and 14–15) and case 18 has two defendants (at least).

39. Cases 6, 9, 13, 16, 18, 21, 22.

40. Cases 5, 13, 22. The other Appendices demonstrate that an international dimension was present in a surprisingly huge number of defamation cases.

41. Cases 14–15.

42. Case 13.

43. Cases 3, 8, 22; see also Appendix 3.2 under France (Lecache case) and United Kingdom (Sereny case).

44. Cases 6, 12, 13, 17, 20; see also partly case 18.

45. Case 6; see also partly case 18.

46. Case 19.

47. Case 15.

48. Cases 2, 3, 8, 10, 11, 16, 22.

49. Case 18.

50. Cases 9, 14.

51. For example, case 4.

52. Case 2.

53. Historical anthropologists could throw light on the hypothetical continuity between the reputation-related conflicts (slander and libel) discussed here and honor-related conflicts (feuds and vendettas) of past centuries.

54. See Henry Rousso, "Justiz, Geschichte und Erinnerung in Frankreich: Überlegungen zum Papon-Prozeß," in Norbert Frei, Dirk van Laak, and Michael Stolleis, eds., *Geschichte vor Gericht: Historiker, Richter und die Suche nach Gerechtigkeit* (Munich: Beck, 2000), 156; and Olivier Dumoulin, *Le rôle social de l'historien: de la chaire au prétoire* (Paris: Albin Michel, 2003), 129–31.

55. For France, cases 4–11 and the seven relevant cases of Appendix 3.2; for the Netherlands, cases 14–18 and the three relevant cases of Appendix 3.2.

56. Applications before the European Court of Human Rights: Appendix 3.1 (case 9) and three cases (Giniewski, Éditions Plon, and Radio France) of Appendix 3.2 (France). For the other countries, see case 21 (United Kingdom) of Appendix 3.1, the *Neue Kronen Zeitung* case (Austria), the Feldek and Hrico cases (Slovakia) of Appendix 3.2, and the Stănescu case (Romania) of Appendix 3.3. Applications before the European Commission of Human Rights: the Panev case (Bulgaria) of Appendix 3.2 and the Middelburg case (Netherlands) of Appendix 3.2.

57. See, among others, Bredin, "Le Droit, le juge et l'historien," 104, 109; Jean Stengers, "L'Historien face à ses responsabilités," *Cahiers de l'école des sciences philosophiques et religieuses*, no. 15 (1994), 23; Jean-Pierre Azéma and Georges Kiejman, "L'Histoire au tribunal," *Le Débat*, no. 102 (November–December 1998), 48.

58. De Baets, *Censorship,*23.

59. Rebuttals *during* the course of the lawsuit: cases 3, 18. In case 3, the defendant became the target of a 160-page pamphlet, published in 1994 by the Holocaust-denying group "Vrij Historisch Onderzoek" ("Free Historical Research")

and reportedly distributed to all libraries and history teachers in Dutch-speaking Belgium. Rebuttals *after* the lawsuit: cases 14–15, and again 18.

60. Threats in cases 15–16; death threats in cases 12 and 15.

61. Case 15 and the De Jong cases of Appendix 3.2.

62. Case 21.

63. Case 21.

64. Cases 1–2.

65. Cases 3, 12, 15.

66. Cases 2, 9, 13–14, 16, 20–21. Cases 9 and 21 became applications before the European Court of Human Rights.

67. Case 10. See *Le Monde* (27 February 1999), 11; Sonia Combe, *Archives interdites: l'histoire confisquée* (originally 1994; Paris: La Découverte, 2001), xvii–xxiii.

68. For the concept- and theory-dependent character of facts, see Chris Lorenz, *De constructie van het verleden: Een inleiding in de theorie van de geschiedenis* (Amsterdam and Meppel: Boom, 1998), 25–60 [German edition: *Konstruktion der Vergangenheit: eine Einführung in die Geschichtstheorie* (Cologne: Böhlau, 1997).]

69. Bredin, "Le Droit, le juge et l'historien," 100, 102–3 (quotation on 111); Gilissen, "La Responsabilité civile et pénale," 311–15, 1010–12, 1016–17, 1038–39; Jean-Noël Jeanneney, *Le Passé dans le prétoire: l'historien, le juge et le journaliste* (Paris: Seuil, 1998), 36; Edelman, "L'Office," 51–58.

70. In case 5, the judge acknowledged that the defendant had the right to judge the complainant's texts but not his behavior. He distinguished between opinions about texts and facts about behavior. See Pierre Assouline, "Enquête sur un historien condamné pour diffamation," *L'Histoire*, no. 68 (June 1984), 100.

71. Case 20.

72. Case 9.

73. Case 10. See *Le Monde* (29 March 1999), 8.

74. Case 11.

75. Case 22.

76. This is especially the case for the Holocaust, considered by the European judges as an established fact. See, for another, Canadian, example (concerning the question whether a document of 1760 was a treaty and whether that treaty was still in effect): Attorney General of Quebec *versus* Régent Sioui, Conrad Sioui, Georges Sioui & Hugues Sioui (1982–90).

77. Regardless even of whether the media mention these facts. Schauer, *Free Speech*, 176–77; Stengers, "L'Historien face à ses responsabilités," 27, 29, 37–38. See also Gilissen, "La Responsabilité civile et pénale," 318, 1034–35.

78. Case 4.

79. Cases 5, 10, 11, 21.

80. Cases 13, 19.

81. Case 21.

82. For the difficult problem of whether speech is a subclass of action or a separate category, see Thomas Scanlon, "A Theory of Freedom of Expression," *Philosophy and Public Affairs*, 1, no. 2 (Winter 1972), 207–9; Schauer, *Free Speech*, 197–98; Barendt, *Freedom of Speech*, 78–88, 172, 174.

83. It is doubtful that judges would accept the good faith defense in negationist cases, that is, the defense that Holocaust deniers hold their conviction
in all honesty.

84. For the European Commission and the European Court, see Appendix
3.6, and also Macovei, *Freedom of Expression*, 7, 19, 43; Mendel, *Study*, 33–34; *Case
Law*, passim. More in general, see Barendt, *Freedom of Speech*, 170–86; Karl Josef
Partsch, "Freedom of Conscience and Expression, and Political Freedoms," in
Henkin, ed., *The International Bill of Rights*, 226–30; Nowak, *U.N. Covenant*, 359–69.
See also Dinah PoKempner, "A Shrinking Realm: Freedom of Expression since
9/11," in Human Rights Watch, *World Report 2007* (Washington: Human Rights
Watch, 2007), 63–85.

85. Barendt, *Freedom of Speech*, 182–83. See also the survey in International
Criminal Tribunal for Rwanda, *Prosecutor v. Ferdinand Nahimana, Jean-Bosco
Barayagwiza, Hassan Ngeze; Case no. ICTR-99-52-T: Judgement and Sentence* (http://
www.grandslacs.net/doc/2905.pdf; 2003), paragraphs 978–1039.

86. See Appendix 3.6 (Faurisson case). The Human Rights Committee, though,
made a critical comment about the French law (paragraph 9.3 and third individual opinion, paragraph 9). See also Mendel, *Study*, 47, 55. Within the European
Union, a proposal is pending to make punishable publicly condoning, denying
or grossly trivializing genocide, crimes against humanity, and war crimes. See
Council of European Union, "Council Framework Decision on Combating Racism and Xenophobia," in Council of European Union, *Press Release 2794th Council Meeting, Justice and Home Affairs* (19–20 April 2007), 23–25.

87. See, for example, Loe de Jong, *Het Koninkrijk der Nederlanden in de Tweede
Wereldoorlog*, vol. 13 (The Hague and Leiden: SDU, 1988), 69–76.

88. Almost five decades ago, magistrate and historian John Gilissen already
defended this right. See his "La Responsabilité civile et pénale," 1006–12, 1021–30,
1039. In "Historians and Moral Evaluations," *History and Theory*, 43, no. 4 (December 2004), 14–16, Richard Vann also asks whether there are "subjects about which
it would be ethically preferable for historians to rein their curiosity or suspend the
application of at least some of the rules of historical method." (quotation on 14.)

89. A rough division would probably locate Leopold von Ranke, Marc Bloch,
Lucien Febvre, Benedetto Croce, Pieter Geyl, Henri Steele Commager, Herbert
Butterfield, Edward Carr, Geoffrey Barraclough, Jean Stengers, and the postmod-
ernists at the side of understanding, and Heinrich von Sybel, Heinrich von Treit-
schke, the Marxists, Lord Acton, Thomas Macauly, Ahmed Kasravi, Golo Mann,
Richard Tawney, Isaiah Berlin, François Bédarida, and Jörn Rüsen at the side of
understanding-*cum*-judging. Many others do not pronounce themselves on the
issue, defend incoherent views, or take an intermediate position. Background to
this discussion is provided by Vann, "Historians and Moral Evaluations," 3–30.

90. Barendt, *Freedom of Speech*, 93–98.

91. The United Nations Human Rights Committee members formulated a
concurring opinion in the *Faurisson* case (Appendix 3.6): "While there is every
reason to maintain protection of *bona fide* historical research against restriction,
even when it challenges accepted historical truths and by so doing offends
people, anti-Semitic allegations of the sort made by the author [i.e., Faurisson],

which violate the rights of others in the way described, do not have the same claim to protection against restriction." See also Mendel, *Study*, 40–41, 44.

92. See also European Court of Human Rights, *Peter Lingens versus Austria* (1975–86) [1986: Lingens's freedom of expression was violated.]

93. Pre–1945 case: John Bryce *versus* George William Rusden (1895).

94. Pre–1945 case: government *versus* Olof Kexel (1768).

95. See also European Court of Human Rights, *Monnat versus Switzerland* (1997–2006) [European Court of Human Rights, 2006: Daniel Monnat's freedom of expression was violated.] In this case, the court said the following about historical truth *en passant* (paragraph 68): "'[A] unique historical truth' that certainly does not exist . . . at the level of historical argument." ("'[U]ne vérité historique unique' qui, de toute façon, n'existe pas . . . au niveau du discours historique.")

96. See also European Court of Human Rights cases of 1999: Arslan *versus* Turkey; Baskaya & Okçuoglu *versus* Turkey; Karataş *versus* Turkey; Okçuoglu *versus* Turkey; Öztürk *versus* Turkey; Polat *versus* Turkey [European Court of Human Rights, 1999: the freedom of expression of Günay Arslan, Fikret Baskaya, and Mehemet Selim Okçuoglu, Hüseyin Karataş, Ahmet Zeki Okçuoglu, Ünsal Öztürk, and Edip Polat was violated.]

97. Pre–1945 case: Emperor Napoleon Bonaparte *versus* René de Chateaubriand (1807) (for comparison of Napoleon with Roman Emperor Nero).

98. Pre–1945 cases: Chancellor Otto von Bismarck *versus* Theodor Mommsen (1882–83); and *Kaiser* Wilhelm II *versus* Ludwig Quidde (1896) (*lèse majesté* for comparison of Wilhelm II with Roman Emperor Caligula).

99. Pre–1945 case: X (on behalf of Emperor Hirohito) *versus* Tsuda Sōkichi (1939–42) (*lèse majesté*).

100. Pre–1945 case: King Fuad I *versus* Muhammad Sabri (ca. 1936) (*re* Khedive Ismail).

101. Pre–1945 case: Communist Party Secretary-General Joseph Stalin *versus* A.G. Slutsky (1931) (*re* Communist Party leader Vladimir Lenin).

102. Pre–1945 case: X *versus* Taha Husayn (1926–27) (*re* Abraham & Ismail, Prophet Mohammed).

103. Cases in United States: Mel Mermelstein *versus* Institute for Historical Review et al. (1979–92); Simon Wiesenthal Center & American Jewish Committee *versus* William David McCalden (1984–92). Cases in Canada: R *versus* Keegstra (1990); R *versus* Zündel (1992); and Citron *versus* Zündel (2002).

104. See also Malcolm Lowes *versus* United Kingdom (1988).

105. See also Malcolm Ross *versus* Canada (1996–2000).

Chapter 4

1. The French original is part of the short story *Sarzan* (originally 1947), in Birago Diop, *Les Contes d'Amadou Koumba* (originally 1961; Paris: Présence Africaine, 1987), 180.

2. Carl Haub, "How Many People Have Ever Lived on Earth?" *Population Today*, 30, no. 8 (November/December 2002), 3–4. Older estimates are 69 billion

(in 1960; by Nathan Keyfitz), 50 billion (in 1980; by Arthur Westing), and 96 billion (in 1999; again by Nathan Keyfitz).

3. The medical profession, for example, considers the patient to be its primary ethical focus. See World Medical Association, *Declaration of Geneva* [also called "Physician's Oath"] (1948, 2005): "The health of my patient will be my first consideration." Another example is the International Federation of Journalists, *Declaration of Principles on the Conduct of Journalists* (1954, 1986), Article 1: "Respect for truth and for the right of the public to truth is the first duty of the journalist."

4. I do not differentiate between "responsibilities," "obligations," and "duties."

5. Antoon De Baets, "Resistance to the Censorship of Historical Thought in the Twentieth Century," in Sølvi Sogner, ed., *Making Sense of Global History: The 19th International Congress of Historical Sciences, Oslo 2000, Commemorative Volume* (Oslo: Universitetsforlaget, 2001), 390.

6. Antoon De Baets, "Human Rights, History of" in Neil Smelser and Paul Baltes, eds., *International Encyclopedia of the Social and Behavioral Sciences*, vol. 10 (Oxford, etc.: Elsevier-Pergamon, 2001), 7013. In my *Censorship of Historical Thought: A World Guide, 1945–2000* (Westport, CT, and London: Greenwood Press, 2002), 24, I also suggested that historians had social obligations regarding past generations.

7. For considerations about future generations, see, for example, Derek Parfit, *Reasons and Persons* (Oxford: Clarendon Press, 1984), 349–441, and John Rawls, *A Theory of Justice* (originally 1971; Cambridge, MA: Cambridge University Press, 1999), 111, 118–21, 183, 251–62, 514. Rawls, for example, maintains: "[I]n first principles of justice we are not allowed to treat generations differently solely on the grounds that they are earlier or later in time" (1999: 260). For an explicit attempt to link future to past generations, see Bruce Auerbach, *Unto the Thousandth Generation: Conceptualizing Intergenerational Justice* (New York: Peter Lang, 1995), 173–206 ("obligations to past generations").

8. In addition, as this Chapter will show, some ideas of my *Declaration* echo the articles of the UNESCO *Declaration* about peace and nondiscrimination.

9. In Arthur Prior's words: "Things that *have* existed do seem to be individually identifiable and discussable in a way in which things that don't yet exist are not (the dead are metaphysically less frightening than the unborn.)" See his *Past, Present and Future* (originally 1967; Oxford: Clarendon Press, 1978), 171.

10. Derek Parfit, "Rationality and the Metaphysics of Time" (manuscript; version August 2006).

11. Parfit, *Reasons and Persons*, 149–86. See also Thomas Nagel, *The View from Nowhere* (New York and Oxford: Oxford University Press, 1986), 228–29; John Martin Fischer, ed., *The Metaphysics of Death* (Stanford: Stanford University Press, 1993), passim; Annette Baier, "The Rights of Past and Future Persons," in Ernest Partridge, ed., *Responsibilities to Future Generations: Environmental Ethics* (New York: Prometheus, 1980), 172–73; Auerbach, *Unto the Thousandth Generation*, 174–75; Ernest Partridge, "Posthumous Interests and Posthumous Respect," *Ethics*, 91, no. 2 (January 1981), 249.

12. See also the discussion of the "non-identity problem" in Parfit, *Reasons and Persons*, particularly on 355–57, 363, 372, 377–78, 523n18.

13. Quoted in Fischer, ed., *Metaphysics of Death*, 95.

14. Parfit, *Reasons and Persons*, 160–86. For an intuitive application of the bias toward the future, see Herbert Butterfield, *The Discontinuities between the Generations in History: Their Effect on the Transmission of Political Experience* (Cambridge: Cambridge University Press, 1971), 9, and Butterfield, "Historiography," in Philip Wiener, ed., *Dictionary of the History of Ideas: Studies of Selected Pivotal Ideas*, vol. 2 (New York: Charles Scribner's Sons, 1974), 472.

15. Parfit, *Reasons and Persons*, 172–74.

16. For the asymmetry between experience and expectation on the one hand, and the expanded difference between both since the early modern period (1500–1800) embodied in the concept of "progress" on the other, see Reinhart Koselleck, "'Space of Experience' and 'Horizon of Expectation': Two Historical Categories" (originally German 1976), in Koselleck, *Futures Past: On the Semantics of Historical Time* (originally German 1979; New York: Columbia University Press, 2004), 259–61, 263–70, 274.

17. This question deals with the dead and not with the dying. Dying and the debate about the right to life and the right to die are different matters.

18. Jacob Rendtorff and Peter Kemp, *Basic Ethical Principles in European Bioethics and Biolaw*, vol. 1 (Copenhagen: Centre for Ethics and Law, and Barcelona: Institut Borja de Bioètica, 2000), 24, 65–70, 348–54.

19. See the text of the World Health Organization in Appendix 5.1 of this book. Chapters 4 and 5 should be read closely together with this appendix where many of the key international instruments mentioned are quoted extensively.

20. Kenneth Iserson, *Death to Dust: What Happens to Dead Bodies?* (Tucson AZ: Galen Press, 1994), 18–19; Parfit, *Reasons and Persons*, 199–217. See also Jay Rosenberg, *Thinking Clearly about Death* (Englewood Cliffs, NJ: Prentice-Hall, 1983), 116–25.

21. For the concept of "dead persons," see *Geneva Conventions I* (1949), Articles 4 and 16, and *II* (1949), Articles 5 and 19–20; *Additional Protocol I to the Geneva Conventions* (1977), Articles 32–34. See also Appendix 5.1. of this book. For a critical note on this use of the concept of "dead persons," see Albin Eser, "Mental Elements: Mistake of Fact and Mistake of Law," in Antonio Cassese, Paola Gaeta, and John Jones, eds., *The Rome Statute of the International Criminal Court: A Commentary*, vol. 1 (Oxford: Oxford University Press, 2002), 923n156.

22. For a critical discussion of the Lockean distinction between persons and human beings, see paragraphs 7 and 10 of Derek Parfit, "Persons, Bodies, and Human Beings," in Dean Zimmerman, Theodore Sider, and John Hawthorne, eds., *Contemporary Debates in Metaphysics* (Oxford: Blackwell, 2007), 177–208.

23. The mirror question reads: "From which moment do we speak of human beings?" Although there is strong disagreement about the ontological status of human zygotes, embryos, and fetuses, a minimal consensus can be found in the viewpoint that they are *potential* human beings (and persons). I think that my Article 1 applies unreservedly to all cases of miscarriage, abortion, or stillbirth and my Article 3 unreservedly applies to stillbirth. Articles 2 and 5 are less strict and depend on the estimated viability of the fetus and on the philosophical and religious views of the parents. See also Ruth Chadwick, "Corpses,

Recycling and Therapeutic Purposes," in Robert Lee and Derek Morgan, eds., *Death Rites: Law and Ethics at the End of Life* (London and New York: Routledge, 1994), 66–68; Manfred Nowak, *U.N. Covenant on Civil and Political Rights: CCPR Commentary* (Kehl am Rhein, Strasbourg, Arlington, VA: Engel, 1993), 285–86.

24. Iserson, *Death to Dust*, 13–18; Lawrence Becker, "Human Being: The Boundaries of the Concept," *Philosophy and Public Affairs*, 4, no. 4 (Summer 1975), 336; see also 352–59, especially 357–58.

25. See also Fred Feldman, *Confrontations with the Reaper: A Philosophical Study of the Nature and Value of Death* (New York and Oxford: Oxford University Press, 1992), 89–124, especially 113–15, see also 148.

26. Palle Yourgrau's solution—reserving the term existence for the living and the term being for the nonliving—is not convincing, because, by doing so, it introduces the new problem of distinguishing the dead from fictional and future human beings. See Yourgrau's "The Dead," *Journal of Philosophy*, 86, no. 2 (February 1987), 89–90.

27. Irving Copi and Carl Cohen, *Introduction to Logic* (originally 1953; Upper Saddle River, NJ: Pearson and Prentice-Hall, 2005), 115–17.

28. For inspiring defenses of the view that the dead have rights, see Raymond Belliotti, "Do Dead Human Beings Have Rights?" *The Personalist*, 60, no. 2 (1979), 201–10; Baier, "The Rights of Past and Future Persons," 171–83; and Loren Lomasky, *Persons, Rights, and the Moral Community* (New York and Oxford: Oxford University Press, 1987), 212–21. Another defense is Tim Mulgan, "The Place of the Dead in Liberal Political Philosophy," *The Journal of Political Philosophy*, 7, no. 1 (1999), 52–70. Louis-Vincent Thomas, *Le Cadavre: de la biologie à l'anthropologie* (Brussels: Éditions Complexe, 1980), 116–21, speaks of "the rights *of* the corpse," but in fact means "the rights *over* the corpse."

29. Joel Feinberg, *Harm to Others* (New York and Oxford: Oxford University Press, 1984), 81, writes that we speak of the dead in the language of loss, although we should speak about destruction, not loss, because there is no survivor to be the proper subject of harm. He adds, however: "[T]his linguistic strictness would deprive us of metaphors of striking aptness and utility."

30. Parfit, *Reasons and Persons*, 357.

31. Alan White, *Rights* (Oxford: Clarendon Press, 1984), 60–62, also 86–89. Mary Midgley calls the duties to the dead "noncontractual"; see her "Duties Concerning Islands" (originally 1983), in Peter Singer, ed., *Ethics* (Oxford: Oxford University Press, 1994), 381.

32. For moderate criticism of the notion of respect for the dead, see Nigel Barley, *Dancing on the Grave: Encounters with Death* (originally 1995; London: Abacus, 1997), 42–43, 136, 164, 205.

33. Antoon De Baets, "How Humanity Stands on Its Dignity," *The Australian* (13 July 2005), 36. For a fuller treatment, see my "A Successful Utopia: The Doctrine of Human Dignity," *Historein: A Review of the Past and Other Stories*, no. 7 (2007), 71–85.

34. The source of contemporary thinking about human dignity is Immanuel Kant's *Grundlegung zur Metaphysik der Sitten* (originally 1785), in *Kant's gesammelte Schriften*, vol. 4, ed. Preußischen Akademie der Wissenschaften (Berlin:

Reimer, 1903), 434–40, especially 436, 438, 440. For Kant, only rational and autonomous beings (persons) possessed dignity, and therefore, by implication, he excluded the dead.

35. Claude Lévi-Strauss, *Tristes tropiques* (Paris: Plon, 1955), 241. See also Johannes Fabian, "How Others Die: Reflections on the Anthropology of Death," in Arien Mack, ed., *Death in American Experience* (New York: Schocken Books, 1973), 189–90 (burials and the hominization process), and Barley, *Dancing on the Grave*, 13–45 (about the emotional universality of death.)

36. Robert Pogue Harrison, *The Dominion of the Dead* (Chicago and London: University of Chicago Press, 2003), xi; and Ewa Domańska, "Necrocracy," *History of the Human Sciences*, 18, no. 2 (2005), 111–22.

37. See Appendix 5.1 herein, under *Geneva Conventions*.

38. For the concept of "outrages upon personal dignity," see Appendix 5.1 herein, under *International Criminal Court*. See also *Geneva Conventions* (1949), Common Article 3.

39. See (chronologically): Joel Feinberg, *Rights, Justice, and the Bounds of Liberty: Essays in Social Philosophy* (Princeton: Princeton University Press, 1980), 173–76 ("dead persons" [originally in a 1971 paper first published in 1974]); Frank Harrison III, "What Kind of Beings Can Have Rights?" *Philosophy Forum*, 12, nos. 1–2 (September 1972), 115, 126; Kenneth Goodpaster, "On Being Morally Considerable," *Journal of Philosophy*, 75, no. 6 (June 1978), 308–25; W.R. Carter, "Once and Future Persons," *American Philosophical Quarterly*, 17, no. 1 (January 1980), 61–66; Peter Singer, "The Concept of Moral Standing," in Arthur Caplan and Daniel Callahan, eds., *Ethics in Hard Times* (New York and London: Plenum Press, 1981), 40–45; Partridge, "Posthumous Interests and Posthumous Respect," 255–59; Rosenberg, *Thinking Clearly about Death*, 116–36, especially 120–23; White, *Rights*, 75–92; Peter Jones, *Rights* (Houndmills, Basingstoke: Macmillan, 1994), 67–71.

40. Joel Feinberg, *Offense to Others* (New York and Oxford: Oxford University Press, 1985), 57; see also 53–57, 70–71, 94–95, 116–17. Similar ideas in Chadwick, "Corpses," 62–63, and Rosenberg, *Thinking Clearly about Death*, 121–22.

41. See the considerable arousal of interest for issues related to the 1990 Native American Graves Protection and Repatriation Act (NAGPRA) in the United States. Other indications: the frequent practice of archaeologists to give nicknames to skeletons (see Paul Bahn, "Do Not Disturb? Archaeology and the Rights of the Dead," *Oxford Journal of Archaeology*, 3, no. 1 [1984], 131); the return of the remains of Saartjie Baartman (1789–1816) from the Musée de l'Homme in Paris to South Africa in April 2002, followed in August 2002 by her solemn reburial (see <http://www.senat.fr/basile>).

42. This argument is developed at length in Partridge, "Posthumous Interests," 259–61; see also Belliotti, "Do Dead Human Beings Have Rights?" 208; Lomasky, *Persons, Rights, and the Moral Community*, 216–17; Christopher Hill, "Some Philosophical Problems about Rights," in Hill, ed., *Rights and Wrongs: Some Essays on Human Rights* (Harmondsworth: Penguin, 1969), 9.

43. The last two assumptions do not cover dead children.

44. Joan Callahan, "On Harming the Dead," *Ethics*, 97, no. 2 (January 1987), 347.

45. Thomas Nagel, *Mortal Questions* (Cambridge: Cambridge University Press, 1979), 5–7; A.I. Melden, *Rights and Persons* (Oxford: Blackwell, 1977), 48–52 ("Deathbed promises"); Yourgrau, "The Dead," 85–86; Roger Scruton, *Modern Philosophy: An Introduction and Survey* (London: Mandarin and Reed International Books, 1996), 307, 312; Raymond Belliotti, *What Is the Meaning of Human Life?* (Amsterdam and Atlanta, GA: Rodopi, 2001), 147–48, 154–55, see also 88–91; Avishai Margalit, *The Ethics of Memory* (Cambridge, MA: Harvard University Press, 2002), 91–94.

46. See Appendix 5.1.

47. See De Baets, "A Successful Utopia."

48. Feinberg, *Rights,* 134; Feinberg, *Harm,* 109–10.

49. Full citations appear in Appendix 5.1.

50. Belliotti ("Do Dead Human Beings Have Rights," 209) identified four "rights" of the dead: "(a) the right to dispose of property; (b) the right to the reputation which is merited by deeds performed when alive; (c) the right to any posthumous award to which a claim of entitlement can justifiably be lodged; (d) the right to specify the burial procedures and handling of one's corpse." Belliotti's first and last "rights" are covered (to a large degree) by my Article 4, and his second and (indirectly) third "rights" by my Articles 6 and 7.

51. For a discussion of the concept of 'balancing of interests,' see Schauer, *Free Speech,* 132–41, and Eric Barendt, *Freedom of Speech* (fully revised and updated second edition; Oxford: Oxford University Press, 2005), 65, 225.

52. William Prosser, "Privacy," *California Law Review,* 48, no. 3 (August 1960), 389–407 (quotation on 389).

53. See also the NAGPRA; International Council of Museums, *Code of Ethics for Museums* (2004), Articles 6.2 and 6.3 ("return and restitution of cultural property"); and Bahn, "Do Not Disturb," 127–39.

54. European Commission of Human Rights, *X versus Federal Republic of Germany* (1981), paragraph 2.

55. For the distinction between coverage and protection, see Frederick Schauer, *Free Speech: A Philosophical Inquiry* (Cambridge: Cambridge University Press, 1982), 89–92.

56. See Barendt, *Freedom of Speech,* 33–34, 238–39; European Court of Human Rights, *Hachette Filipacchi Associés versus France* (2007).

57. Prosser, "Privacy," 398, 400–401, 422–23. Although I advocate the thesis that the dead possess (posthumous) dignity, privacy, and reputation, I do not assign honor to them, because the concept of honor is the result of a capacity for self-reflection (see Chapter 3), which the dead lack.

58. See David Flaherty, "Privacy and Confidentiality: The Responsibilities of Historians," *Reviews in American History,* 8, no. 3 (September 1980), 419–29.

59. See also Feinberg, *Rights,* 175–76; Feinberg, *Harmless Wrongdoing* (New York and Oxford: Oxford University Press, 1988), 254–56; Robert Wennberg, "The Moral Standing of the Dead and the Writing of History," *Fides et Historia,* 30, no. 2 (Summer-Fall 1998), 51–63.

60. John David Viera, "Images as Property," in Larry Gross, John Stuart Katz, and Jay Ruby, eds., *Image Ethics: The Moral Rights of Subjects in Photographs, Film,*

and Television (New York and Oxford: Oxford University Press, 1988), 150–52 (discussing the Elvis Presley cases [1977, 1980]); Barendt, *Freedom of Speech,* 266 (discussing Martin Luther King Jr. Center for Social Change *versus* American Heritage Products [1982]).

61. The communal character of "heritage" is the reason why it is the overlapping characteristic in the declarations about future and past generations and why it took so long before I integrated it in Table 4.1.

62. Iserson, *Death to Dust,* 516–32.

63. The use of dead bodies for educational purposes is allowed, if exercised with respect. Objections against medical or forensic research into dead bodies are varied. The principle of the relatives' free and informed consent may be overruled solely to find evidence in cases of suspected unnatural death. For an overview of medical and legal aspects, mentioning many historical controversies, see Dorothy Nelkin and Lori Andrews, "Do the Dead Have Interests? Policy Issues for Research after Life," *American Journal of Law and Medicine,* 24, nos. 2–3 (Summer–Fall 1998), 261–91. See also Thomas Grey, *The Legal Enforcement of Morality* (New York: Knopf, 1983), 16–19, 103–53 ("treatment of the dead"); Feinberg, *Offense,* 72–77, 94–95; Iserson, *Death to Dust,* 100, 153–54, 514; Chadwick, "Corpses," 65–69.

64. This definition of "quasi-right" comes from Grey, *Legal Enforcement,* 16; see also Hugh Bernard, *The Law of Death and Disposal of the Dead* (New York: Oceana Publications, 1966), 12–17; Iserson, *Death to Dust,* 556–59; Chadwick, "Corpses," 61–62; Nelkin and Andrews, "Do the Dead Have Interests," 282, 284–85.

65. For a good overview of the cultural diversity of attitudes toward death, see Barley, *Dancing on the Grave,* 27, 37, 61–76, 101, 152–53, 219 (giving examples of myths about the origins of death and about why people die.) See also International Committee of the Red Cross, *Operational Best Practices Regarding the Management of Human Remains and Information on the Dead by Non-Specialists* (<http://www.icrc.org>; 2004), 16–20. For the view that archivating is like an act of burial, see Achille Mbembe, "The Power of the Archive and Its Limits," in Carolyn Hamilton, et al., eds., *Refiguring the Archive* (Cape Town: David Philip, 2002), 21–22; for the view that historical writing is like a funerary rite, see Michel de Certeau, *L'écriture de l'histoire* (Paris: Gallimard, 1975), 117–20.

66. Definition adapted from NAGPRA, section 2.1. See also Iserson, *Death to Dust,* 525–28; Barley, *Dancing on the Grave,* 205.

67. Robert Hertz, "A Contribution to the Study of the Collective Representation of Death" (originally French, 1907), in Hertz, *Death and the Right Hand* (Aberdeen: Cohen & West, 1960), 27–86.

68. For an analysis of effigies as substitutes, representations, and doubles of the dead, see Carlo Ginzburg, "Representation: The Word, the Idea, the Thing" (originally French 1991), in Ginzburg, *Wooden Eyes: Nine Reflections on Distance* (originally Italian, 1998; New York: Columbia University Press, 2001), 63–78, 201–7. My definition of the dead as past human beings helps explaining why so many representations of the dead are anthropomorphic, but it is less compatible with nonanthropomorphic representations.

69. See also UNIDROIT, *Convention Providing a Uniform Law on the Form of an International Will* (1973), Annex, here Articles 1–6. For caselaw about wills, see European Commission of Human Rights, *X versus Federal Republic of Germany* (1981), cited above, and European Court of Human Rights, *Pla and Puncernau versus Andorra* (2004). The latter case concerned the exclusion of an adopted child from an inheritance on the basis of an interpretation of a 1939 will.

70. See also S.C. Humphreys, "Death and Time," in S.C. Humphreys and Helen King, eds., *Mortality and Immortality: The Anthropology and Archaeology of Death* (London: Academic Press, 1981), 271, 273.

71. For this, see, e.g., Jay Winter, *Sites of Memory, Sites of Mourning: The Great War in European Cultural History* (Cambridge: Cambridge University Press, 1995), chapter 1.

72. James Frazer, *The Golden Bough*, vol. 2, *Taboo and the Perils of the Soul* (originally 1890; London: Macmillan, 1914), 138–45 (names of mourners), 349–74 (names of the dead), 363–65 (historical knowledge; quotation on 363). For the tabooing of names of the dead and the use of necronyms (names expressing kinship relations between persons and their deceased relatives), see Claude Lévi-Strauss, *La Pensée sauvage* (Paris: Plon, 1962), 253–65. See also Barley, *Dancing on the Grave*, 31, 139. Some cultures also practice group burial; see S.C. Humphreys, "Introduction," and "Death and Time," both in Humphreys and King, eds., *Mortality and Immortality*, 6, 10–11, 270; Barley, *Dancing on the Grave*, 79, 108, 158–59.

73. For reflections on the photography of dead bodies and on the relationship between photography and death, see Susan Sontag, *On Photography* (New York: Farrar, Straus and Giroux: 1977), 15, 19–21, 70–71, 105–7; Roland Barthes, *La chambre claire: Note sur la photographie* (Paris: Gallimard-Seuil, 1980), 44–46, 123–24, 143–47, 171.

74. Barendt, *Freedom of Speech*, 244–46, also 63; Simon Davies, "Private Matters," *Index on Censorship*, 29, no. 3 (May–June 2000), 44. For an example of a balancing test resulting in silence, see Rudi van Doorslaer and Etienne Verhoeyen, *De moord op Lahaut* [The murder of Lahaut] (Louvain: Kritak, 1985 [French translation appeared in 1987]), 186–87. A member of parliament and a leading Belgian communist, Julien Lauhaut shouted "Vive la république" during King Baudouin's enthronement in 1950. A week later, Lahaut was assassinated. The murder was not solved. Although officially closed in 1962, the famous case continued to appeal to the imagination. While researching their book, the authors discovered the name of the murderer (the latter had died in 1977), but they decided not to mention it in order not to offend the family who had collaborated actively with them. In 2002, a member of parliament disclosed the name. The example shows that the practical circumstances in which the test is executed can be complicated (the circumstances were: [a] the possible involvement of the monarchy in the murder and the public interest, in this eventuality, in disclosing the murderer's name; [b] an actively collaborating family to whom the authors were much indebted; and [c] the possibility that third parties eventually disclose the omitted fact). For another case in which a historian preferred to remain silent, see Jean Stengers, "L'Historien face à ses

responsabilités," *Cahiers de l'école des sciences philosophiques et religieuses*, no. 15 (1994), 38.

75. For a critical assessment of the concepts of heritage, patrimony, and legacy, see David Lowenthal, *Possessed by the Past: The Heritage Crusade and the Spoils of History* (New York, etc.: The Free Press, 1996).

76. See Appendix 5.1.

77. See United Nations, *Declaration of Basic Principles of Justice for Victims of Crime and Abuse of Power* (1985), Principle 2: "The term 'victim' also includes, where appropriate, the immediate family or dependants of the direct victim and persons who have suffered harm in intervening to assist victims in distress or to prevent victimization." See also Principle 12(b).

78. See George Sher, "Ancient Wrongs and Modern Rights" (originally 1980), in Peter Laslett and James Fishkin, eds., *Justice between Age Groups and Generations* (New Haven and London: Yale University Press, 1992), 48–61, and criticism of his view by Peter Laslett, "Is There a Generational Contract?" in the same volume, 39–43. See also Jeremy Waldron, "Superseding Historic Injustice," *Ethics*, 103, no. 1 (October 1992), 4–28. There is no room here to outline the different views on rectifying historical or intergenerational injustice. For the United Nations debate about impunity following periods of slavery, colonialism, and wars of conquest, see, for example, Sub-Commission on the Promotion and Protection of Human Rights, *Resolution 2002/5* (2002). The basic general document is *Final Report on the Question of the Impunity of Perpetrators of Human Rights Violations (Economic, Social and Cultural Rights)*, prepared by Mr. El Hadji Guissé, Special Rapporteur (E/CN.4/Sub.2/1997/8; 1997).

79. For a collection of essays on this topic, see Fischer, ed., *Metaphysics of Death*.

80. Similar ideas in United Nations, *Principles on the Effective Prevention and Investigation of Extra-Legal, Arbitrary and Summary Executions* (1989). Also in United Nations, *Manual on the Effective Prevention and Investigation of Extra-Legal, Arbitrary and Summary Executions* (1991), chapter 5 ("Human remains"), especially part 3 ("Model Protocol for a Legal Investigation of Extra-Legal Arbitrary and Summary Executions ['Minnesota Protocol']"), part 4 ("Model Autopsy Protocol"), and part 5 ("Model Protocol for Disinterment and Analysis of Skeletal Remains"). The introduction to the Model Autopsy Protocol states: "Historians, journalists, attorneys, judges, other physicians and representatives of the public may also use this model autopsy protocol as a benchmark for evaluating an autopsy and its findings."

81. Occasional cannibalism practiced for survival in life-threatening circumstances is not included here. For examples of war crimes trials involving charges of cannibalism, necrophagy, mutilation of dead bodies, or refusal of honorable burial, see "Case no. 82: Trial of Max Schmid—United States General Military Government Court at Dachau, Germany, 19th May, 1947," in *Law Reports of Trials of War Criminals*, vol. 13 (London: United Nations War Crimes Commission, 1949), 151–52. Not only is the Schmid trial briefly analyzed here, so are four cases of Japanese perpetrators. For examples of the mutilation of dead bodies during the genocide in Rwanda in 1994, see International Criminal Tribunal for Rwanda, *Prosecutor versus Jean-Paul Akayesu;*

Case no. ICTR-96-4-T: Judgement (1998), paragraph 120 and note 54; see also paragraphs 159, 161, 280, 288; International Criminal Tribunal for Rwanda, *Prosecutor versus Eliézer Niyitegeka; Case no. ICTR-96-14-T: Judgement and sentence* (2003), paragraphs 273, 287, 312–13, 316.

82. International Committee of the Red Cross, *Operational Best Practices*, 10.

83. For examples of dead bodies that were first buried in mass graves, then excavated and mutilated, and eventually reburied in new, remote mass graves so as to erase evidence of the crime and make impossible every form of mourning during the 1995 genocide in Srebrenica, see International Criminal Tribunal for the Former Yugoslavia, *Prosecutor versus Radislav Krstić; Case no. IT-98-33-T: Judgement* (2001), paragraph 596.

84. On 27 September 2006, the International Criminal Tribunal for the former Yugoslavia sentenced Momčilo Krajišnik, a former member of the Bosnian Serb leadership, to 27 years' imprisonment for crimes against humanity. These crimes included, among others, his government's deliberate policy of destroying cultural monuments and sacred sites of importance to the Muslim and Croat populations (museums, archives, libraries, mosques, Catholic churches) in many Bosnian municipalities. It was the first sentence in history in which the destruction of cultural property without overriding military necessity formed major evidence for the existence of an intent to persecute particular groups, which is a crime against humanity. See International Criminal Tribunal for the Former Yugoslavia, *Prosecutor v. Momčilo Krajišnik; Case no. IT-00-39-T: Judgement* (2006), paragraphs 5, 780–83, 836–40.

85. Articles 19.3 and 21 of the *International Covenant on Civil and Political Rights* list the reasons why such ceremonies could be restricted: see Appendix 5.1.

86. See, for example, Lévi-Strauss, *Tristes tropiques*, 242: "Some societies refuse rest [to their dead], they mobilize them: sometimes literally, as is the case with cannibalism and necrophagy when they are based on the ambition to incorporate the virtues and powers of the deceased" (my translation). See also Iserson, *Death to Dust*, 38–39, 366–80, 404–7; Barley, *Dancing on the Grave*, 198–200.

87. Paul Barber, *Vampires, Burial and Death: Folklore and Reality* (New Haven and London: Yale University Press, 1988), 5–9, 61–63; Elias Canetti, *Crowds and Power* (originally German, 1960; New York: Farrar Straus Giroux, 1984), 66–67, 262–77; Clare Gittings, *Death, Burial and the Individual in Early Modern England* (London and Sydney: Croom Helm, 1984), 60–85; Human Rights Office of the Archdiocese of Guatemala, ed., *Guatemala: Never Again! Recovery of Historical Memory Project* (New York: Maryknoll, 1999), 14–22, 173–74; Iserson, *Death to Dust*, 510–12, 559; Catherine Merridale, *Night of Stone: Death and Memory in Russia* (London: Granta Books, 2000), 55–57; J. Middleton, "Anthropology of Ancestors," in Smelser and Baltes, eds., *International Encyclopedia*, vol. 1, 494–96; Hans Schreuer, "Das Recht der Toten: Eine germanistische Untersuchung," *Zeitschrift für Vergleichende Rechtswissenschaft*, 33 (1916), part 1, 359–67; Thomas, *Le Cadavre*, 36–39, 64–67, 105–7, 109–11, 116–21; Katherine Verdery, *The Political Lives of Dead Bodies: Reburial and Postsocialist Change* (New York: Columbia University Press, 1999), 97; and Jean-Pierre Vernant, *Mortals and Immortals: Collected Essays* (Princeton, NJ: Princeton University Press, 1991), 39, 67–69, 87–88, 188.

88. Criminals (traitors, murderers), heretics, the executed, witches, sorcerers, suicides, prostitutes, slaves, the eccentric, the disfigured, the mentally ill, those suffering a contagious or incurable disease, the unbaptized, those who died in a catastrophe, those undergoing an abnormal or exceptional death, the aborted, the stillborn, the strangers, and the poor. In some cultures, dying without (male) offspring is punished with the delay or cancellation of a funeral.

89. Mark Connelly, "Funerals," in Nicholas Cull, David Culbert, and David Welch, eds., *Propaganda and Mass Persuasion: A Historical Encyclopedia, 1500 to the Present* (Santa Barbara, CA, Denver, CO, Oxford: ABC-Clio, 2003), 139–41.

90. Vernant, *Mortals and Immortals*, 72.

91. Parfit, *Reasons and Persons*, 159, 357, 480–86. Tyler Cowen and Derek Parfit, "Against the Social Discount Rate," in Laslett and Fishkin, eds., *Justice between Age Groups and Generations*, 144–61, discuss and discard twelve defenses of the SDR.

92. See also Belliotti, "Do Dead Human Beings Have Rights," 209–10 (discussing the posthumous defamation of Rocky Marciano and Cicero), and Lomasky, *Persons, Rights, and the Moral Community*, 218.

Chapter 5

1. *Popol Vuh: The Sacred Book of the Ancient Quiché Maya* (English translation Delia Goetz and Sylvanus Morley; London: William Hodge, 1951), 205.

2. "Pamphlet by Henry Festing Jones: Charles Darwin and Samuel Butler—A Step towards Reconciliation; Published by A.C. Fifield, 1911," reprinted in Nora Barlow, ed., *The Autobiography of Charles Darwin, 1809–1882* (London: Collins, 1958), 197–98.

3. "Mes larmes ne la ressusciteront pas. C'est pourquoi je pleure," as quoted in Robert Sabatier, *Dictionnaire de la mort* (Paris: Albin Michel, 1967), 276.

4. The corresponding articles in the *Universal Declaration of Human Rights* are 12, 18, and 19. Chapters 4 and 5 should be read closely together with Appendix 5.1. of this book where many of the key international instruments mentioned are quoted extensively.

5. Galen Strawson, "Blood and Memory: Do We Have a Duty of Remembrance to the Dead?" *The Guardian* (4 January 2003).

6. John Sutton, "Memory," in Donald Borchert, ed., *Encyclopedia of Philosophy*, vol. 6 (Detroit: Thomson/Gale, 2006), 122–23; Greg Miller, "How Are Memories Stored and Retrieved?" *Science*, 309 (1 July 2005), 92.

7. Simon Blackburn, *The Oxford Dictionary of Philosophy* (Oxford and New York: Oxford University Press, 1994), 238.

8. Karl Josef Partsch, "Freedom of Conscience and Expression, and Political Freedoms," in Louis Henkin, ed., *The International Bill of Rights: The Covenant on Civil and Political Rights* (New York: Columbia University Press, 1981), 217; Manfred Nowak, *U.N. Covenant on Civil and Political Rights: CCPR Commentary* (Kehl am Rhein, Strasbourg, Arlington, VA: Engel, 1993), 339.

9. *Black's Law Dictionary*, B.A. Garner, ed. (originally 1891; St. Paul, MN: West Group, 2004), 1126, defines "opinion" as "a person's thought, belief or inference . . ." For Article 19's definition, see Chapter 3, note 8.

10. In a personal communication to the author (October 2003), legal scholar Toby Mendel, Head of Law Programme of the Global Campaign for Freedom of Expression *Article 19,* also subsumed memories within opinions.

11. United Nations Human Rights Committee, *General Comment 10 (International Covenant on Civil and Political Rights): Freedom of Expression* (1983).

12. Nowak, *U.N. Covenant,* 295.

13. See, e.g., *Amnesty International Reports* (London: Amnesty International) of *1977,* 301–2; *1978,* 158; *1985,* 210; *1989,* 118, 251; *1990,* 41.

14. The right to peaceful assembly is Article 20 of the *Universal Declaration of Human Rights* and Article 21 of the *International Covenant on Civil and Political Rights.*

15. Robert Merton, *On the Shoulders of Giants: A Shandean Postscript* (New York: Free Press; London: Collier-Macmillan, 1965), 180 (quotation in Latin). On the ideas of debt and cultural memory, see Michael Schudson, "Dynamics of Distortion in Collective Memory," in Daniel Schacter, ed., *Memory Distortion: How Minds, Brains, and Societies Reconstruct the Past* (Cambridge, MA, and London: Harvard University Press, 1995), 346–47. For a contemporary defense of the debt idea, see Robert Pogue Harrison, *The Dominion of the Dead* (Chicago and London: University of Chicago Press, 2003). Remember also Gilbert Chesterton's words from 1908: "Tradition means giving votes to the most obscure of all classes, our ancestors. It is the democracy of the dead."

16. The classic example is Pericles's funeral oration in 431 BCE for the Athenian soldiers who had died at the opening battles of the Peloponnesian war, in Thucydides, *The Peloponnesian War, Book II,* ed. J.S. Rusten (Cambridge: Cambridge University Press, 1989), paragraphs 34–47.2, pages 52–58 (text), 135–79 (commentaries).

17. In The Hague on 11 March 2003.

18. The arguments of the first two groups correspond to the "metaphysical motives" in Table 1.3 of this book.

19. Aleksander Solzhenitsyn, *The Gulag Archipelago 1918–1956: An Experiment in Literary Investigation* (originally Russian, 1973; New York: Harper & Row, 1974), quotations on v (dedication) and vi (author's note). For the discussion of a duty to remember, see Vladimir Jankélévitch, *L'Imprescriptible* (Paris: Seuil, 1986); Tzvetan Todorov, *Les Abus de la mémoire* (Paris: Arléa, 1995) [English: "The Abuses of Memory," *Common Knowledge,* 5, no. 1 (Spring 1996), 6–26]; Todorov, *Mémoire du mal, tentation du bien: Enquête sur le siècle* (Paris: Laffont, 2000), 173–91; Todorov, "The Uses and Abuses of Memory," in Howard Marchitello, ed., *What Happens to History? The Renewal of Ethics in Contemporary Thought* (New York and London: Routledge, 2001), 11–22; Henry Rousso, *La Hantise du passé* (Paris: Textuel, 1998), 42–47; Paul Ricœur, *La Mémoire, l'histoire, l'oubli* (Paris: Seuil, 2000), 105–11, 471–80, 585–89; Alain Finkielkraut, *Une Voix vient de l'autre rive* (Paris: Gallimard, 2000), chapter 1; Avishai Margalit, *The Ethics of Memory* (Cambridge, MA: Harvard University Press, 2002), 70–83; René Rémond, *Quand l'État se mêle de l'Histoire* (Paris: Stock, 2006); Emmanuel Terray, *Face aux abus de mémoire* (Arles: Actes Sud, 2006).

20. See, for example, Comité pro Justicia y Paz de Guatemala, *Human Rights in Guatemala* ([Geneva]: Comité pro Justicia y Paz de Guatemala, 1984), 18: "[T]he elders of the community are murdered with exceptional cruelty in order to destroy the people's links with their past. . . . [T]he elders are the trustees of the people's history, culture and beliefs, and responsible for transmitting them to coming generations." This idea is also expressed in Human Rights Office of the Archdiocese of Guatemala, ed., *Guatemala: Never Again! Recovery of Historical Memory Project* (New York: Maryknoll, 1999), 48, and *Guatemala: Memoria del silencio: Informe de la Comisión para el Esclarecimiento Histórico,* vol. 5, *Conclusiones y recomendaciones* (Guatemala: Oficina de Servicios para Proyectos de las Naciones Unidas, 1999), paragraph 62.

21. *Hampâté Bâ* (1900–91) ("Quand un vieillard meurt, c'est une bibliothèque qui brûle"): probably pronounced before a UNESCO meeting around 1960. *Rojas* (1882–1957) ("Cada vez que un viejo de mas de ochenta años se va para el silencio, es como si se quemara una biblioteca de cosas tradicionales"): attributed to him by Atahualpa Yupanqui (1908–92).

22. Thomas Paine, *The Rights of Man* (originally 1791; London: Dent, and New York: Dutton, 1969), 13.

23. Karl Marx, *Der Achtzehnte Brumaire des Louis Bonaparte* (originally 1852; Hamburg: Meissner, 1885), 7 ("Die Tradition aller todten Geschlechter lastet wie ein Alp auf dem Gehirne der Lebenden.")

24. Friedrich Nietzsche, *The Use and Abuse of History* (originally *Vom Nutzen und Nachteil der Historie für das Leben: Zweite Unzeitgemässe Betrachtung,* 1874; English edition originally 1949; New York: Liberal Arts Press, 1957), 12–22.

25. *Historians:* for example, Allan Megill, "Some Aspects of the Ethics of History Writing: Reflections on Edith Wyschogrod's *An Ethics of Remembering,*" in David Carr, Thomas Flynn, and Rudolf Makkreel, eds., *The Ethics of History* (Evanston, IL: Northwestern University Press, 2004), 52, and Jörn Rüsen, "Responsibility and Irresponsibility in Historical Studies: A Critical Consideration of the Ethical Dimension in the Historian's Work," in Carr, Flynn, and Makkreel, eds., *Ethics,* 203. *Archivists:* for example, Perrine Canavaggio, "Introduction," *Comma: International Journal on Archives,* no. 2 (2004), 9–13.

26. See also Judy Barsalou and Victoria Baxter, "The Urge To Remember: The Role of Memorials in Social Reconstruction and Transitional Justice," *United States Institute of Peace Stabilization and Reconstruction Series,* no. 5 (<http://www.usip.org>; January 2007), 3, 4 ("The dark side of memorialization . . . involves efforts to use memories of the past to fan the flames of ethnic hatred, consolidate a group's identity as victims, demarcate the differences among identity groups, and reify grievances. Wittingly or unwittingly, interested parties around the world use memorial sites to seek absolution, lodge accusations against their enemies, establish competing claims of victimhood, or promote ideological agendas.").

27. Megill, "Some Aspects," 65–66, 69.

28. United Nations Human Rights Committee, *General Comment 22 (International Covenant on Civil and Political Rights): The Right to Freedom of Thought, Conscience and Religion (Article 18)* (1993).

29. Partsch, "Freedom of Conscience," 218; see also Nowak, *U.N. Covenant,* 314.

30. Monica Macovei, *Freedom of Expression: A Guide to the Implementation of Article 10 of the European Convention on Human Rights* (originally 2001; Strasbourg: Council of Europe, 2004), 8 and 15.

31. Eric Barendt, *Freedom of Speech* (fully revised and updated second edition; Oxford: Oxford University Press, 2005), 93–98. See also Priscilla Hayner, *Unspeakable Truths: Facing the Challenge of Truth Commissions* (New York and London: Routledge, 2002), 185.

32. Marie Smyth in 1998, as quoted in Article 19, *"Who Wants to Forget?" Truth and Access to Information about Past Human Rights Violations* (London: Article 19, 2000), 5.

33. Adam Phillips, "The Forgetting Museum," *Index on Censorship,* 34, no. 2 (2005), 36.

34. Arthur Danto, "Prudence, History, Time, and Truth," in Carr, Flynn, and Makkreel, eds., *Ethics,* 82.

35. Peter Burke, "History as Social Memory," in Thomas Butler, ed., *Memory: History, Culture and the Mind* (Oxford and New York: Blackwell, 1989), 97, 110.

36. Roger Markwick, *Rewriting History in Soviet Russia: The Politics of Revisionist Historiography, 1956–1974* (Houndmills and New York: Palgrave 2001), 290n25.

37. "Das Recht auf Geschichte: Kontroversen in der CSSR um die Charta 77," *Osteuropa: Zeitschrift für Gegenwartsfragen des Ostens,* 36 (1986), A370–84.

38. Adolf Juzweńko, "The Right to Historical Truth," *Index on Censorship,* 17, no. 9 (1988), 10–15.

39. Michael Schoenhals, "The 1978 Truth Criterion Controversy," *China Quarterly,* no. 125 (March 1991), 243–68; Schoenhals, "Sun's Fight for Press Freedom," *Index on Censorship,* 18, no. 8 (1989), 12–14.

40. See also Antoon De Baets, "Resistance to the Censorship of Historical Thought in the Twentieth Century," in Sølvi Sogner, ed., *Making Sense of Global History: The 19th International Congress of Historical Sciences, Oslo 2000, Commemorative Volume* (Oslo: Universitetsforlaget, 2001), 389–409.

41. Robert Darnton, "Poland Rewrites History," *New York Review of Books* (16 July 1981), 8.

42. For many examples of attempts to censor truth commissions, see Antoon De Baets, "Truth Commissions," in Derek Jones, ed., *Censorship: A World Encyclopedia,* vol. 4 (London and Chicago: Fitzroy Dearborn, 2001), 2459–62; updated regularly in the *Annual Reports* of the Network of Concerned Historians (<http://www.concernedhistorians.org>).

43. Truth and Reconciliation Commission of South Africa, *Report,* vol. 1 (Cape Town: Truth and Reconciliation Commission of South Africa, 1998), 111–12.

44. Quoted in Bernard Williams, *Truth & Truthfulness: An Essay in Genealogy* (Princeton and Oxford: Princeton University Press, 2002), 243.

45. Herbert Butterfield, "Historiography," in Philip Wiener, ed., *Dictionary of the History of Ideas: Studies of Selected Pivotal Ideas,* vol. 2 (New York: Charles

Scribner's Sons, 1973–74), 467, 496, 498. Reviewed by Antoon De Baets, "The Grandeur of Historiography," *Storia della Storiografia*, no. 57 (2007), 141–47.

46. For an evaluation of the idea of truth, see Simon Blackburn, *Truth: A Guide for the Perplexed* (originally 2005; Harmondsworth: Penguin, 2006). For a history of truth, see Williams, *Truth & Truthfulness* (but consult his remarks on the feasibility of a history of truth on 61, 271, 285n17, and 300n31), and Felipe Fernández-Armesto, *Truth: A History and A Guide for the Perplexed* (London, etc.: Bantam, 1997). For a history of the right to the truth, see (a) Juan Méndez, "The Right to Truth," in Christopher Joyner and Chérif Bassiouni, eds., *Reigning in Impunity for International Crimes and Serious Violations of Fundamental Human Rights: Proceedings of the Siracusa Conference, 17–21 September, 1998* (St Agnes: Erès, 1998), 255–78; (b) "Legal Brief *Amicus Curiae* Presented by the International Commission of Jurists before the Inter-American Court of Human Rights in the Case of Efraín Bámaca Velásquez vs. Guatemala," *The Review*, nos. 62–63 (September 2001), 129–58; (c) Jean-Marie Henckaerts and Louise Doswald-Beck, eds., *Customary International Humanitarian Law*, vol. 2: *Practice*, part 2 (Cambridge: Cambridge University Press, 2005), 2302–27 ("enforced disappearance"), 2655–2741 ("the dead"), 2742–74 ("missing persons")—to be read in conjunction with the extensive commentaries on the 1949 *Geneva Conventions* and their two 1977 *Protocols* by the International Committee of the Red Cross (the official custodian of these conventions and protocols); (d) Yasmin Naqvi, "The Right to the Truth in International Law: Fact or Fiction?" *International Review of the Red Cross*, 88, no. 862 (June 2006), 245–73; (e) Office of the United Nations High Commissioner for Human Rights, *Study on the Right to the Truth* (E/CN.4/2006/91; 2006) and *Right to the Truth* (<http://www.ohchr.org>; A/HRC/5/7; 2007). For a history of the governmental duties to investigate and prosecute, see Diane Orentlicher, "Settling Accounts: The Duty to Prosecute Human Rights Violations of a Prior Regime," *Yale Law Journal*, 100 (1991), 2537–2615.

47. *International Covenant on Civil and Political Rights* (1966), Article 15(2).

48. United Nations, *Convention on the Non-applicability of Statutory Limitations to War Crimes and Crimes against Humanity* (1968), Article 1. Useful reflections on imprescriptibility and retroactive justice in Ruti Teitel, *Transitional Justice* (Oxford: Oxford University Press, 2000), 15–16, 20–21, 33–34, 62–66, 138–41.

49. United Nations, *Declaration on the Protection of All Persons from Enforced Disappearance* (1992), Article 17; *International Convention for the Protection of All Persons from Enforced Disappearance* (2006), preamble, Articles 8, 24(2).

50. Diane Orentlicher, *Impunity: Report of the Independent Expert to Update the Set of Principles to Combat Impunity* (E/CN.4/2005/102; 2005), paragraph 63; Office of the United Nations High Commissioner for Human Rights, *Study on the Right to the Truth*, 8.

51. United Nations, *Convention on the Rights of the Child* (1989), Article 9. Similar ideas in *Geneva Conventions Protocol II* (1977), Article 4.

52. United Nations General Assembly, *Resolution 3220 (XXIX)* ["Assistance and Co-operation in Accounting for Persons Who Are Missing or Dead in Armed Conflicts"] (1974)—followed by similar resolutions in later years. See also Idem,

Principles of International Co-operation in the Detection, Arrest, Extradition and Punishment of Persons Guilty of War Crimes and Crimes against Humanity (1973).

53. See Appendix 5.1.

54. United Nations Human Rights Committee, *General Comment 6 (International Covenant on Civil and Political Rights): Right to Life* (1982).

55. United Nations Human Rights Committee, *María del Carmen Almeida de Quintero and Elena Quintero de Almeida versus Uruguay: Decision of 21 July 1983* (CCPR/C/19/D/107/1981; Communication no. 107/1981), paragraph 14. For other early mentions of the right to know, see *Study on Amnesty Laws and Their Role in the Safeguard and Promotion of Human Rights: Preliminary Report by Mr. Louis Joinet, Special Rapporteur* (E/CN.4/Sub.2/1985/16; 1985), paragraph 81; and "Legal Brief," 135–37.

56. Inter-American Court of Human Rights, *Velásquez Rodríguez Case: Judgment of July 29, 1988* (<http://www.corteidh.or.cr>; 1988), paragraphs 166–81, 184 (quotation), 194. See also United Nations Human Rights Committee, *General Comment 26 (International Covenant on Civil and Political Rights): Continuity of Obligations* (1997).

57. For leading jurisprudence on the right to the truth from international courts, see the notes of Office of the United Nations High Commissioner for Human Rights, *Study on the Right to the Truth,* and, *Right to the Truth.* The right to the truth also played an important role in the case about the disappearance of Alejandra Aguiar de Lapacó in Argentina: the Argentinian government eventually acknowledged and guaranteed as a principle her mother's imprescriptible right to the truth (and right to mourn), regardless of previous prosecutions of, and amnesties for, the perpetrators in question; see Inter-American Commission on Human Rights, *Report no. 21/00; Case 12.059: Carmen Aguiar de Lapacó versus Argentina* (http://www.cidh.org/casos/99.eng.htm; 1999). For European cases establishing a right to mourn, see European Court of Human Rights, *Płoski versus Poland* (2002), paragraphs 35–39; *Éditions Plon versus France* (2004), paragraph 47; *Hachette Filipacchi Associés versus France* (2007), paragraph 46.

58. *Question of Human Rights and States of Emergency: Eighth Annual Report Presented by Mr. Leandro Despouy, Special Rapporteur* (E/CN.4/Sub.2/1995/20; 1995), paragraph 54. For the question of the nonderogable character of its complement (the duty to investigate and prosecute), see Orentlicher, "Settling Accounts," 2606–12.

59. For the right to know as understood as access to information, see, for example, Thomas Blanton, "The World's Right To Know," *Foreign Policy* (July-August 2002), 50–58. Access to information is both narrower than the right to know (see text) and broader (its scope encompasses not only information about human rights abuses, but also information about scandals, disasters, corruption, reproductive health, and so on).

60. Naqvi, "The Right to the Truth," 249, 265–66, 268.

61. Nowak, *U.N. Covenant,* 343–44; Barendt, *Freedom of Speech,* 108–12, 434–35.

62. Andreas Guadamuz, "Habeas Data: An Update on the Latin America Data Protection Constitutional Right" (<http://www.bileta.ac.uk/01papers/guadamuz.html>; Edinburgh: University of Edinburgh, 2001).

63. See Article 19, *Defamation ABC: A Simple Introduction to Key Concepts of Defamation Law* (2006), 8. For examples, see European Court of Human Rights, *Özgür Gündem versus Turkey: Judgement* (2000), paragraph 43; Inter-American Court of Human Rights, *Marcel Claude Reyes and Others versus Chile: Judgment* (2006), paragraphs 72–73, 77, 84–86, 101.

64. International Committee of the Red Cross, *The Missing and Their Families* (2003), 6.

65. Inter-Parliamentary Union, *Universal Declaration on Democracy* (<http://www.ipu.org>; 1997), Articles 14, 17.

66. An example, Mozambique, in Lyn Graybill, "Pardon, Punishment, and Amnesia: Three African Post-Conflict Methods," *Third World Quarterly*, 25, no. 6 (2004), 1125–27.

67. Méndez, "The Right to Truth," 256.

68. Similar ideas in *Declaration of the Rights of the Child* (1959), Article 3; *Convention on the Rights of the Child* (1989), Articles 7–9.

69. See also preamble and Articles 24–25. Similar ideas in United Nations, *Declaration on the Protection of All Persons from Enforced Disappearance* (1992), Articles 4, 9, 13, 20(1); United Nations, *Guiding Principles on Internal Displacement* (1998).

70. This is an update of the "Set of Principles for the Protection and Promotion of Human Rights through Action to Combat Impunity" [the so-called "Joinet Principles"], in *Question of the Impunity of Perpetrators of Human Rights Violations (Civil and Political): Revised Final Report Prepared by Mr. Joinet* (E/CN.4/Sub.2/1997/20/Rev.1; 1997), Annex II. See also Diane Orentlicher, *Independent Study on Best Practices, Including Recommendations, to Assist States in Strengthening Their Domestic Capacity to Combat All Aspects of Impunity* (E/CN.4/2004/88; 2004), paragraphs 14–23; Orentlicher, *Impunity: Report,* paragraphs 15, 17–22, 63.

71. According to the *Principles to Combat Impunity,* truth commissions are "official, temporary, non-judicial fact-finding bodies that investigate a pattern of abuses of human rights or humanitarian law, usually committed over a number of years."

72. According to the *Principles to Combat Impunity,* archives refer to "collections of documents pertaining to violations of human rights and humanitarian law from sources including (a) national governmental agencies, particularly those that played significant roles in relation to human rights violations; (b) local agencies, such as police stations, that were involved in human rights violations; (c) state agencies, including the office of the prosecutor and the judiciary, that are involved in the protection of human rights; and (d) materials collected by truth commissions and other investigative bodies." See also Chapter 2 of this book.

73. See also Principles 3–4, 24. Similar ideas in United Nations, *Declaration of Basic Principles of Justice for Victims of Crime and Abuse of Power* (1985), Principles 4–17, 19, 21. For commemorations and collective funerals, see International Committee of the Red Cross, *Operational Best Practices Regarding the Management of*

Human Remains and Information on the Dead by Non-Specialists (<http://www.icrc. org>; 2004), 18–20.

74. Similar ideas in *Geneva Conventions Protocol I* (1977), Articles 53 and 85.4(d), and *Protocol II* (1977), Article 16; and *International Criminal Court Statute* (1998), Articles 8(2)(b)(ix) and 8(2)(e)(iv). See also UNESCO, *Convention Concerning the Protection of the World Cultural and Natural Heritage* (1972), Article 1; UNESCO, *Convention on the Protection of the Underwater Cultural Heritage* (2001); UNESCO, *Convention for the Safeguarding of the Intangible Cultural Heritage* (2003), Article 2; UNESCO, *Declaration Concerning the Intentional Destruction of Cultural Heritage* (2003). See also *Treaty on the Protection of Artistic and Scientific Institutions and Historic Monuments (Roerich Pact)* (1935); *Convention for the Protection of Cultural Property in the Event of Armed Conflict* and its protocols (1954, 1999); UNESCO, *Convention on the Means of Prohibiting and Preventing the Illicit Import, Export and Transfer of Ownership of Cultural Property* (1970); and UNIDROIT, *Convention on Stolen or Illegally Exported Cultural Objects* (1995).

75. Similar ideas in *Versailles Treaty* (1919), Articles 225–26; *Geneva Convention I* (1949), Articles 15–17; *Geneva Convention II* (1949), Articles 18–21; *Geneva Convention III* (1949), Articles 120–23; *Geneva Convention IV* (1949), Articles 16, 26, 129–31, 136–41; "List of Customary Rules of International Humanitarian Law," *International Review of the Red Cross*, 87, no. 857 (March 2005), rules 112–17. See also International Committee of the Red Cross, *Operational Best Practices*, 9–10.

76. Similar ideas in *Geneva Conventions Protocol I* (1977), Article 17; "List of Customary Rules," rules 112–13, 115–17; *United Nations Declaration on the Rights of Indigenous Peoples* (General Assembly, Resolution 61/295; 2007), Article 12; *Principles and Guidelines for the Protection of the Heritage of Indigenous People* (2000), Principles 13, 19, 21, 25.

77. Similar ideas in *Geneva Conventions* (1949), Common Article 3; *Geneva Convention III* (1949), Article 14; *Geneva Convention IV* (1949), Article 27; *Geneva Conventions Protocol I* (1977), Articles 75, 85; *Geneva Conventions Protocol II* (1977), Article 4.

78. Knut Dörmann, *Elements of War Crimes under the Rome Statute of the International Criminal Court: Sources and Commentary* (Cambridge: Cambridge University Press, 2003), 314, 323.

79. See also Articles 2.5, 3.7, 4.4.

80. Similar ideas in the remaining articles; see also World Archaeological Congress, *First Code of Ethics* ([1990]), Principle 3 and Rule 5; and World Archaeological Congress, *The Tamaki Makau-rau Accord on the Display of Human Remains and Sacred Objects*, Principles 1–6.

Chapter 6

1. "Science sans conscience n'est que ruine de l'âme." François Rabelais, *Pantagruel: Édition critique sur le texte de l'édition publiée à Lyon en 1542 par François Juste* (Paris: Honoré Champion, 1997), 110. The texts of all codes of ethics mentioned in Chapter 6 (and many others) are reproduced in the ethics section of

the Network of Concerned Historians (NCH) website (<http://www.concerned-historians.org>).

2. See also Richard Vann, "Historians and Moral Evaluations," *History and Theory*, 43, no. 4 (December 2004), 2–3, 6.

3. Carl Mitcham, "Ethical Issues in Pseudoscience: Ideology, Fraud, and Misconduct," in William Williams, ed., *Encyclopedia of Pseudoscience: From Alien Abductions to Zone Therapy* (Chicago and London: Fitzroy Dearborn, 2000), xv–xvi.

4. Pierre Nora, *Les Lieux de mémoire*, vol. 1 (Paris: Gallimard, 1984), xvii–xlii; René Rémond, *Quand l'État se mêle de l'Histoire* (Paris: Stock, 2006), 96–97.

5. Chris Lorenz, "Will the Universities Survive the European Integration? Higher Education Policies in the EU and in the Netherlands Before and After the Bologna Declaration," *Sociologia Internationalis*, 44, no. 1 (2006), 123–53.

6. UNESCO, *Recommendation Concerning the Status of Higher-Education Teaching Personnel* (<http://www.unesco.org>; 1997), Article 22(k). See also International Association of Universities, *Statement on Academic Freedom, University Autonomy and Social Responsibility* (<http://www.unesco.org/iau>; 1998), and many regional instruments. Specifically for history, see also Council of Europe (Parliamentary Assembly), *History and the Learning of History in Europe: Recommendation 1283* (<http://www.assembly.coe.int>; 1996), paragraph 14(xi) ("A code of practice for history teaching should be drawn up in collaboration with history teachers, as well as a European Charter to protect them from political manipulation") and paragraph 15(iii) ("The Assembly . . . recommends that the Committee of Ministers . . . ensure that the right of historians to freedom of expression is protected").

7. Ahmed Baghli, Patrick Boylan, and Yani Herreman, *History of ICOM (1946–1996)* (Paris: International Council of Museums, 1998), 51–52. For the code itself, see International Council of Museums, *Code of Ethics for Museums* (<http://www.icom.museum>; earlier versions: 1986, 2001; 2004).

8. World Archaeological Congress, *Vermillion Accord on Human Remains* (1989), and *First Code of Ethics* [1990], and *The Tamaki Makau-rau Accord on the Display of Human Remains and Sacred Objects* (n.d.) (<http://www.worldarchaeologicalcongress.org>).

9. Yvonne Bos-Rops, "Een mooi beroep verdient een code" (A nice profession merits a code), *Archievenblad*, 101, no. 1 (1998), 20–21. The code itself: International Council on Archives, *Code of Ethics* (<http://www.ica.org>; 1996).

10. Carol Barker and Matthew Fox, *Classified Files: The Yellowing Pages—A Report on Scholars' Access to Government Documents* (New York: The Twentieth-Century Fund, 1972), 61–62.

11. John Gilissen, "La Responsabilité civile et pénale de l'historien," *Revue belge de philologie et d'histoire*, 38(1960), part 2, 1037–39. For other early attempts see Charles Samaran, ed., *L'Histoire et ses méthodes* (Paris: Gallimard, 1961), xii–xiii (eleven principles of historical method), and David Fischer, *Historians' Fallacies: Toward a Logic of Historical Thought* (New York, etc.: Harper Torchbooks, 1970) (a brilliant book exposing 112 fallacies to which historians succumb).

12. American Historical Association, *Statement on Standards of Professional Conduct* (<http://www.historians.org>; 1987; amended eight times between May 1987 and January 2003, wholly revised January 2005). For pre–1987 discussions see, for example, Sheldon Hackney, and others, *Report of the American Historical Association Committee on the Rights of Historians* (<http://www.historians.org>; 1974)—the result of discussions started in 1970. Four societies affiliated to the American Historical Association issued more specialized guidelines: see NCH website.

13. Australian Council of Professional Historians Associations, *Code of Ethics and Professional Standards for Professional Historians in Australia* (<http://www.historians.org.au>; 2001); Australian Historical Association, "AHA Code of Conduct," *History Australia: The Australian Historical Association Bulletin*, 3, no. 1 (June 2006), 31.1–31.2 (originally published in 2003; see also <http://www.theaha.org.au>).

14. Schweizerische Gesellschaft für Geschichte/Société suisse d'histoire, *Ethik-Kodex / Code d'éthique* (<http://www.sgg-ssh.ch>; 2004).

15. The NCH website contains oral history codes for Australia, New Zealand, South Africa, the United Kingdom, and the United States.

16. International Committee of Historical Sciences, *Constitution* (<http://www.cish.org>), Article 1.

17. Rolf Torstendahl, "History, Professionalization of," in Neil Smelser and Paul Baltes, eds., *International Encyclopedia of the Social and Behavioral Sciences*, vol. 10 (Oxford, etc.: Elsevier-Pergamon, 2001), 6868.

18. See Thomas Nagel, *The View from Nowhere* (New York and Oxford: Oxford University Press, 1986), 164–88; Derek Parfit, *Reasons and Persons* (Oxford: Clarendon Press, 1984), 452–53.

19. Torstendahl, "History, Professionalization of," 6865.

20. "AHA Announces Changes in Efforts Relating to Professional Misconduct" (Washington: American Historical Association Press Release, 5 May 2003); William Cronon, "A Watershed for the Professional Division" (Washington: American Historical Association, September 2003).

21. Eric Barendt, *Freedom of Speech* (fully revised and updated second edition; Oxford: Oxford University Press, 2005), 213; see also 217, 220–21.

22. Robert Merton, "The Normative Structure of Science" (originally 1942), in Merton, *The Sociology of Science: Theoretical and Empirical Investigations* (Chicago and London: University of Chicago Press, 1973), 267–78; Philip Altbach, "The Academic Profession," in Altbach, ed., *International Higher Education: An Encyclopedia*, vol. 1 (New York and London: Garland, 1991), 43–44.

23. For this insight, see, e.g., Theo Thomassen, "Archivists between Knowledge and Power: On the Independence and Autonomy of Archival Science and the Archival Profession," *Arhivski Vjesnik* (Zagreb), no. 42 (1999), 149–67.

24. International Federation of Journalists, *Declaration of Principles on the Conduct of Journalists* (originally 1954; <http://www.ifj.org>, 1986), Principle 6; Barendt, *Freedom of Speech*, 422–23, 435–41.

25. Council of Europe (Committee of Ministers), *Recommendation No. R (2000) 7 of the Committee of Ministers to Member States on the Right of Journalists Not To Disclose Their Sources of Information* (including *Principles Concerning the*

Right of Journalists Not To Disclose Their Sources of Information) (<http://www. assembly.coe.int>; 2000). The European Court of Human Rights has confirmed the right to nondisclosure of sources (most notably in *Goodwin versus the United Kingdom* [1996]).

26. *Principles Concerning the Right of Journalists,* Principles 1 and 3.

27. African Commission on Human and People's Rights, *Declaration of Principles on Freedom of Expression in Africa* (<http://www.achpr.org>; 2002), Principle 15; Inter-American Commission on Human Rights, *Inter-American Declaration of Principles on Freedom of Expression* (<http://www.cidh.oas.org>; 2000), Principle 8.

28. For discussion of a controversial 1970 case in the United States involving privileged access to classified governmental sources (private papers, memoirs, etc.), and the subsequent excessive use in a monograph of these sources and of eighty personal interviews without annotation, without any attribution to authors, and without direct quotations from them, see: Barker and Fox, *Classified Files,* 78–81.

29. The judges of the European Court of Human Rights would generally not require a hard truth defense from journalists, but would require less demanding defenses (such as good faith). See Monica Macovei, *Freedom of Expression: A Guide to the Implementation of Article 10 of the European Convention on Human Rights* (originally 2001; Strasbourg: Council of Europe, 2004), 10.

30. See also John Lere and Bruce Gaumnitz, "The Impact of Codes of Ethics on Decision Making: Some Insights from Information Economics," *Journal of Business Ethics,* 48 (2003), 373–74, and Bos-Rops, "Een beroepscode," 228.

31. Edward Shils, *The Calling of Education: The Academic Ethic and Other Essays on Higher Education,* ed. Steven Grosby (Chicago: Chicago University Press, 1997), 9–13; Karl Popper, "The Moral Responsibility of the Scientist," in Paul Weingartner and Gerhard Zecha, eds., *Induction, Physics, and Ethics: Proceedings and Discussions of the 1968 Salzburg Colloquium in the Philosophy of Science* (Dordrecht: Reidel, 1970), 335.

32. "Wisdom obligates," a dictum of André Mercier's, in his "Science and Responsibility," in Weingartner and Zecha, eds., *Induction,* 342.

33. Not all articles of this code have been exhaustively discussed in previous chapters. Guidance will be found in Chapter 1 for Articles 1, 3, 5–7, 12–14, and 18–19; in Chapter 2 for Articles 7, 10–11, and 18; in Chapter 3 for Articles 4, 9, 11–13, and 15; in Chapter 4 for Articles 4, 9, and 11; in Chapter 5 for Articles 4, 6, 9, and 15–19; and in Chapter 6 for Articles 1–3, 5, 7–8, 11, 14, and 20.

Epilogue

1. My translation of a passage in the Dutch version of Imre Kertész, *Valaki más* (Budapest: Magvető, 1997).

2. Paul Ricœur, "Coming to Terms with Time," *UNESCO Courier,* 44, no. 4 (April 1991), 14.

3. Cited in Günter Grass, "I remember," *Index on Censorship,* 30, no. 1 (2001), 66.

BIBLIOGRAPHY

Note: This bibliography overlaps only partially with references given in chapter notes. The first part encompasses either sources such as conventions, court decisions, codes of ethics, or commentaries on them. As for court decisions, see also the notes of Chapters 2 and 3 and Appendices 3.1–3.6. The second part attempts to list essential works: either titles mentioned in the notes or classical works that were actively used as a background to the present book. All websites given throughout this book were last accessed on 1 December 2008. Many sources are brought together on the website of the *Network of Concerned Historians* (http://www.concernedhistorians.org), often in English as well as in French and Spanish.

Sources

American Association of University Professors. *1940 Statement of Principles on Academic Freedom and Tenure, with 1970 Interpretive Comments* (originally 1940; http://www.aaup.org; 1990).

American Historical Association. *Statement on Standards of Professional Conduct* (originally 1987; http://www.historians.org; 2005).

Article 19 (Global Campaign for Free Expression). *Defamation ABC: A Simple Introduction to Key Concepts of Defamation Law* (http://www.article19.org; 2006).

———. *Defining Defamation: Principles on Freedom of Expression and Protection of Reputation* (http://www.article19.org; 2000).

———. *The Public's Right to Know: Principles of Freedom of Information Legislation* (http://www.article19.org; 1999).

———. *Rights vs Reputations: Campaign against the Abuse of Defamation and Insult Laws* (http://www.article19.org; 2003).

———. "Themes and Issues." In Article 19 (Global Campaign for Free Expression). *Information. Freedom and Censorship: World Report* (originally 1988; London: Article 19, 1991), 409–40.

———. *"Who Wants to Forget?" Truth and Access to Information about Past Human Rights Violations* (http://www.article19.org; 2000).

Banisar, David. *Freedom of Information Around the World 2006: A Global Survey of Access to Government Records Laws* (http://www.freedominfo.org; Washington: Freedominfo.org; 2006) [and previous editions of this survey which have appeared under various names since 2000].

Berne Convention for the Protection of Literary and Artistic Works (originally 1886; http://www.wipo.int; 1979).

Black's Law Dictionary. Ed. B.A. Garner (originally 1891; St. Paul, MN: West Group, 2004).

Case Law Concerning Article 10 of the European Convention on Human Rights (Strasbourg: Council of Europe [Directorate General of Human Rights], 2001).

"Case no. 82: Trial of Max Schmid: United States General Military Government Court at Dachau, Germany, 19th May, 1947." In *Law Reports of Trials of War Criminals*, vol. 13 (London: United Nations War Crimes Commission, 1949), 151–52.

Cassese, Antonio, Paola Gaeta, and John Jones, eds. *The Rome Statute of the International Criminal Court: A Commentary*, vol. 1 (Oxford: Oxford University Press, 2002).

Council of Europe (Committee of Ministers). *History and the Learning of History in Europe: Reply to Recommendation 1283 (Doc. 7639)* (http://www.assembly.coe.int; 1996).

———. *Recommendation No. R (2000) 7 of the Committee of Ministers to Member States on the Right of Journalists Not to Disclose Their Sources of Information* (http://www.assembly.coe.int; 2000) [including *Principles Concerning the Right of Journalists Not to Disclose Their Sources of Information*].

Council of Europe (Parliamentary Assembly). *History and the Learning of History in Europe: Recommendation 1283* (http://www.assembly.coe.int; 1996).

———. *History and the Learning of History in Europe: Report (Doc. 7446)* (http://www.assembly.coe.int; 1995) [including *Colloquy on the Learning of History in Europe* (http://www.assembly.coe.int; 1996)].

De Baets, Antoon. *Censorship of Historical Thought: A World Guide, 1945–2000* (Westport, CT, and London: Greenwood Press, 2002).

———. "A Declaration on the Responsibilities of the Present Generations toward Past Generations." *History and Theory*, 43, no. 4 (December 2004), 130–64.

Dörmann, Knut. *Elements of War Crimes under the Rome Statute of the International Criminal Court: Sources and Commentary* (Cambridge: Cambridge University Press, 2003).

European Court of Human Rights. *Application of D[avid] I[rving] versus Germany* (http://www.echr.coe.int; 1996).

———. *Application of Garaudy versus France* (http://www.echr.coe.int; 2003).

———. *Case of Lehideux and Isorni versus France: Judgement* (http://www.echr.coe.int; 1998).

———. *Case of Lingens versus Austria: Judgement* (http://www.echr.coe.int; 1986).

———. *Case of Rotaru versus Romania: Judgement* (http://www.echr.coe.int; 2000).

Examination of the Alignment of the Laws on Defamation with the Relevant Case-Law of the European Court of Human Rights, Including the Issue of Decriminalisation of Defamation (Strasbourg: Council of Europe [Steering Committee on the Media and New Communication Services], 2006).

Henckaerts, Jean-Marie, and Louise Doswald-Beck, eds. *Customary International Humanitarian Law*, vol. 2: *Practice*, part 2 (Cambridge: Cambridge University

Press, 2005), 2302–27 ("enforced disappearance"), 2655–2741 ("the dead"), 2742–74 ("missing persons").

Henkin, Louis, ed. *The International Bill of Rights: The Covenant on Civil and Political Rights* (New York: Columbia University Press, 1981), 185–245.

Huskamp Peterson, Trudy. *Final Acts: A Guide to Preserving the Records of Truth Commissions* (Washington: Woodrow Wilson International Center Press, and Baltimore: Johns Hopkins University Press, 2005).

———. "Temporary Courts, Permanent Records." *United States Institute of Peace Special Report*, no. 170 (http://www.usip.org; August 2006).

InterAction Council of Former Heads of States and Governments. *A Universal Declaration of Human Responsibilities* (http://www.interactioncouncil.org; 1997).

Inter-American Commission on Human Rights. *Report no. 21/00; Case 12.059: Carmen Aguiar de Lapacó versus Argentina* (http://www.cidh.org/casos/99. eng.htm; 1999).

Inter-American Court of Human Rights. *Velásquez Rodríguez Case: Judgment of July 29, 1988* (http://www.corteidh.or.cr; 1988).

International Commission of Jurists. "Legal Brief *Amicus Curiae* Presented by the International Commission of Jurists before the Inter-American Court of Human Rights in the Case of Efraín Bámaca Velásquez vs. Guatemala." *The Review* (Geneva: International Commission of Jurists), nos. 62–63 (September 2001), 129–58.

International Committee of Historical Sciences. *Constitution* (originally 1926; http://www.cish.org; 2005).

International Committee of the Red Cross. *1949 Conventions and Additional Protocols and their Commentaries* (http://www.icrc.org/ihl; 1949 and 1977).

———. *Operational Best Practices Regarding the Management of Human Remains and Information on the Dead by Non-specialists* (http://www.icrc.org; 2004).

International Council on Archives. *Code of Ethics* (http://www.ica.org; 1996).

International Criminal Court. *Statute* (http://www.icc-cpi.int; 1998).

———. (Assembly of States Parties to the Rome Statute of the International Criminal Court). "Elements of Crimes." In International Criminal Court. *First Session: Official Records* (http://www.icc-cpi.int; ICC-ASP/1/3; 2002), 108–55.

International Criminal Tribunal for the Former Yugoslavia. *Prosecutor v. Momčilo Krajišnik; Case no. IT-00-39-T: Judgement* (http://www.un.org/icty; 2006).

International Criminal Tribunal for Rwanda. *Prosecutor versus Ferdinand Nahimana, Jean-Bosco Barayagwiza, Hassan Ngeze; Case no. ICTR-99-52-T: Judgement and Sentence* (http://www.grandslacs.net/doc/2905.pdf; 2003).

International Federation of Journalists. *Declaration of Principles on the Conduct of Journalists* (originally 1954; http://www.ifj.org; 1986).

International Law Commission. *Draft Declaration on Rights and Duties of States* (http://untreaty.un.org; 1949).

Inter-Parliamentary Union. *Universal Declaration on Democracy* (http://www. ipu.org; 1997).

Joint Declaration by the UN Special Rapporteur on Freedom of Opinion and Expression, the OSCE Representative on Freedom of the Media and the OAS Special Rapporteur on Freedom of Expression (http://www.article19.org; 2000).

"List of Customary Rules of International Humanitarian Law." Annex to Jean-Marie Henckaerts. "Study on Customary International Humanitarian Law." *International Review of the Red Cross*, 87, no. 857 (March 2005), 198–212.

Macovei. Monica. *Freedom of Expression: A Guide to the Implementation of Article 10 of the European Convention on Human Rights* (originally 2001; Strasbourg: Council of Europe, 2004).

Mendel, Toby. *Study on International Standards Relating to Incitement to Genocide or Racial Hatred—For the UN Special Advisor on the Prevention of Genocide* (N.p.; April 2006).

Native American Graves Protection and Repatriation Act (http://www.cr.nps.gov/nagpra; 1990).

Network of Concerned Historians (http://www.concernedhistorians.org).

Nowak, Manfred. *U.N. Covenant on Civil and Political Rights: CCPR Commentary* (Kehl am Rhein, Strasbourg, and Arlington, VA: Engel, 1993).

Office of the United Nations High Commissioner for Human Rights. *Right to the Truth: Report of the Office of the High Commissioner for Human Rights* (http://www.ohchr.org; A/HRC/5/7; 2007).

———. *Study on the Right to the Truth: Report of the Office of the United Nations High Commissioner for Human Rights* (http://www.ohchr.org; E/CN.4/2006/91; 2006).

Orentlicher, Diane. *Impunity: Report of the Independent Expert to Update the Set of Principles to Combat Impunity* (http://www.ohchr.org; E/CN.4/2005/102; 2005).

———. *Independent Study on Best Practices, Including Recommendations to Assist States in Strengthening Their Domestic Capacity to Combat All Aspects of Impunity* (http://www.ohchr.org; E/CN.4/2004/88; 2004).

———. "Settling Accounts: The Duty to Prosecute Human Rights Violations of a Prior Regime." *Yale Law Journal*, 100, no. 8 (June 1991), 2537–2615.

Organization of American States (General Assembly). *Right to the Truth* (Resolution 2175 [XXXVI-O/06]) (http://www.oas.org; 2006).

———. *Right to the Truth* (Resolution 2267 [XXXVII-O/07]) (http://www.oas.org; 2007).

———. *Right to Truth* (Resolution 2406 [XXXVIII/08]) (http://www.oas.org; 2008).

UNESCO. *Declaration on the Responsibilities of the Present Generations towards Future Generations* (http://www.unesco.org; 1997).

———.*Recommendation Concerning the Status of Higher-Education Teaching Personnel* (http://www.unesco.org; 1997).

UNIDROIT. *Convention Providing a Uniform Law on the Form of an International Will* (http://www.unidroit.org; 1973).

United Nations. *Convention on the Non-applicability of Statutory Limitations to War Crimes and Crimes against Humanity* (http://www.ohchr.org; 1968).

———. *Convention on the Prevention and Punishment of the Crime of Genocide* (http://www.ohchr.org; 1948).

———. *Declaration of Basic Principles of Justice for Victims of Crime and Abuse of Power* (http://www.ohchr.org; 1985).

————. *International Covenant on Civil and Political Rights* (http://www.ohchr. org; 1966).

————. *International Covenant on Economic, Social and Cultural Rights* (http:// www.ohchr.org; 1966).

————. *Manual on the Effective Prevention and Investigation of Extra-Legal, Arbitrary and Summary Executions* (1991), chapter 5 ("human remains").

————. *Universal Declaration of Human Rights* (http://www.ohchr.org; 1948).

————. *Vienna Convention on Succession of States in Respect of State Property, Archives and Debts* (http://untreaty.un.org; 1983).

United Nations Commission on Human Rights. *Final Report on the Question of the Impunity of Perpetrators of Human Rights Violations (Economic, Social and Cultural Rights), Prepared by Mr. El Hadji Guissé, Special Rapporteur* (http:// www.ohchr.org; E/CN.4/Sub.2/1997/8; 1997).

————. *Question of the Impunity of Perpetrators of Human Rights Violations (Civil and Political): Revised Final Report Prepared by Mr. Joinet* (http://www.ohchr. org; E/CN.4/Sub.2/1997/20/Rev.1; 1997).

————. *Right to the Truth: Resolution 2005/66* (http://www.ohchr.org; 2005).

————. *Updated Set of Principles for the Protection and Promotion of Human Rights Through Action to Combat Impunity* (http://www.ohchr.org; E/ CN.4/2005/102/Add.1; 2005).

United Nations Committee on Economic, Social and Cultural Rights, *General Comments to the International Covenant on Economic, Social and Cultural Rights* (http://www2.ohchr.org/english/bodies/cescr/comments.htm): *Comment 13* (right to education) (1999); *Comment 17* (right of everyone to benefit from the protection of the moral and material interests resulting from any scientific, literary or artistic production of which he is the author) (2005).

United Nations General Assembly. *Basic Principles and Guidelines on the Right to a Remedy and Reparation for Victims of Gross Violations of International Human Rights Law and Serious Violations of International Humanitarian Law: Resolution 60/41* (http://www.un.org/ga; 2006).

————. *Resolution 3220 (XXIX)* ["Assistance and Co-operation in Accounting for Persons Who Are Missing or Dead in Armed Conflicts"] (http://www. un.org/ga; 1974).

United Nations Human Rights Committee. *Communication no. 107/1981* (María del Carmen Almeida de Quintero and Elena Quintero de Almeida *versus* Uruguay) (http://www1.umn.edu/humanrts/undocs/allundocs.html; CCPR/C/ 19/D/107/1981; decision 1983).

————. *Communication no. 550/1993* (Faurisson *versus* France) (http://www1. umn.edu/humanrts/undocs/allundocs.html; CCPR/C/58/D/550/1993; decision 1996).

————. *General Comments to the International Covenant on Civil and Political Rights* (http://www.ohchr.org/english/bodies/hrc/comments.htm): *Comment 6* (right to life) (1982); *Comment 10* (freedom of expression) (1983); *Comment 11* (prohibition of propaganda for war and inciting national, racial or religious hatred) (1983); *Comment 16* (the right to respect of privacy, family, home, and correspondence, and protection of honour and reputation) (1988); *Comment*

22 (the right to freedom of thought, conscience, and religion) (1993); *Comment 26* (continuity of obligations) (1997).

United Nations Human Rights Council. *Right to the Truth: Decision 2/105* (http://www.ohchr.org; 2006).

World Archaeological Congress. *First Code of Ethics* (http://www.worldarchaeologicalcongress.org; [1990]).

———. *The Tamaki Makau-rau Accord on the Display of Human Remains and Sacred Objects* (http://www.worldarchaeologicalcongress.org; n.d.).

———. *Vermillion Accord on Human Remains* (http://www.worldarchaeologicalcongress.org; 1989).

World Press Freedom Committee. *Insult Laws: An Insult to Press Freedom* (http://www.wpfc.org; Reston, VA: World Press Freedom Committee, 2000).

———. *It's a Crime: How Insult Laws Stifle Press Freedom: A 2006 Status Report* (http://www.wpfc.org; Reston, VA: World Press Freedom Committee, 2006).

Literature

Altbach, Philip. "The Academic Profession." In *International Higher Education: An Encyclopedia*, edited by Altbach. Vol. 1 (New York and London: Garland, 1991), 23–45.

"Archives and Human Rights." *Comma: International Journal on Archives*, 4, no. 2 (2004) (theme issue).

Auerbach, Bruce. *Unto the Thousandth Generation: Conceptualizing Intergenerational Justice* (New York: Peter Lang, 1995).

Bahn, Paul. "Do Not Disturb? Archaeology and the Rights of the Dead." *Oxford Journal of Archaeology*, 3, no. 1 (1984), 127–39.

Baier, Annette. "The Rights of Past and Future Persons." In *Responsibilities to Future Generations: Environmental Ethics*, edited by Ernest Partridge (New York: Prometheus, 1980), 171–83.

Barendt, Eric. *Freedom of Speech* (fully revised and updated 2nd ed.; Oxford: Oxford University Press, 2005).

Barley, Nigel. *Dancing on the Grave: Encounters with Death* (originally 1995; London: Abacus, 1997).

Barros, Carlos, ed. *Actas del II Congreso Internacional "Historia a Debate,"* vol. 2, *Nuevos paradigmas* (Santiago de Compostela: Historia a Debate, 2000), 195–211 ("el historiador y el poder") and 233–59 ("el historiador, la ética y el compromiso social").

Barsalou, Judy, and Victoria Baxter. "The Urge to Remember: The Role of Memorials in Social Reconstruction and Transitional Justice." *United States Institute of Peace Stabilization and Reconstruction Series*, no. 5 (http://www.usip.org; January 2007).

Bédarida, François. "L'Histoire entre science et mémoire?" (originally 1996). In *L'Histoire aujourd'hui*, edited by Jean-Claude Ruano-Borbalan (Auxerre: Éditions Sciences humaines, 1999), 335–42.

———. "L'Historien régisseur du temps? Savoir et responsabilité." *Revue historique*, 122, no. 605 (1998), 3–24.

———. "Le Métier d'historien aujourd'hui." In *Être historien aujourd'hui*, edited by René Rémond (Paris: UNESCO and Érès, 1988), 283–303.

———. "The Modern Historian's Dilemma: Conflicting Pressures from Science and Society." *Economic History Review*, 40, no. 3 (1987), 335–48.

———. "Les Responsabilités de l'historien 'expert.'" In *Passés recomposés: champs et chantiers de l'histoire*, edited by Jean Boutier and Dominique Julia (Paris: Autrement. 1995), 136–44.

———. "Temps présent et présence de l'histoire." In *Écrire l'histoire du temps présent: en hommage à François Bédarida*, edited by Institut d'Histoire du Temps Présent (Paris: CNRS Éditions, 1993), 391–402.

———, ed. "The Social Responsibility of the Historian." *Diogenes*, 168 (1994) (theme issue).

Belliotti, Raymond. "Do Dead Human Beings Have Rights?" *The Personalist*, 60, no. 2 (April 1979), 201–10.

———. *What Is the Meaning of Human Life?* (Amsterdam and Atlanta, GA: Rodopi, 2001).

Berlin, Isaiah. "Historical Inevitability." In Berlin, *Four Essays on Liberty* (originally 1954; Oxford: Oxford University Press, 1969), 41–117.

Bernheim, Ernst. *Lehrbuch der Historischen Methode und der Geschichtsphilosophie* (originally 1889; Leipzig: von Duncker & Humblot, 1903).

Bevir, Mark, *The Logic of the History of Ideas* (Cambridge, Cambridge University Press, 1999), 265–308 ("distortions").

Black, Jeremy. *Using History* (London: Hodder Arnold, 2005).

Blackburn, Simon. *Truth: A Guide for the Perplexed* (originally 2005; Harmondsworth: Penguin, 2006).

Bloch, Marc. *Apologie pour l'histoire ou métier d'historien* (originally 1949; Paris: Colin, 1967).

Bredin, Jean-Denis. "Le Droit, le juge et l'historien." *Le Débat*, no. 32 (November 1984), 93–111.

Broad, William, and Nicholas Wade. *Betrayers of the Truth* (New York: Simon and Schuster, 1982).

Brown, Elizabeth. "Falsitas pia sive reprehensibilis: Medieval Forgers and Their Intentions." In *Fälschungen im Mittelalter*, vol. 1 (Hannover: Hahnsche Buchhandlung, 1988), 101–19.

Brugioni, Dino. *Photo Fakery: The History and Techniques of Photographic Deception and Manipulation* (Dulles, VA: Brassey's, 1999).

Brush, Stephen. "Should the History of Science Be Rated X?" *Science*, 183, no. 4130 (22 March 1974), 1164–72.

Butler, Thomas, ed. *Memory: History, Culture and the Mind* (Oxford and New York: Blackwell, 1989).

Butterfield, Herbert. "Historiography." In *Dictionary of the History of Ideas: Studies of Selected Pivotal Ideas*, edited by Philip Wiener. Vol. 2 (New York: Charles Scribner's Sons, 1974), 464–98 [electronic version on http://etext.virginia.edu].

———. "Official History: Its Pitfalls and Criteria" (originally 1949). In Butterfield, *History and Human Relations* (London: Collins, and New York: Macmillan, 1951), 182–224.

Callahan, Joan. "On Harming the Dead." *Ethics*, 97, no. 2 (January 1987), 341–52.

Carr, David, Thomas Flynn, and Rudolf Makkreel, eds. *The Ethics of History* (Evanston, IL: Northwestern University Press, 2004).

Carr, Edward. *What Is History?* (originally 1961; Harmondsworth: Penguin, 1973).

Carroll, Robert Todd. *The Skeptic's Dictionary: A Collection of Strange Beliefs, Amusing Deceptions, and Dangerous Delusions* (Hoboken, NJ: Wiley, 2003).

Carter, W.R. "Once and Future Persons." *American Philosophical Quarterly*, 17, no. 1 (January 1980), 61–66.

Chadwick, Ruth. "Corpses, Recycling and Therapeutic Purposes." In *Death Rites: Law and Ethics at the End of Life*, edited by Robert Lee and Derek Morgan (London and New York: Routledge, 1994), 54–71.

Clanchy, M.T. *From Memory to Written Record, England 1066–1307* (originally 1979; Oxford: Blackwell, 1993).

Cole, Elizabeth, and Judy Barsalou. "Unite or Divide? The Challenges of Teaching History in Societies Emerging from Violent Conflict." *United States Institute of Peace Special Report*, no. 163 (http://www.usip.org; June 2006).

Cole, Robert, ed. *International Encyclopedia of Propaganda* (Chicago and London: Fitzroy Dearborn, 1998).

Coliver, Sandra, ed. *Striking a Balance: Hate Speech, Freedom of Expression and Non-discrimination* (London: Article 19, 1992).

Constable, Gilles. "Forgery and Plagiarism in the Middle Ages." *Archiv für Diplomatik: Schriftgeschichte, Siegel- und Wappenkunde*, 29 (1983), 1–41.

Corino, Karl, ed. *Gefälscht! Betrug in Politik, Literatur, Wissenschaft, Kunst und Musik* (originally 1988; Reinbek: Rowohlt, 1992).

Dance, Edward. "Clio Abused." In Dance, *History the Betrayer: A Study in Bias* (originally 1960; London: Hutchinson, 1964), 53–78.

Danto, Arthur. "Prudence, History, Time, and Truth." In *The Ethics of History*, edited by David Carr, Thomas Flynn, and Rudolf Makkreel (Evanston, IL: Northwestern University Press, 2004), 76–88.

Davies, Simon. "Private Matters." *Index on Censorship*, 29, no. 3 (May–June 2000), 36–44.

De Baets, Antoon. "Archaeology." "Archives." "History: Historians." "History: Rewriting History." "History: School Curricula and Textbooks." "Holocaust: Denying the Holocaust." "Truth Commissions." In *Censorship: A World Encyclopedia*, edited by Derek Jones (London and Chicago: Fitzroy Dearborn, 2001), vol. 1, 73–82; vol. 2, 1056–59, 1062–73, 1079–80; vol. 4, 2459–62.

———. "Censorship." In *Encyclopedia of Western Colonialism since 1450*, edited by Thomas Benjamin. Vol. 1 (Macmillan/Thomson Gale: Detroit, MI, etc., 2007), 199–204.

———. "Censorship and Historical Writing." In *A Global Encyclopedia of Historical Writing*, vol. 1, edited by Daniel Woolf (New York: Garland, 1998), 149–50.

———. "Censorship and History (1945–present)." In *The Oxford History of Historical Writing*, edited by Axel Schneider and Daniel Woolf. Vol. 5, *1945 to Present* (Oxford: Oxford University Press, [2010] chapter 4, forthcoming).

———. "Defamation Cases against Historians." *History and Theory*, 41, no. 3 (October 2002), 346–66.

———. "Exile and Acculturation: Refugee Historians since the Second World War." *International History Review*, 28, no. 2 (June 2006), 316–49.

———. "Historiography in the Service of Authoritarianism and Dictatorships." In *The Oxford History of Historical Writing*, edited by Attila Pók, Stuart Macintyre, and Juan Maiguashca. Vol. 4, *1800 to 1945* (Oxford: Oxford University Press, [2010] chapter 7, forthcoming).

———. "Human Rights, History of." In *International Encyclopedia of the Social and Behavioral Sciences*, edited by Neil Smelser and Paul Baltes. Vol. 10 (Oxford, etc.: Elsevier-Pergamon, 2001), 7012–18.

———. "The Impact of the *Universal Declaration of Human Rights* on the Study of History," *History and Theory*, 48, no.1 (February 2009).

———. "The Network of Concerned Historians: A Decade of Campaigning." *History Australia: The Australian Historical Association Bulletin*, 3, no. 1 (2006), 16.1–16.4 [also published as "The Organization that Fights for Human Rights for Historians." *History News Network* (http://hnn.us/articles/16382.html; 10 October 2005)].

———. "A Organizaçâo do esquecimento: Historiadores perseguidos e censurados na Africa, Asia e América Latina." *Revista de história* (São Paulo), no. 134 (1996), 95–103.

———. "Resistance to the Censorship of Historical Thought in the Twentieth Century." In *Making Sense of Global History: The 19th International Congress of Historical Sciences, Oslo 2000, Commemorative Volume*, edited by Sølvi Sogner (Oslo: Universitetsforlaget, 2001), 389–409.

———. "A Successful Utopia: The Doctrine of Human Dignity." *Historein: A Review of the Past and Other Stories* (Athens), no. 7 (2007), 71–85.

———. "The Swiss Historical Society's Code of Ethics: A View from Abroad." *Schweizerische Zeitschrift für Geschichte / Revue suisse d'histoire / Rivista storica svizzera*, 55, no. 4 (2005), 451–62.

Dewey, John. "Academic Freedom" (1902) in *John Dewey: The Middle Works, 1899–1924*, edited by Jo Ann Boydston. Vol. 2, 1902–1903 (Carbondale and Edwardsville: Southern Illinois University Press, and London and Amsterdam: Feffer & Simons, 1976), 53–66.

Dolby, Riki. *Uncertain Knowledge: An Image of Science for a Changing World* (Cambridge: Cambridge University Press, 1996).

Dumoulin, Olivier. *Le rôle social de l'historien: de la chaire au prétoire* (Paris: Albin Michel, 2003).

Dworkin, Ronald. "We Need a New Interpretation of Academic Freedom." In *The Future of Academic Freedom*, edited by Louis Menand (Chicago: University of Chicago Press, 1996), 181–98.

Eco, Umberto. "Fakes and Forgeries." In Eco, *The Limits of Interpretation* (originally Italian 1990; Bloomington and Indianapolis, IN: Indiana University Press, 1990), 174–202.

———. "The Force of Falsity." In Eco, *Serendipities: Language & Lunacy* (New York: Columbia University Press, 1998), 1–21.

Edelman, Bernard. "L'Office du juge et l'histoire." *Droit et société: revue internationale de théorie du droit et de sociologie juridique*, 14, no. 38 (1998), 47–58.

Eich, Hermann. *Die mißhandelte Geschichte: historische Schuld- und Freisprüche* (Munich: Deutscher Taschenbuch Verlag, 1983).

Erdmann, Karl, Jürgen Kocka, and Wolfgang Mommsen. *Toward a Global Community of Historians: The International Historical Congresses and the International Committee of Historical Sciences, 1898–2000* (originally German, 1987; New York and Oxford: Berghahn, 2005).

Evans, Richard. "History, Memory, and the Law: The Historian as Expert Witness," *History and Theory*, 41, no. 3 (October 2002), 326–45.

Fälschungen im Mittelalter (Hannover: Hahnsche Buchhandlung, 1988), vol. 1.

Feder, Kenneth. *Frauds, Myths, and Mysteries: Science and Pseudoscience in Archaeology* (originally 1990; Mountain View, CA, London, and Toronto: Mayfield, 1999).

Feinberg, Joel. *Harm to Others* (New York and Oxford: Oxford University Press, 1984).

———. "Limits to the Free Expression of Opinion." In *Philosophy of Law*, edited by Feinberg and Hyman Gross (Encino, CA, and Belmont, CA: Dickenson, 1975), 135–51.

———. *Offense to Others* (New York and Oxford: Oxford University Press, 1985).

———. *Rights, Justice, and the Bounds of Liberty: Essays in Social Philosophy* (Princeton: Princeton University Press, 1980).

Fernández-Armesto, Felipe. *Truth: A History and a Guide for the Perplexed* (London, etc.: Bantam, 1997).

Ferro, Marc. *Comment on raconte l'histoire aux enfants à travers le monde entier* (Paris: Payot, 1981) [English translation: *The Use and Abuse of History, or How the Past Is Taught* (originally 1984; London and Boston: Routledge, 2003)].

———. *L'Histoire sous surveillance: science et conscience de l'histoire* (Paris: Calmann-Lévy, 1985).

———. *Les Tabous de l'histoire* (Paris: Nil Éditions, 2002).

Finley, Moses. *The Use and Abuse of History* (London: Chatto & Windus, and New York: Viking, 1986).

Fischer, David Hackett. *Historians' Fallacies: Toward a Logic of Historical Thought* (New York, etc.: Harper Torchbooks, 1970).

Fischer, John Martin, ed. *The Metaphysics of Death* (Stanford: Stanford University Press, 1993).

Flaherty, David. "Privacy and Confidentiality: The Responsibilities of Historians." *Reviews in American History*, 8, no. 3 (September 1980), 419–29.

Fowler, Don. "Uses of the Past: Archaeology in the Service of the State." *American Antiquity*, 52, no. 2 (1987), 229–48.

Frazer, James. *The Golden Bough: A Study in Magic and Religion.* Vol. 2, *Taboo and the Perils of the Soul* (originally 1890; London: Macmillan, 1914), 138–45 ("mourners tabooed"), 349–74 ("names of the dead tabooed").

Frei, Norbert, Dirk van Laak, and Michael Stolleis, eds. *Geschichte vor Gericht: Historiker, Richter und die Suche nach Gerechtigkeit* (Munich: Beck, 2000).

Fresco, Nadine. "Les Redresseurs de morts." *Les Temps Modernes,* 35, no. 407 (June 1980), 2150–2211.

Fuld, Werner. *Das Lexikon der Fälschungen: Fälschungen, Lügen und Verschwörungen aus Kunst, Historie, Wissenschaft und Literatur* (Frankfurt am Main: Eichborn, 1999).

Garton Ash, Timothy. "The Truth about Dictatorship." *New York Review of Books,* 45, no. 3 (19 February 1998), 35–40.

Gathercole, Peter, and David Lowenthal, eds. *The Politics of the Past* (London: Unwin Hyman, 1990).

Geyl, Pieter. *The Use and Abuse of History* (New Haven, CT: Yale University Press, 1955).

Gilissen, John. "La Responsabilité civile et pénale de l'historien." *Revue belge de philologie et d'histoire,* 38 (1960), part 1, 295–329; part 2, 1005–1039.

Ginzburg, Carlo. "Checking the Evidence: The Judge and the Historian." *Critical Inquiry,* 18, no. 1 (Autumn 1991), 79–92.

González Quintana, Antonio. "Archives of the Security Services of Former Repressive Regimes." *Janus: Archival Review,* 2 (1998), 7–25 [also at http://www.unesco.org].

———. "Los Archivos de la represión: balance y perspectivas." *Comma: International Journal on Archives,* no. 2 (2004), 59–74.

"The Good of History: Ethics. Post-structuralism and the Representation of the Past." *Rethinking History,* 2, no. 3 (1998), 309–424 (theme issue).

Goodpaster, Kenneth. "On Being Morally Considerable." *Journal of Philosophy,* 75, no. 6 (June 1978), 308–25.

Gordon, David. *Self-determination and History in the Third World* (Princeton, NJ: Princeton University Press, 1971).

Grafton, Anthony. *Forgers and Critics: Creativity and Duplicity in Western Scholarship* (Princeton, NJ: Princeton University Press, 1990).

Grey, Thomas. *The Legal Enforcement of Morality* (New York: Knopf, 1983).

Gross, Hyman. *A Theory of Criminal Justice* (New York: Oxford University Press, 1979).

Gustavson, Carl. "A Most Dangerous Product: History" (originally 1976). In *The Vital Past: Writings on the Uses of History,* edited by Stephen Vaughn (Athens, GA: University of Georgia Press, 1985), 249–58.

Harrison, Robert Pogue. *The Dominion of the Dead* (Chicago and London: University of Chicago Press, 2003).

Harrison III, Frank. "What Kind of Beings Can Have Rights?" *Philosophy Forum,* 12, nos. 1–2 (September 1972), 113–29.

Hartog, François, and Jacques Revel, eds. *Les Usages politiques du passé* (Paris: Éditions de l'École des Hautes Études en Sciences Sociales, 2001).

Haub, Carl. "How Many People Have Ever Lived on Earth?" *Population Today*, 30, no. 8 (November-December 2002), 3–4 [originally: *Ibidem*. February 1995].

Haywood, Ian. *Faking It: Arts and the Politics of Forgery* (Brighton: Harvester Press, 1987).

"L'Histoire face au politique." *Politique Africaine*, no. 46 (June 1992) (theme issue).

"Historians and Ethics." *History and Theory*, 43, no. 4 (December 2004) (theme issue).

"Historical Consciousness and Political Action." *History and Theory*, 17, no. 4 (December 1978) (theme issue).

"History Falsified." *Index on Censorship*, 14, no. 6 (December 1985), 1–54; 15, no. 2 (February 1986), 9–22; 15, no. 4 (April 1986), 24–30 (theme issues).

"History's Ethical Crisis." *Journal of American History*, 90, no. 4 (March 2004) (theme issue).

Hobsbawm, Eric. "Introducing: Inventing Traditions." In *The Invention of Tradition*, edited by Eric Hobsbawm and Terence Ranger (Cambridge: Cambridge University Press, 1983), 1–14.

Hoff-Wilson, Joan. "Access to Restricted Collections: The Responsibility of Professional Historical Organizations." *American Archivist*, 46, no. 4 (Fall 1983), 441–47.

Hovannisian, Richard, ed. *Remembrance and Denial: The Case of the Armenian Genocide* (Detroit: Wayne State University, 1998).

Iggers, Georg. "The Uses and Misuses of History: the Responsibility of the Historian, Past and Present." In *Making Sense of Global History: The 19th International Congress of Historical Sciences, Oslo 2000, Commemorative Volume*, edited by Sølvi Sogner (Oslo: Universitetsforlaget, 2001), 311–19.

Ignatieff, Michael. "Articles of Faith." *Index on Censorship*, 25, no. 5 (September–October 1996), 110–22.

Iserson, Kenneth. *Death to Dust: What Happens to Dead Bodies?* (Tucson, AZ: Galen Press, 1994).

Jaubert, Alain. *Le Commissariat aux archives: les photos qui falsifient l'histoire* (Paris: Barrault, 1986) [English translation: *Making People Disappear: An Amazing Chronicle of Photographic Deception* (Washington and London: Pergamon-Brassey, 1989)].

Jeanneney, Jean-Noël. *Le Passé dans le prétoire: l'historien, le juge et le journaliste* (Paris: Seuil, 1998).

Jones, Derek, ed. *Censorship: A World Encyclopedia*. 4 vols. (London and Chicago: Fitzroy Dearborn, 2001).

Jones, Mark, ed. *Fake? The Art of Deception* (Berkeley and Los Angeles: University of Los Angeles Press, 1990).

Jonker, Ed. "Geen etiquette. wel ethiek." [No to etiquette. yes to ethics.] *Tijdschrift voor Geschiedenis*, 118, no. 4 (December 2005), 572–80.

Kant, Immanuel. *Grundlegung zur Metaphysik der Sitten* (originally 1785). In *Kant's gesammelte Schriften*, edited by Preußischen Akademie der Wissenschaften. Vol. 4 (Berlin: Reimer, 1903), 385–464.

———. "On a Supposed Right to Lie from Altruistic Motives" (originally German, 1785). In *Ethics*, edited by Peter Singer (Oxford: Oxford University Press, 1994), 280–81.

Kiejman, Georges. "L'Histoire devant ses juges." *Le Débat*, no. 32 (November 1984), 112–25.

Kocka, Jürgen. "Objektivitätskriterien in der Geschichtswissenschaft." In Kocka, *Sozialgeschichte* (Göttingen: Vandenhoeck & Ruprecht, 1977), 40–47.

Koselleck, Reinhart. "'Space of Experience' and 'Horizon of Expectation': Two Historical Categories" (originally German, 1976). In Koselleck, *Futures Past: On the Semantics of Historical Time* (originally German, 1979; New York: Columbia University Press, 2004), 255–75.

Ku Chieh-kang (Gu Jiegang). *The Autobiography of a Chinese Historian, Being the Preface to A Symposium on Ancient Chinese History (Ku Shih Pien)* (translation and annotation: Arthur Hummel; Leyden: Brill, 1931).

LaFollette, Marcel. *Stealing into Print: Fraud, Plagiarism, and Misconduct in Scientific Publishing* (Berkeley and Los Angeles: University of California Press, 1992).

Langlois, Charles-Victor, and Charles Seignobos. *Introduction aux études historiques* (originally 1898; Paris: Éditions Kimé, 1992).

Lasswell, Harold, Daniel Lerner, and Hans Speier, eds. *Propaganda and Communication in World History*. 3 vols. (Honolulu: University of Hawaii Press, 1979–80).

Leerssen, Joep, and Ann Rigney, eds. *Historians and Social Values* (Amsterdam: Amsterdam University Press, 2000).

Le Goff, Jacques. *Histoire et mémoire* (Paris: Gallimard, 1988).

Lévi-Strauss, Claude. *La Pensée sauvage* (Paris: Plon, 1962).

Lewis, Bernard. *History Remembered, Recovered, Invented* (originally 1975; Princeton, NJ: Princeton University Press, 1987).

Lomasky, Loren. *Persons, Rights, and the Moral Community* (New York and Oxford: Oxford University Press, 1987).

Lowenthal, David. "Fabricating Heritage." *History & Memory*, 10, no. 1 (Spring 1998), 5–25.

Maier, Charles. "Doing History, Doing Justice: The Narrative of the Historian and of the Truth Commission." In *Truth versus Justice: The Morality of Truth Commissions*, edited by Robert Rotberg and Dennis Thompson (Princeton and Oxford: Princeton University Press, 2000), 261–78.

Malik, Kenan. "Beyond Tolerance and the Intolerable." *Index on Censorship*, 35, no. 1 (2006), 154–59.

———. "Don't Incite Censorship." *Index on Censorship*, 36, no. 2 (2007), 81.

Mallon, Thomas. *Stolen Words: Forays into the Origins and Ravages of Plagiarism* (New York: Ticknor & Fields, 1989).

Marchitello, Howard, ed. *What Happens to History? The Renewal of Ethics in Contemporary Thought* (New York and London: Routledge, 2001).

Margalit, Avishai. *The Ethics of Memory* (Cambridge, MA: Harvard University Press, 2002).

McNamara, Lawrence. "History, Memory, and Judgment: Holocaust Denial, the History Wars and Law's Problems with the Past." *The Sydney Law Review*, 26, no. 3 (September 2004), 353–94.

McNeill, William. "Mythistory, or Truth, Myth, History, and Historians." *American Historical Review*, 91, no. 1 (February 1986), 1–10.

Megill, Allan. "Some Aspects of the Ethics of History Writing: Reflections on Edith Wyschogrod's *An Ethics of Remembering*." In *The Ethics of History*, edited by David Carr, Thomas Flynn, and Rudolf Makkreel (Evanston, IL: Northwestern University Press, 2004), 45–75.

"Memory and Forgetting." *Index on Censorship*, 30, no. 1 (January–February 2001), 38–96 (theme issue).

Méndez, Juan. "Responsibility for Past Human Rights Violations: An Emerging 'Right to the Truth.'" In *Truth and Justice: In Search of Reconciliation in Suriname*, edited by Alfredo Forti and Georgine de Miranda (San José [Costa Rica]: Inter-American Institute of Human Rights. 1999), 43–52.

———. "The Right to Truth." In *Reigning in Impunity for International Crimes and Serious Violations of Fundamental Human Rights: Proceedings of the Siracusa Conference, 17–21 September, 1998*, edited by Christopher Joyner and Chérif Bassiouni (St Agnes: Erès, 1998), 255–78.

Merton, Robert. "The Normative Structure of Science" (originally 1942). In Merton, *The Sociology of Science: Theoretical and Empirical Investigations* (Chicago and London: University of Chicago Press, 1973), 267–78.

Meyer, Lukas. "Intergenerational Justice" (originally 2003; version 2008). In *The Stanford Encyclopedia of Philosophy*, edited by Edward Zalta (http://plato. stanford.edu; Stanford: Stanford University Press).

The Misuses of History (Strasbourg: Council of Europe [Council for Cultural Co-operation], 2000).

Misztal, Barbara. "Memory and Democracy," *American Behavioral Scientist*, 48, no. 10 (June 2005), 1320–38.

Mitcham, Carl. "Ethical Issues in Pseudoscience: Ideology, Fraud, and Misconduct." In *Encyclopedia of Pseudoscience: From Alien Abductions to Zone Therapy*, edited by William Williams (Chicago and London: Fitzroy Dearborn, 2000), xii–xvii.

Momigliano, Arnaldo. "Ancient History and the Antiquarian" (originally 1950). In Momigliano, *Studies in Historiography* (London: Weidenfeld and Nicolson, 1966), 1–39.

Monmonier, Mark. *How to Lie with Maps* (Chicago and London: University of Chicago Press, 1991).

Nagel, Thomas. "Death." In Nagel, *Mortal Questions* (Cambridge: Cambridge University Press, 1979), 1–10.

———. *The View from Nowhere* (New York and Oxford: Oxford University Press, 1986).

Naqvi, Yasmin. "The Right to the Truth in International Law: Fact or Fiction?" *International Review of the Red Cross*, 88, no. 862 (June 2006), 245–73.

Neier, Aryeh. "What Should Be Done about the Guilty?" *New York Review of Books*, 37, no. 1 (1 February 1990), 32–35.

Nekrich, Aleksandr. *Forsake Fear: Memoirs of an Historian* (translated by Donald Lineburgh; Boston, etc.: Unwin Hyman, 1991).

Nelkin, Dorothy, and Lori Andrews. "Do the Dead Have Interests? Policy Issues for Research after Life." *American Journal of Law and Medicine*, 24, nos. 2–3 (Summer–Fall 1998), 261–91.

Nerson, Roger. "Le Respect par l'historien de la vie privée de ses personnages." In *Mélanges offerts au professeur Louis Falletti* (Paris: Dalloz, 1971), 449–71.

Nietzsche, Friedrich. *The Use and Abuse of History* (originally *Vom Nutzen und Nachteil der Historie für das Leben: Zweite Unzeitgemässe Betrachtung*, 1874; English edition originally 1949; New York: Liberal Arts Press, 1957).

Nora, Pierre. *Les Lieux de mémoire*, vol. 1 (Paris: Gallimard, 1984), xvii–xlii [English translation: "Between Memory and History: *Les Lieux de Mémoire*." *Representations*, no. 26 (Spring 1989) 7–25].

Orwell, George. *1984* (London: Secker & Warburg, 1949).

Ouy, Gilbert. "Les Faux dans les archives et les bibliothèques." In *L'Histoire et ses méthodes*, edited by Charles Samaran (Paris: Gallimard, 1961), 1367–83.

Parfit, Derek. "Persons, Bodies, and Human Beings." In *Contemporary Debates in Metaphysics*, edited by Dean Zimmerman, Theodore Sider, and John Hawthorne (Oxford: Blackwell, 2007), 177–208.

———. *Reasons and Persons* (Oxford: Clarendon Press, 1984).

Partridge, Ernest. "Posthumous Interests and Posthumous Respect." *Ethics*, 91, no. 2 (January 1981), 243–64.

Plumb, John. *The Death of the Past* (London: Macmillan, and Boston: Houghton Mifflin, 1969).

PoKempner, Dinah. "A Shrinking Realm: Freedom of Expression since 9/11." In Human Rights Watch, *World Report 2007* (Washington: Human Rights Watch, 2007), 63–85.

"Politiques de l'oubli." *Le Genre humain*, 18 (October 1988) (theme issue).

Popper, Karl. *Conjectures and Refutations: The Growth of Scientific Knowledge* (originally 1963; London: Routledge & Kegan Paul, 1974).

———. *Logic of Scientific Discovery* (originally German, 1934; originally English 1959; London: Hutchinson, 1980).

———. "The Moral Responsibility of the Scientist." *Encounter*, 32, no. 3 (March 1969), 52–57 [also in Paul Weingartner and Gerhard Zecha, eds. *Induction, Physics, and Ethics: Proceedings and Discussions of the 1968 Salzburg Colloquium in the Philosophy of Science* (Dordrecht: Reidel, 1970), 329–36].

Pork, Andrus. "History, Lying and Moral Responsibility." *History and Theory*, 29, no. 3 (October 1990), 321–30.

Prosser, William. "Privacy." *California Law Review*, 48, no. 3 (August 1960), 383–423.

Rémond, René. *Quand l'État se mêle de l'Histoire* (Paris: Stock, 2006).

"Rewriting History." *Index on Censorship*, 24, no. 3 (May–June 1995), 24–98 (theme issue).

Ricœur, Paul. "Coming to Terms with Time." *UNESCO Courier*, 44, no. 4 (April 1991), 11–15.

———. *La Mémoire, l'histoire, l'oubli* (Paris: Seuil, 2000).

Rorty, Richard. "Afterword." In *Historians and Social Values*, edited by Joep Leerssen and Ann Rigney (Amsterdam: Amsterdam University Press, 2000), 197–203.

Samaran, Charles, ed. *L'Histoire et ses méthodes* (Paris: Gallimard, 1961).

Scammell, Michael. "Censorship and Its History: A Personal View." In Article 19, *Information, Freedom and Censorship: World Report* (London: Article 19, 1988), 1–18.

Scanlon, Thomas. "A Theory of Freedom of Expression." *Philosophy and Public Affairs*, 1, no. 2 (Winter 1972), 204–226.

Schauer, Frederick. *Free Speech: A Philosophical Inquiry* (Cambridge: Cambridge University Press, 1982).

Scholars at Risk, *Standards on International Academic Freedom, Institutional Autonomy and Responsibility: A Summary of Existing Statements* (working paper, 20 pages; New York: Scholars at Risk, March 2007).

Schöpflin, George. "The Functions of Myth and a Taxonomy of Myths." In *Myths and Nationhood*, edited by Geoffrey Hosking and George Schöpflin (London: Hurst, 1997), 19–35.

Schreuer, Hans. "Das Recht der Toten: Eine germanistische Untersuchung." *Zeitschrift für Vergleichende Rechtswissenschaft*, 33 (1916), part 1, 333–432; 34 (1916), part 2, 1–208.

Schudson, Michael. "Dynamics of Distortion in Collective Memory." In *Memory Distortion: How Minds, Brains, and Societies Reconstruct the Past*, edited by Daniel Schacter (Cambridge, MA, and London: Harvard University Press, 1995), 346–64.

Sen, Amartya. "History and the Enterprise of Knowledge," *New Humanist*, 116, no. 2 (Summer 2001), 4–8.

Sher, George. "Ancient Wrongs and Modern Rights" (originally 1980). In *Justice between Age Groups and Generations*, edited by Peter Laslett and James Fishkin (New Haven and London: Yale University Press, 1992), 48–61.

Shermer, Michael, and Alex Grobman. *Denying History: Who Says the Holocaust Never Happened and Why Do They Say It?* (Berkeley, Los Angeles, London: University of California Press, 2000).

Shils, Edward. "Academic Freedom." In *International Higher Education: An Encyclopedia*, edited by Philip Altbach. Vol. 1 (New York and London: Garland, 1991), 1–22.

———. *The Calling of Education: The Academic Ethic and Other Essays on Higher Education*, edited by Steven Grosby (Chicago: University of Chicago Press, 1997).

Smith, Wilfred C. "A Human View of Truth." *Studies in Religion: A Canadian Journal*, 1, no. 1 (1971), 6–24.

Sophocles. *The Theban Plays: King Oedipus; Oedipus at Colonus; Antigone*. Translated E.F. Watling (Harmondsworth: Penguin, 1947, 1974), here *Antigone* (originally 442–41 BCE).

Stengers, Jean. "L'Historien face à ses responsabilités." *Cahiers de l'école des sciences philosophiques et religieuses*, no. 15 (1994), 19–50.

Stoerger, Sharon. "History Ethics." (originally 2002; http://www.web-miner. com/historyethics.htm; 2005).

Stump, David. "Pseudoscience." In *New Dictionary of the History of Ideas,* edited by Maryanne Horowitz. Vol. 5 (Detroit. MI: Scribner's, 2005), 1950–51.

Sutton, John. "Memory." In *Encyclopedia of Philosophy,* edited by Donald Borchert. Vol. 6 (Detroit, MI: Thomson/Gale, 2006), 122–28.

Teitel, Ruti. *Transitional Justice* (Oxford: Oxford University Press, 2000).

Terray, Emmanuel. *Face aux abus de mémoire* (Arles : Actes Sud, 2006).

Thomas, Louis-Vincent. *Le Cadavre: de la biologie à l'anthropologie* (Brussels: Éditions Complexe, 1980).

Thomassen, Theo. "Archivists between Knowledge and Power: On the Independence and Autonomy of Archival Science and the Archival Profession." *Arhivski Vjesnik* (Zagreb), no. 42 (1999), 149–67.

Todorov, Tzvetan. *Les Abus de la mémoire* (Paris: Arléa, 1995) [English: "The Abuses of Memory." *Common Knowledge,* 5, no. 1 (Spring 1996), 6–26].

———. "The Uses and Abuses of Memory." In *What Happens to History? The Renewal of Ethics in Contemporary Thought,* edited by Howard Marchitello (New York and London: Routledge, 2001), 11–22.

Torstendahl, Rolf. "History, Professionalization of." In *International Encyclopedia of the Social and Behavioral Sciences,* edited by Neil Smelser and Paul Baltes. Vol. 10 (Oxford, etc.: Elsevier-Pergamon, 2001), 6864–69.

Trigger, Bruce. *A History of Archaeological Thought* (Cambridge: Cambridge University Press, 1989).

Truzzi, Marcello. "Pseudoscience." In *The Encyclopedia of the Paranormal,* edited by Gordon Stein (Amherst, NY: Prometheus, 1996), 560–74.

"The Uses and Misuses of History and the Responsibilities of the Historians, Past and Present." In *Making Sense of Global History: The 19th International Congress of Historical Sciences, Oslo 2000, Commemorative Volume,* edited by Sølvi Sogner (Oslo: Universitetsforlaget, 2001), 309–409.

Vann, Richard. "Historians and Moral Evaluations." *History and Theory,* 43, no. 4 (December 2004), 3–30.

Vansina, Jan. *Oral Tradition As History* (originally, French 1961; originally, English 1965; London: James Currey, 1985).

Vidal-Naquet, Pierre. *Assassins of Memory: Essays on the Denial of the Holocaust* (originally French, 1987; New York: Columbia University Press, 1992).

Voss, Ingrid. "Le Comité International des Sciences Historiques face aux défis politiques des années trente." *Bulletin du Comité International des Sciences Historiques,* no. 19 (1993), 159–73.

Waldron, Jeremy. "Superseding Historic Injustice." *Ethics,* 103, no. 1 (October 1992), 4–28.

Weber, Max. "Wissenschaft als Beruf." In Weber, *Wissenschaft als Beruf 1917/1919; Politik als Beruf 1919. Max Weber Gesamtausgabe.* Vol. I/17, edited by Wolfgang Mommsen and Wolfgang Schluchter (Tübingen: Mohr & Siebeck, 1992), 71–111.

Wennberg, Robert. "The Moral Standing of the Dead and the Writing of History." *Fides et Historia*, 30, no. 2 (Summer-Fall 1998), 51–63.

Wiener, Jon. *Historians in Trouble: Plagiarism, Fraud, and Politics in the Ivory Tower* (New York and London: The New Press, 2005).

Williams, Bernard. *Truth & Truthfulness: An Essay in Genealogy* (Princeton and Oxford: Princeton University Press, 2002).

Williams, Glanville. *The Mental Element in Crime* (Jerusalem: Magnes Press, 1965).

Williams, William, ed. *Encyclopedia of Pseudoscience: From Alien Abductions to Zone Therapy* (Chicago and London: Fitzroy Dearborn, 2000).

Winkler, Karin. "Historians and Ethics." *Chronicle of Higher Education* (6 July 1994), A17–18.

Wolfe, Bertram. "Totalitarianism and History." In *Totalitarianism,* edited by Carl Friedrich (originally 1954; New York and Cambridge, MA: Cambridge University Press, 1964), 262–77.

Woolf, Daniel. "Historiography." In *New Dictionary of the History of Ideas,* edited by Maryanne Horowitz. Vol. 1 (Detroit, MI: Scribner's, 2005), xxxv–lxxxviii.

Wyschogrod, Edith. *An Ethics of Remembering: History, Heterology, and the Nameless Others* (Chicago: University of Chicago Press, 1998).

Yerushalmi, Yosef, et al. *Usages de l'oubli* (Paris: Seuil, 1988).

INDEX